SISIRKUMAR MITRA taught history at Rabindranath Tagore's international university Visva-Bharati, Santiniketan, West Bengal, for eight years. Then a call from within took him to Sri Aurobindo Ashram, Pondicherry. He is now Academic Member and Professor, History of Civilisation, Sri Aurobindo International Centre of Education, an extension of Sri Aurobindo Ashram in the field of education. Among his published works are *Resurgent India, The Dawn Eternal—The Secret of India's Evolution, A Marvel of Cultural Fellowship, History as the Future, Sri Aurobindo and Indian Freedom, Sri Aurobindo and the New World, Sri Aurobindo—A Homage* (With Prof. Tan Yun-Shan), *Evolution of India—Its Meaning, The Liberator.*

INDIA
VISION AND FULFILMENT

INDIA
VISION AND FULFILMENT

SISIRKUMAR MITRA

D. B. TARAPOREVALA SONS & CO. PRIVATE LTD.

210 D. Naoroji Road -   -   -   - Bombay 1

PRINTED IN INDIA

Printed by P. H. Raman at Associated Advertisers & Printers, 505, Tardeo Arthur
Road, Bombay 34 and published by Russi J. Taraporevala for D. B. Taraporevala
Sons & Co. Private Ltd.

Preface

THE VERY first thing to say about the book is that its central theme as also the main lines of its elaboration is inspired by Sri Aurobindo's thought. It is an attempt at a study, from the standpoint of evolutionary history, of the growth and expansion of Indian culture as a motivating force in the progress of man towards his divine destiny, envisaged in the Master's vision of the Future.

And from this vision the book derives its title, its coherence, its ensemble. The chapters tend to focus this vision on India's endeavours through the ages to develop her life—spiritual, cultural, social and political—towards its perfect form in the future in which all creative expressions will find their oneness in the oneness of the Spirit. Therefore, the movement of India's soul was also towards unity and fellowship, and was not confined to her frontiers; it expanded far beyond and touched the mind and heart of almost the whole of humanity—a fact of great importance to the future remaking of man. Spiritual forces are at work to prepare man for his divine destiny. History takes on its true meaning when it visions this march of man in all its phases.

Written at different times, the chapters may at the first blush appear to be lacking in organic unity, but a closer view will bring to the fore a common historical background and an intimate co-relation. Certain repetitions may be noticed, but they are deliberate and intended to stress certain important aspects of the subjects in which the various creative endeavours of India, and the world generally, have been studied in relation to man's ultimate growth into a greater life in the future.

The world today is in the throes of a new birth. The widespread gloom and the terrible misery and the desolation of the present signalise, not the success but the desperate death-struggle of the forces of Darkness that sway the world-order today. Their movements are like the deepening of night just before daybreak, the maddened sweep and moan of a storm dying down. Even now, these forces have begun to flag and stagger, and the time is not far when they, and those that are yet stubborn in their resistance, will be completely annihilated. For, the forces of Light are bound

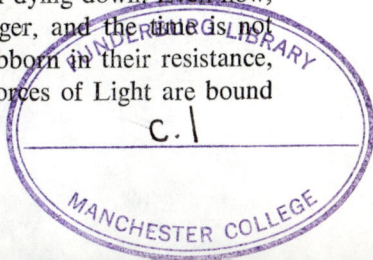

to triumph, and the full manifestation of the Divine is a certainty. The earth must cease to be dominated by the Asuras. It is God's kingdom, and he must come down and repossess it and be its sole Ruler.

It is for man to receive the Call and respond to it by taking an active part in the spiritual remaking of the world, the highest privilege he can ever have in his earthly sojourn. The Knowledge that India, the pioneer of this new adventure, has preserved through the ages, has been possessed and revealed today for the liberation of man into the truth, bliss and freedom of a higher existence, a diviner perfection which it is his destiny to attain as the very end and consummation of his life on earth.

The book seeks among other things to be a pointer to that phase of India's historic development which carries in it the mighty seed of a world transformation. It traces the evolution of her great past in order to show how her soul speaks through it into a greater future, a future big with the destiny of the entire humanity. The vision that India holds before man today is the vision of a new world, a new heaven on earth. And this because the time has come for man to be ready for the divine fulfilment of his earthly life. In fact, there are signs today of how that great event begins. 'Never in history has there been a greater age than now.'

Except Chapters 4 and 5, all the other chapters were read through by Sri Aurobindo and approved by him for publication. The author however has incorporated in them, particularly in Chapter 6, many new facts of great importance and of historical value that came his way later.

The author's grateful thanks are due to Messrs. D. B. Taraporevala Sons & Co. Private Limited, Bombay, the pioneer book-publishers of India, for having brought out the book to commemorate Sri Aurobindo's birth centenary on 15 August 1972.

Sri Aurobindo Ashram   SISIRKUMAR MITRA
Pondicherry 2
India

Contents

Illustrations

(between pages 128 and 129)

Illustrations

1

The Vision[1]

THE PAST of India has yet to be deeply looked into and properly appraised. The spiritual adventures that she has undertaken throughout the ages, especially in the early days of her history, cannot be said to have been studied in all their deeper implications, at least in their bearings on her destiny. It is therefore necessary to emphasise that an insight into and a correct re-visioning of the cultural achievements of the race in their true perspective are indispensable to the future rebuilding of India, to the understanding of the forces that are to bring about a resurgence of her soul.

It is said that India has a message for humanity. There is no doubt that she has. But scarcely has any attempt been made to have an exact idea of the real character of that message. A spiritual message is a vague term. Such evangels about the ancient wisdom of India some of her great sons have already delivered to the world in her recent past. And India has, because of them, begun to figure more prominently before the seeing mind of humanity. But the inner India, her soul, has yet to say her last liberating Word, the Word that shall bring into birth a new world and solve for ever the problems of mankind.

The story is indeed a romantic one of how India carried on her epic quest into the profundities of life and God and everything that inwardly or outwardly concerned the terrestrial exist-

---

1. Unacknowledged quotations in this chapter and also in all subsequent ones, are from Sri Aurobindo's works listed under References at the end of each chapter.

ence of man. The fruits of her unique *tapasya*[2] for millenniums are treasured in her sacred literature and in other relics and antiquities; but they are reflected more unmistakably in the very life of the people, in the continuously enlarging tradition of the Godward endeavours of their soul. Her earliest days, however, were the most glorious, when she had the deepest of her spiritual experiences, when she saw the supreme Reality manifesting itself in every form of creation, when she saw in man his divinity, and proclaimed that man could become that divinity, become a god, become one with God, become the ineffable Brahman.[3]

But India's was not an exclusive spirituality. To her the powers of matter, life and mind were no less real than those of the Spirit; and in the search after their truth her seers discovered that in them is inherent the Spirit which is seeking to unfold itself in the earth-nature. Life, mind and body were therefore regarded as the field and condition for the Spirit to fulfil itself in the terrestrial existence of man. Thus did India make the first attempt to solve the most vital of problems, the problem of harmony between life and spirit, of which the vision came to her seers almost at the very dawn of her history.

This treatise is an attempt at something like an aerial survey of India's endeavour through the ages to realise that ideal in all her inner and outer adventures through which she has now grown in sufficient power and potentiality, not only to see and possess the deeper truth of the Ideal but to show to humanity the Way which will lead it to the attainment of its highest spiritual destiny. This is the mission which India has borne through the ages, 'preserving the Knowledge that preserves the world.'

I

It cannot be said that Indian history so far has given due importance to its earliest period, which, according to Sri Aurobindo's revealing exegesis, was the most brilliant and creative in the world of the spirit. Indeed whatever efforts in the same sphere India made in the subsequent epochs have, all of them, been inspired by the truths that had come to the intuitive vision of her early seers.

---

2. Spiritual effort.
3. The Supreme Reality.

The beginning of this spiritual age in India is shrouded in the dim past. The date with which the Rig Veda Samhita is usually associated represents the close of a long period of vigorous and incomparable inward pursuits of which an idea may be found in the opulent imagery and mystic symbolism of the sublimest truths, seen by the Rishis[4] and expressed in the *riks*.[5] There is reason, however, to believe that greater ages of Intuition, of the luminous Dawns of the Forefathers, had preceded the Rig Vedic times, and that the entire secret of their esoteric teachings was not probably revealed even to the Rishis of the Rig Veda who were perhaps not ready for it. Yet the Rig Veda has every claim to be regarded as the most authentic document recording the Aryan Fathers' deepest experiences of the higher truths whose golden light opened to them the path of the gods.

The end of human life was to these mystics a divine outflowering. 'Life is therefore a movement from mortality to immortality, from mixed light and darkness to the splendour of a divine Truth whose home is above in the infinite but which can be built up here in man's soul and life, a battle between the children of Light and the sons of Night, a getting of treasure, of the wealth, the booty given by the gods to the human warrior, a journey and a sacrifice.' If a state of permanent living in light, in truth, in bliss, in freedom and in immortality is his ultimate destiny, man will have to attain that in his life by overcoming the limitations imposed on him by the forces of darkness, division and falsehood.

The Vedic idea of sacrifice with the soul of man as the enjoyer of its fruits points to the path that leads to this conquest. Of all his gains and works, of all that he himself is and has, man must make an offering to the powers of the Godhead, the powers of Consciousness, the gods, who recognise in the soul of man their brother and ally and desire to help and increase him by themselves increasing in him so as to exalt and enrich his world with their light, strength and beauty. It is not, therefore, that it is man only who invokes the gods to descend into his world, into him in response to his sacrifice. The gods also have need of man to whose awakened soul they send their call to combine with them against the sons of Darkness and Division who hold their sway over the earth. And victory in this battle—an ultimate certainty—

---

4. Seers.
5. Hymns of the Rig Veda.

means a new birth for man, a divine becoming; for, liberated from his bondage to the lower nature, man becomes ready for a divine manifestation.

The sacrifice is also a journey, an upward journey, which man undertakes in quest of his supreme goal. And as he does that, he grows from one state into a still higher one till he finds himself before the full Ray of the Light, and in possession of all the treasures of heaven. 'Become high-uplifted, O Strength, pierce all veils, manifest in us the things of the Godhead,' was the constant prayer of the Vedic seekers. And sacrifice is the way by which the fruit, 'the raining of the world of light,' can be obtained. The ascent towards the light will fulfil its purpose only when the descent takes place bringing into the lower the pure experience of the higher. But the effective descent would mean a global widening, an increasing on every side into the wholeness of the world of light. Sacrifice in its inner sense is a glad, ungrudging and aspiring renunciation of the lower and finite for the attainment of the higher and infinite. An offering of all one's possessions and powers to the Supreme from whom they are derived is the means to the realisation of the Supreme and the enjoyment of the bliss of His Light, Love and infinite plenitude. And the mystic Fire, the fire of the awakened Psyche, is the priest and leader of this sacrifice. In an undeveloped man, this Fire smoulders under a heap of gross vital-physical preoccupations; only in those who have developed their spiritual consciousness and awakened to a high sense of their divine destiny it flames up and mounts towards the unwalled heavens of the Spirit. It rises, a quenchless, indomitable Seer-Will, *kavikratu,* cleaving through all the planes of consciousness, devouring all the desires of man, consuming all the rank weeds of his ignorance, till it lands the soul, free and immune, upon the shoreless ocean of immortality. But for this Fire, the soul would have remained pent up in an eternal inconscience. It is the great vicar of evolutionary sacrifice, the intrepid pilot of the soul's voyage towards infinity.

The life of the Vedic Aryans was, every moment of it, a ceaseless effort to live up to the ideal of sacrifice, to think of it, to prepare for it and then to perform it in an effective manner. Indeed it was their sole concern, the dominant idea behind all their activities and nothing existed for them which had no connection with this supreme work of life. For the initiates, it was an inner, esoteric

discipline. For the common run, it took the form of rites by per-
forming which they might open to the truths implied in the Vedic
symbols. The Fire in man must therefore burn and burn continuously. Its flames must rise higher and higher carrying up the
sacrifice, stair by stair, so that man may grow in his spirit and
be able to attain the highest end of his earthly existence. This is
the integral vision envisaged in the Veda. If by sacrifice the lower
elements of man's earthly existence are conquered and made
amenable to the influence of the Light which will take them up
into itself, into their respective higher terms from which they
originated, it is again, by the same act that the Divine manifests
in the human vehicle, enlarging it into the infinity of his own
being.

To the Vedic seers came intuitive visions of the Infinite
Light of heaven and of its three modes of self-unfoldment, *ritam,
satyam, brihat,* 'the Right, the True, the Vast.' The force of these
visions impelled the soul of India to grow and expand both in her
inner and outer life, the two aspects being one in the oneness of
the Spirit. Ritam, says Sri Aurobindo, is the action of the Divine
knowledge, will and joy in the lines of the Truth, the play of the
truth-consciousness. These lines of the Truth later became the
lines of the Dharma[6] which connect the individual soul with its
godhead. Satyam is the dynamic essence of the truth-consciousness
which has to permeate the being and convert it into its substance.
Brihat is the infinity of Sachchidananda[7] out of which the other
two proceed and in which they are founded. Man's divine perfection towards which the force of these visions secretly prepares
him lies in the fulfilment of the infinite possibilities of his terrestrial existence, indicated by them. These visions are the spiritual
foundations of the culture of India and the world. And in these
visions was born the soul of India with its undying quest for the
Infinite.

The Vedic seers discovered the essential nature of the terrestrial existence as Sachchidananda veiled in the phenomenal oppo-
sitions of matter, life and mind, but compelling in the earth-nature
an effort to cleave through these contrary conditions and eventually
arrive at its own unveiled Splendour, the Perfection implicit in it.

---

6. Rule of ideal living, the right line of self-development towards perfection in the Spirit.
7. The Supreme Reality as self-existent Being, Consciousness and Bliss.

These conditions have grown and developed in the earth to create in it the necessary field for a greater Manifestation. They are derived in the lower planes from their original spiritual principles in the higher hemisphere; Mind from the light of the Truth-Consciousness, Life from the energy of the Consciousness-Force, Matter from the primal substance of Existence. The mystics had the vision of the plane of the Truth-Consciousness whose power is as well inherent in the earth as the above principles but is not, like them, active in it, and whose descent into the earth would quicken that Manifestation towards which man is progressing in his evolution.

The manifestation would therefore mean not only the descent of the Light on earth but also the ascent of man into a higher than his present mental plane of consciousness. It is this higher plane which is the link between the lower hemisphere of life, mind, body and the higher hemisphere of Sachchidananda. 'Man ascending thither strives no longer as a thinker but is victoriously the seer; he is no longer this mental creature but a divine being. His will, life, thought, emotion, sense, act are all transformed into values of all-puissant Truth and remain no longer an embarrassed or a helpless tangle of mixed truth and falsehood. He moves lamely no more in our narrow and grudging limits but ranges in the un-obstructed Vast; toils and zigzags no longer amid these crooked-nesses, but follows a swift and conquering straightness; feeds no longer on broken fragments, but is suckled by the teats of the Infinity. Therefore he has to break through and out beyond these firmaments of earth and heaven; conquering firm possession of the solar worlds, entering on to his highest Height he has to learn how to dwell in the triple principles of Immortality.' Thus in the psychological and therefore the real implication of the Vedic teaching, life with all its powers is affirmed, accepted and cherish-ed as a field for the gods' adventure, for a divine efflorescene. If man is of the earth, he is also of heaven; and his godhead will be reborn in him when 'Heaven and Earth equalised join hands in the bliss of the Supreme.'

With this integral vision of the Infinite and of an infinite existence for man as the perennial source of inspiration, India started on her quest of that which would bring her its realisation in the life of the race. This movement from the Rig Vedic times traced not a straight line but a curve, luminous all through because of its origin in the light to which it was naturally inclined to return, and it proceeded in a downward course with the purpose of illumining the different parts and planes of man's being so that he might he prepared for the perfection that was to come to him in the future. It is not that India could always hold fast to this ideal; but the great epochs of her history are those in which she turned her eyes towards it and strove with all her soul to actualise it in the life of the race, to give form to its truth in the varied expressions of her creative life. For, it is to this sublime seeing of the early fathers that the mind of India does rightly trace all its philosophy, religion, the essential things of culture, the beginnings of the future spirituality of her people.

The curve of the adventure of India's soul showed the first sign of a downward tendency when the Vedic age of Intuition was passing into the Upanishadic age of intuitive Thought, in which was already faintly foreshadowed the coming reign of Reason. And this adventure was, as it has ever been in later times, a necessity for her growth towards the future which was to be greater than the past. In the Veda intuition had a freer play, since mind and life were then plastic enough to its influence and action. In the Upanishads mind evinced an increasing tendency towards an independent and exclusive self- development and absorbed whatever intuition had to offer for its as well as life's illumination. Nevertheless, there must have been a strong basis of life-force for the vigorous spiritual efforts that were made by the Vedantic mystics. People lived a rich and robust life, and a harmony there surely was between it and the intense seeking after truth that was so much in evidence among the kings and nobles no less than among the sages and saints of the time. Royal courts and forest hermitages were humming with these activities; and such glowing examples were not solitary as those of the *rajarshis* or sage-kings like Janaka ruling over a vast empire and at the same time living the unfettered, luminous life of the Spirit; and of *brahmarshis* or kings of sages like Yajnavalkya—perhaps the greatest figure in the Upanishads—to whom truth was greater than anything else, and yet who accepted with both hands worldly possessions along with spiritual riches. Among other noted monarchs of this age were Pravahana Jaivali, Ajatashatru and Ashvapati Kaikeya, who managed the affairs of their States, led armies into the battlefield and were at the same time widely known as great teachers of *brahma vidya*.[8]

But how did they discover this harmony? By knowledge, which to the Upanishadic seers was always knowledge by an identity with the object of knowledge in a higher than the mental plane of consciousness. It is while engaged in the pursuit of this truth of knowledge that the seers realised that knowledge of the Self is the highest knowledge, and that 'the Self in man is one with the universal Self of all things and that this Self again is the same as God and Brahman, a transcendent Being or Existence, and they beheld, felt, lived in the inmost truth of all things in the universe and the inmost truth of man's inner and outer existence by the light of this one and unifying vision.' The Upanishads say that *ananda*, 'delight', is the essential nature of the Self, and it is from this delight hidden in the self that the world came into existence and by delight it is sustained and led to its goal.

Harmony among our parts of nature is emphasised in the Upanishads as a basic necessity in spiritual life. And this harmony may be brought about by an inward concentration which will put us into touch with our psychic centre in the inner heart connected through a hundred channels with the lines of our individual consciousness. The psychic represents the Transcendent in the universal Nature and is intended to manifest on earth the Transcendent through its universalised individuality of mind, life and body. It is the golden nucleus of our evolving personality. This is a distinctive contribution of Indian thought. The West could not go beyond the conception of the constructed individual, mind being to her the highest power possible to man; whereas in India the Spirit is held to be the highest truth of man, and through it is realised his infinite possibility. Integration of all his powers to the psychic, an aspect of the Spirit in Man, would mean the building up of a perfect personality ready for ascension into higher heights of his being. As the seeker opens into the power of the psychic principle in him, he becomes capable of drawing down into himself from higher Nature such forces as may purify and exalt their lower counterparts in him and with an affinity established between his inner nature and the outer, the seeker rises into

---

8. The Knowledge of the Supreme Reality.

a higher consciousness and from there into the yet higher of the Transcendent which is the ultimate goal of the Upanishadic teaching. And to that end, all egoistic impulses, all sordid attachments must be completely eliminated from his nature. 'Life has to be transcended in order that it may be freely accepted; the works of the universe have to be overpassed in order that they may be divinely fulfilled.'

The whole view comprised by the oneness of life and spirit was there, but the greater urge that characterised the period was always towards the realisation of the transcendent Truth, through which new riches of world-knowledge, God-knowledge and Self-knowledge came into the possession of the early mystics. If the Vedic basis was in the main psycho-physical, in which life was not only recognised but emphasised as the condition for a greater life, the Upanishadic was fundamentally psycho-spiritual. Yet the latter was little more than a restatement in less symbolic but more intelligible terms of the truths expressed in the former. 'The Upanishads did not deny life, but held that the world is a manifestation of the Eternal, of Brahman, all here is Brahman, all is in the Spirit and the Spirit is in all, the self-existent Spirit has become all these things and creatures; life too is Brahman, the life-force is the very basis of our existence, the life-spirit, *Vayu*, is the manifest and evident Eternal, *pratyaksham brahman*. But it affirmed that the present way of existence of man is not the highest or the whole; his outward mind and life are not all his being; to be fulfilled and perfect he has to grow out of his physical and mental ignorance into spiritual self-knowledge.' The most inspiring record of revelatory knowledge, the Upanishads have throughout the ages exercised their profound influence upon almost every sphere of man's spiritual, religious and cultural life both in India and abroad.

II

During the age of the Spirit, the Veda and the Vedanta affirmed this ideal, giving to the Indian mind through the universality of their teachings that peculiar synthetic cast which became so clearly defined in its catholic outlook, especially on matters concerning the social and religious welfare of the people. The age

of Dharma that followed witnessed the working of a comprehensive plan to bring about an integral development of man's individual and collective existence. It was marked by such constructive efforts as resulted in the fixing of the external forms of Indian
life and culture in their broad and large lines. The Vedantic soul
of India begins to take its body, but it is a body which is, or has
always tended to be, one with its soul, because the body here
has no meaning without its indwelling Spirit. It is this idea that
governed every kind of social thinking in ancient India: law-
makers and psychologists were ever alive to the fact that everything in life acquires its value only when it helps and converges
on the attainment by man of his spiritual perfection. This is why,
recognising the complexity of human nature, they tried to discover its right place in the cosmic movement and give its full
legitimate value to each part of man's composite being and
many-sided aspiration and find out the key to their unity.

The result of this endeavour was the laying down of the
four fundamental motives of human living, *artha, kama, dharma,*
and *moksha,* man's vital interests and needs, his desires, his
ethical and religious seeking, his ultimate spiritual aim and
destiny. The other institution, evolved as a corollary to the above,
was that of the four stages of life. The first was the period of
education and preparation based on this idea of life; the second,
a period of normal living to satisfy human desires and interests
under the moderating rule of the ethical and religious part in
us; the third, a period of withdrawal and spiritual preparation;
and the last, a period of renunciation of life and release into the
spirit.

It is clear from the above two basic conceptions of the
ancient Indian social theory, more so from the first, that it
accepted and provided for a disciplined satisfaction of the claims
of man's vital, physical and emotional being, since the ego-life
of *kama* and *artha,* desire and self-interest, must be lived and
the forces it evolves brought to fulness, so that the eventual aim
of a going beyond may be accomplished with less difficulty; the
claims of his ethical and religious being governed by a knowledge
of the law of God and Nature and man, because *dharma* is not
merely a religious creed but a complete rule of ideal living by
which life is to be guided in its fulfilment, each individual growing into his perfection, and to that end, developing his creative

faculties, which will bring well-being not only to him but also to his society; the claims of his spiritual longing for liberation, for the Law, Dharma, and its observance is neither the beginning nor the end of man; beyond it is the great spiritual freedom which man must claim as the ultimate end of his existence. An integration to this supreme goal of the whole tendency of man comprised by *kama, artha* and *dharma,* seems to be the ideal emphasised by the social thinkers of India.

This was, indeed, a very great attempt to build a synthesis, and although in later days an over-emphasis on the last aim and the consequent neglect of the others disturbed the social equilibrium for a while, it cannot however be denied that the steadfast following of all these aims by the people produced vast results, so brilliantly described in the great epics. In the *Ramayana* the ethical side of man's nature is given an extreme importance and its fulfilment is sought through the sincere performance of the duties formulated by the ancients. It pictures an age of heroic action and of an early and finely moral civilisation; whereas the *Mahabharata* reflects a puissant intellectualism, the victorious and manifold mental activity of the age, which gives its character to the culture then prevalent in the country. Heroic action there was, but it had in it more of thought than in the *Ramayana.*

There is no doubt that all the human activities depicted in these two grand expressions of the creative soul of India were inspired by the ancient ideals, although a tendency towards external formation and construction both in the social and mental life, for which the periods mainly stood, detracted from their effort to re-vision the past in its true light. Hence the curve of India's adventure went further down making an arc from where it had started and remained confined for a time to the region of the mind; but, we may repeat, the curve was a luminous one, and the mind of India was sustained by its innate spiritual inclination, of which an outstanding evidence in the latter period is the supreme truth revealed in the Gita, in which a harmony is built of the three great means and powers, Love, Knowledge and Work, the dynamic sublimations of the power of heart, of mind and of life, through which the soul of man can directly approach and cast itself into the Eternal. Here the harmony aimed at reaches its highest point when by a complete self-giving to the Godhead man becomes the fit instrument for a divine manifestation.

In the age of Dharma man was a full-fledged mental being—
his intellect was keen and capacious and masterful; but it had
already begun to turn a red eye on life, to dominate and dragoon
it into its fixed moulds. Itself a prisoner of its own principles
and creeds, it sought to impose the same captivity upon life's
free and fluid movements and stood in the way of its higher
progress. Shri Krishna—a unique figure in the history of human
evolution—came at this stage and tried to break down these in-
flexible barriers of the mind and release it into a loftier atmosphere, an ample light, and a more plastic assimilation. He represents an unparalleled harmonisation of the salient strands of
all forms of past spiritual culture and exalted it not only to a very
high plane of universal vision but also to a mighty effectuation.
He restored to man the idea of Purushottama, the integral Divine,
and emancipated the soul from the rigour and rigidity of the
mind into the luminous vastness and perfection of the Overmind.
Indeed, he stands as the trumpet-voiced herald of the Overmental
fulfilment.

But the Overmind is not the summit of human ascension.
There is the Supermind, the supreme Gnosis, and it is the destiny
of man to rise into its unbarred Light and all-creative Truth-Will.
To this plane of all-comprehending and all-originating consciousness Shri Krishna points a finger of light. But work continues, time ripens and humanity prepares for the advent—we had
almost said the acknowledgement—of the next supreme Leader.

The essential idea in the age of Dharma was to bring to
bear upon the creative powers of mind and life the past spiritual
experiences of the race. But the attempt was made, as naturally,
through the exercise of the ethical and intellectual faculties both of
which developed out of a deep understanding of man's inner profundities. But however high and pure their standards, they are
born of the powers and impulses of the mind. Be they the four
motives or the *ashramas*,[9] they, all of them, belonged to the same
category of human creation as the cultures characterised by them
and embodied in the epics. So in those early days, the mind of
India went through its first round of experiences ample enough
to enable it to be ready for the great classical age that came as
a flowering of the intellectuality of the previous epochs into a

---

9. The four stages of life.

curiosity and care of detail in the varied expressions of the cultural life of the people.

In the later days of the age of Dharma the mind of India was found to be almost entirely engrossed in the formalistic interpretation of the ideals and institutions of the race, and man's right to follow them was more restricted than before. The result was that a spirit of revolt began to show itself in the rise of many dogmas and creeds, and society ceased to function as a cohesive force in the collective life of the people. Moreover, life betrayed a tendency towards hedonistic pursuits. It was at this critical juncture of India's history that the Buddha came and delivered his message of Freedom, freedom from ignorance and suffering, from all social and religious aberrations, even from one's own self, into an utter transcendence above and an overflowing love and compassion below. A way out into the vastness of a Beyond, and an oceanic heart of equality and active love for all, are his greatest gifts to humanity.

This message of freedom and the powerful impact of the Buddha's love unclamped the creative energy of India which found an almost immediate expression in an outburst of cultural activity which has no parallel in all history. It was, indeed, a veritable spring-tide of Indian culture when the genius of the race broke into a myriad forms great, grand and glorious. It inundated the whole country and brimmed over to many distant lands and peoples. India's gospel of universal love echoed in China and Japan and Palestine and even Alexandria. The seeds of a world fraternity were sown, and a noble gesture was made towards human unity. But the deeper meaning of the Buddha's advent is that the compassion he incarnated was the compassion of the Divine for His creatures, His Grace, as it were, in which was hidden the assurance to man that he as a race is destined to a high spiritual achievement.

Buddhism, however, represents an important phase in the spiritual life of India. Of the two directions in which the mind of India seemed to be moving about the time when Buddhism began to be a force in the cultural life of the people, the one is the expression of its creative genius and the other is the denying of life as being a bondage and an obstacle to spiritual pursuits. But both of these were recognised in the age of Dharma. The former was regarded as one of the varied motivations of human personality whose fruition was necessary for the all-round growth of man, for which ample provision was made in the laws that were meant to guide the social evolution of the race. This tendency, moreover, received a great impetus when by its insistence on freedom Buddhism liberated the social life of India from many of its cramping evils and thereby created conditions favourable to the growth and advancement of culture. The latter tendency might be traced to the longing for release from this mundane existence into the Spirit, the Beyond: broadly indicated in the ideals of *moksha*[10] and *sanyasa,*[11] it had not a little to do with the Buddhistic conception of Nirvana. When the true seeker found that religion was compromising with life, subjecting its high spirit to the satisfaction of the latter's unspiritual demands and was thereby deteriorating into soulless forms of mere externalia and priestly obscurantism, so much in evidence about the time of the Buddha's advent, it was but natural that he should think of nothing else but an ascetic withdrawal from life in order to be able to live exclusively in the spirit, in the pure truth of religion —an idea which may have derived some sustenance from one of the trends of the Upanishadic teaching.

But this attitude, as indisputable objective proofs testify, did not very much or materially affect the abundant vitality and creative energy that were so boldly exhibited by the race in its continuous cultural endeavours for centuries, all through sustained by its inborn spirituality, an echo of which rings in the voice of Ashoka proclaiming and practising the ideal of universal fellowship. Indeed, the deeper springs of Ashoka's love for humanity and interest in its religious welfare underlying his efforts are to be found not so much in his adherence to the ethical conception of the *Dhamma*[12] as in the natural spiritual disposition of the country to which he belonged. And the creative activities of the age almost everywhere in their wide range reflected this tendency. The light of the Spirit was touching mind and life and was also in some instances guiding their movements, but it did not rule them as a governing principle, perhaps because they were not ready, and needed more experience for their fuller expression in the Spirit.

---

10. Spiritual liberation.
11. Ascetic renunciation.
12. Code of ideal conduct in Buddhism.

Perfection is attainable by man only when he has presented himself to subject every member of his being to the absolute rule of the Divine.

III

The classical was an age of scholars, legislators, dialecticians and philosophical formalisers. It witnessed the creative and aesthetic enthusiasm of the race pouring itself into things material, into the play of the senses, into the pride and beauty of life. The arts of painting, architecture, dance, drama, all that can minister to the needs of a great and luxurious civic life, received a strong impetus which brought them to their highest technical perfection. 'It is a period of logical philosophy, of science, of art and the developed crafts, law, politics, trade, colonisation, the great kingdoms and empires with their ordered and elaborate administrations, the minute rule of the Shastras in all departments of thought and life, an enjoyment of all that was brilliant, sensuous, agreeable, a discussion of all that could be thought and known, a fixing and systematising of all that could be brought into the compass of intelligence and practice,—the most splendid, sumptuous and imposing millennium of Indian culture.' Never in her history has India seen such a many-sided blossoming of her force of life. Culturally, she has never been so rich, so colourfully creative. And no other age has given her such a plethora of experiences. Indeed, she needed them or rather Nature wanted her to have them, so that India might grow in her being and prepare for the new and greater age of the Spirit that was to have followed the classical period. It goes without saying that from the vigorous efforts made in this age to give form to the various impulses of life, the mind of India had also its due share of growth and experience.

It is in this great age—of which the highest point was reached in the Gupta times—that classical sublimities found their marvellous expression in the poetry and drama of its representative literary mouthpiece, Kalidasa, and in those of the galaxy of its poets and dramatists, the recension of the epics was completed, most of the Puranas were written, the *Dhamasutras* were codified, the Smritis were given their present form, the Sankhya and

Mimamsa philosophies were systematised, the *Shilpashastra* (Fine Arts), the *Kamasutra* (Eugenics, Erotics and allied subjects), the *Arthashastra* and the *Shukraniti* (Polity) were written, the ancient Indian ideas on Astronomy, Physics, Chemistry, Botany, Zoology, Medicine and Mineralogy were rendered into their respective treatises through which they are known today, the masterpieces of art at Ajanta, Bagh, Ellora, etc., were produced, the famous figure of the Buddha was evolved along with the Shikhara and other distinctive characteristics of India's temple, cave and secular architecture, the international centre of learning at Nalanda flourished. The encyclopaedic character of the scientific learning of the age was represented among others by Varahamihira, a master-scientist, whose *Brihatsamhita* is a veritable mine of authoritative information on almost every branch of Science.

In such an age, when life seems to have been lived in its fulness, it is but natural that the curve of India's adventure should go further down in its circular movement reaching a region in which it found itself in touch with the material basis of life. Here the mind of India was seeking to infuse its light of the Spirit into the materialised vitality of man, and was trying to have an insight into the truth of matter. Thus behind these activities of life, the old spirituality of the race kept the lamp of its soul burning. Its most vivid expression is found in the works of art of this period which exhibit a marvellous blending of the two main tendencies of the Indian mind, its love of life based on an understanding of its varied motivations, and its quest of God, the Spirit, the Self of things with the life as the field and means of its manifestation.

The art-creations of this age are indeed a striking example of the peculiar aesthetic bent of India defining itself in the effort of the artist to suggest through the form his inner visions and experiences rather than any external idea of the things seen by him. The artists were to go through a course of spiritual discipline and were in many instances known as *shilpi-yogins*.[13] But they did not confine themselves to the depicting of the sacred subjects.[14] The secular scenes at Ajanta and Bagh, done by monk-artists, show the accuracy of their knowledge of earthly life; yet the figures

---

13. Mystic artists.
14. Briefly dealt with in Chapter 4.

of women in them in the peculiar *tribhanga* (the triple bend) pose indicate a wonderful harmony between such contrary feelings as nonchalance and voluptuousness, both losing themselves in an utter spirit of self-surrender that has surely about it something beyond the concerns of the earth. These frescoes as also those in the same style and of the same period found in other parts of the country are verily marvels of ancient Indian painting. Apart from their classical excellence for which they are famous all the world over, they are characterised by a suggestion of the unity of life and spirit, the vision of which came to the seeker-artists of the age. Painting is naturally the most sensuous of the arts. But the painters of these works succeeded wonderfully in spiritualising this sensuous appeal by making the most vivid outward beauty of their pictures a revelation of subtle spiritual emotion so that the soul and the sense are in harmony in the deepest and finest richness of both and united in their satisfied consonant expression of the inner significance of things and life. In the art of sculpture of the period the most remarkable achievements are the figures of the Bodhisattvas and the Dhyani Buddha. The former represents a marvellous blending of the feeling of detachment from the outer world and the feeling of an infinite compassion for suffering creatures; the latter symbolise the greatest ideal which Indian sculpture ever attempted to express—a serene triumph over life and death and time, a beatific communion of the individual with the universal Soul in a vast, radiant, victorious calm but vibrant with the mighty rhythms of the Eternal.

The spiritual seeking of India took a particular turn about the close of this period when there was a movement preparing the country for a greater age in which her gains through the cultivation and development of her moral, intellectual and material powers in the previous times would be all equally harmonised and made real in the world of the spirit. To all appearances, Shankara did show the promise of being a precursor of that great age in India. But he did not seem to have the complete vision, the whole view of the larger integral ideal of ancient India, the supreme truth of which was a harmony between life and spirit, a mediation between earth and heaven. Shankara took the obviously materialistic character of the culture of the period for a tendency towards deterioration; neither did he visualise the past history of India from a wider perspective. Disgusted, perhaps, with certain

aberrations in the religious life of the people, he sought release
into the realm of the Spirit, leaving the impure Life bound to the
more impure Matter to run for ever the vicious round of its
earthly existence. He affirmed the impermanence of life, and tried
to substantiate this pessimistic view in the light of his own interpretation of the ancient scripture. *Moksha,* liberation from the
bondage of life, he preached with all the vehemence he could
command, and his success meant the failure of the country to
grow in readiness for the greater future that had been the underlying intention of all its past endeavours.

Though supreme in his own way, Shankara proved unequal
to the task that lay before him of furthering the cause of
the country towards the fulfilment of its highest destiny. Rather,
his negative philosophy contributed, however indirectly, to the
strengthening of the forces of disintegration that had been at work
in the country during the post-classical age and a foreign invasion
destroyed whatever possibility there was of a new awakening. It must however be conceded that the efforts of Shankara
were responsible for one and a great good. If his denunciation of life had the effect of emasculating the race, as before
him the similar teaching of the Buddha had done, his emphasis,
however exclusive, on the absolute aspect of the One Reality,
helped the bewildered and groping mind of India to revert to its
ancient affirmation and experience of Advaita, the One Reality
without a second.

IV

But these strivings and the consequent preparation of the country
for a new outlook did not all end only in the negation of life.
Nurtured by the country's age-old spirituality, they flowered into
a vigorous revival of the self-same tendency that expressed itself
so remarkably in the teachings of the mystics, in the Vaishnavic[15]
movements and in the cults of the Tantras.[16] The medieval saints
proclaimed that truth is greater than religion, of which the forms
also are one in the very core of their teachings. They affirmed to
the people, irrespective of caste, creed or race, that life was

---

15. Relating to the cult of devotion, a branch of Hinduism.
16. Cult of the worship of the Power-aspect of the Supreme.

a necessary condition for man's growth into a greater life for which an absolute concordance between his inner and outer existence was indispensable. And mystical experience by living inward and through the fervour of devotion was, according to them, the only way by which that harmony could be discovered.

This as well as the Vaishnavic and the Tantrik cults had all of them their roots in the past. The Upanishadic origin of Vaishnavism and Tantrikism is now established beyond doubt, though there is an opinion that their genesis may be traced to even earlier dates. Through its intimate contact with the forces of life during the classical age the country became conscious of newer possibilities that were considered realisable by man if he could accept the whole of himself including his vital and sensuous natures as the field for his spiritual pursuits. And both of these cults restarted in the post-classical age with this refreshing and wider outlook.

Vaishnavism received a great impetus during the classical age, especially during the Gupta period when its main scriptures, the Bhagvata and the epics underwent a redaction into their present forms. Through these powerful literary influences the Vaishnavism of the North spread to the South where it took a more intellectual form but was equally, if not more, productive in the cultural life of the people which expressed itself amazingly in a vast literature and in the arts, particularly in the gorgeous massiveness of its architecture in which the creative soul poured out the whole of its wealth, all inspired by and articulating an outburst of bhakti,[17] so rapturously sung by the Alvar saints.

The heyday of Vaishnavism, however, is witnessed in the very life and teachings of Shri Chaitanya of Bengal. Here the aim was to sublimate the vital impulses of man through the intensity of devotion into an absolute adoration of the Divine. But it could not go beyond an inner psychic experience of the inner Divine, and whenever a great externalisation was attempted, we know what happened—vitalistic deterioration, corruption and eventual decay. Besides, an entirely spiritual integration was not possible in Vaishnavism in which man sought an eternal nearness to the Divine in his world of Light and not an absolute union with Him, which was a conception of later Vedanta. Nevertheless, it was the

17. Loving and devoted worship of God.

heart here that received the light and found its fruition; and the curve of India's adventure, though yet bound to the levels of the earth, had, it seems, begun to look towards heaven dreaming of the eternal Brindavan[18] and of its establishment in terrestrial life as the consummation of man's spiritual endeavour.

In a sense Tantrikism may be said to have made a nearer approach to the ideal towards which the soul of India has been moving throughout her history. It also is a remarkable flowering of the Indian spirit and another indication of the spiritual renaissance that was to have taken place as the crowning fruit of the creative efforts of India terminating with the classical age during which Tantrikism became another dominant cult, and many of its scriptures including the *Chandi,* the quintessence of Tantrik thought, were written in Bengal.

Tantrikism sought to raise the whole man into the divine perfection as envisaged in the Veda. Regarding life as the cosmic play of the Divine, it postulates a purpose in the play which is possible of fulfilment only in man, who alone of all creations has the unique privilege of awakening to the power of Consciousness latent in him as it is latent in everything else in the universe. Man is a microcosm in himself, having in him all the forces which in their action and interaction constitute the cosmic phenomenon. And when that potential power sleeping at the base of his physical system is roused, it proceeds upward through the centres or planes of the forces rendering them dynamic with its own power, so that they converge in all their new-found strength on the realisation by him of a state in which he possesses and becomes possessed by a higher consciousness.

This ascending urge in man represents his evolutionary possibility, the secret aspiration of his soul towards liberation into a greater life; and when stirred into activity by man becoming conscious of it and responding to its impulsion, it rises up and establishes a free contact between the lower and higher worlds, and passing through all the centres of the being sublimates, polarises and affiliates them to the Transcendent above. The sadhana here is more synthetic, but an absolute self-surrender to the Will of Mahamaya, the supreme Shakti,[19] is imperatively

---

18. The heaven of Beauty and Bliss where Shri Krishna is in eternal play with free souls.
19. Power of the Supreme.

necessary. Like the Upanishads the Tantras also aim at Transcendence, although their idea of Shakti has been generally understood to mean *Prakriti,* the Will-in-Power executive in the universe, who instead of being a Power of *Chit,* Consciousness or *Purusha,* is herself the controller of Purusha or Shiva. Thus, it is a cosmic force whose invocation by the seeker for ascent into higher states usually results in a widening of his consciousness, in the awakening in him of luminous powers, that are often the experiences in the intermediate stages, before the transcendent is reached in which Purusha and Prakriti become one in the supreme Brahman.

The Tantras aim not only at the liberation (*mukti*) into the Brahman but also at a liberated enjoyment of the delight (*ananda*) of the universal Play of the supreme Shakti. The Tantriks[20] started with life and tried to delve deeper into its secret so as to find its unity with the Spirit. They had the vision of the Light, but what they were able to bring down into life was not the creative light of the Consciousness-Force—the supreme dynamic source of harmony and perfection—but an aspect of it through the universal force of Nature, which illumined their being but did not, as indeed it could not, transform its parts. Hence their highest aim, except in rare instances, remained far from complete realisation. 'And in the end, as is the general tendency of Prakriti, Tantrik discipline lost its principle in its machinery and became a theme of formulae and occult mechanism still powerful when rightly used but fallen from the clarity of their original intention.' Nevertheless it is the most daring of spiritual experiments ever undertaken by mankind, and its practice produced a rich harvest of psychological experience of almost every part and plane of man's being, so much so that a conception of their integrality and wholeness was felt to be a necessity in the later spiritual endeavours of the race.

The spiritual mind of India derives not a little of its synthetic cast from the culture of the Tantras. Bengal, the earliest to take it up, developed it by going through every aspect of its discipline and achieved a success almost unique in her religious history. It contributed very largely to her remarkable creative activities in the realm of art and learning, which are witnessed more particularly in the Pala period when Mahayana Buddhism was prevailing in the country only as another name for Tantrikism. Throughout

---

20. Followers of the Tantras.

her history Bengal may be said to have been growing in her consciousness of Shakti, which is believed to be a chief source of inspiration of many of her fruitful cultural efforts. And it would not be entirely incorrect to say that even in modern times the cultural and religious movements in Bengal, many of them, have had distinctive elements of Tantrik idealism as their guiding motive. It is in them as well as in what was done before in the same direction that the meaning is to be sought of the tendencies of the race and of the possibilities of their fruition in the future.

In the days of the decline when everything seemed discouraging for a renewal of the country's destiny it was the Tantrik thought, no less than the practice of its cults, that kept alive the fire of the nation's soul, and when the opportune moment came we find it leaping up into a flaming aspiration towards the Light as seen by the ancient fathers. At this momentous period the curve of India's adventure, for the first time since it began, shows signs of an upward movement. It seems to have caught a very faint glimpse of the same kind of light as it had started from and gravitates towards its divine glory to describe a full circle.

Tantrikism, combining as it does different means and methods of man's inner striving, rekindled in the being of the race all its past seekings and helped to canalise them towards the fulfilment of its highest spiritual destiny. If it could not achieve its great aim in the long period of its influence and popularity for reasons already stated, it must at least be given the credit of having conduced in a great measure to the readiness of the country for the perfection that was to come to it in the future.

V

But the Tantras were not the only source from which the inspiration was drawn for the rebuilding of India in modern times. The earliest movement,[21] started in the last century, looked to Vedanta and, in the light of its teachings, affirmed its ideal, although its inaugurator, it may be noted, had in himself the Tantrik inclinations. This great soul was the first in modern India to turn his

---

21. This and the later movements have been more objectively dealt with in the last chapter of the author's book, *A Marvel of Cultural Fellowship.*

eyes, as also the eyes of his countrymen, from the glamour of foreign ideals that were then slavishly imitated, towards all that was truly glorious in their own past. That he and those who followed him did have a glimpse of the truth of the soul of India is testified to in the endeavours that were made one after another to repossess that truth, stripped of its old forms, and to rebuild on it her life and society. The keynote of their call was an insistence on the need of the race to awaken to its inherent spirituality and make that the very governing principle of all its activities. This urge was by itself the first sign, in modern times, of India returning to her own self and, therefore, preparing for a renewal of her destiny.

We find this renascent spirit defining itself in almost every form of the cultural and religious activity of the time in which the contribution of Vaishnavism also is not negligible. Its literature, art and poetry reflected this new idealism. The political endeavours, too, of the period were not a little inspired by it, by the vision of India the Mother, and their inner motive was always to rehabilitate her intrinsic, therefore spiritual, greatness which, they believed, was possible only in an atmosphere of freedom. It is true that an ascetic tendency is perceptible in the aim of the more recent of the religious movements, but a deeper insight into the lives and teachings of the two great personalities, associated with it, reveals that they represented the awakened soul of the race, that they were immeasurably higher than the work that stands in their names, and that everything they did envisaged a most stupendous work for the spiritual uplift of India and the world.

A child of the Mother, Shri Ramakrishna possessed 'a colossal spiritual capacity by which he mastered in an incredibly short time the truths, himself having practised them, of every religion and of every form of spiritual discipline, and drove straight to the divine realisation, taking, as it were, the kingdom of heaven by violence.' His was a finger of light that pointed India onward along the timeless path of the Spirit, by which only, as he and his great disciple insisted again and again, could she arrive at the goal assigned to her by the Dispenser of her destiny.

But Shri Ramakrishna's was an inner realisation of the inner Divine, and life was to him a necessary field for that. Indeed, life has no meaning if it cannot be an expression of the Spirit.

The truth of life, therefore, lies in the discovery by man of his own divinity. Shri Ramakrishna saw the oneness of the Divine and His Creative Force and called upon man to turn towards Her and live in Her. That is why Dakshineshwar[22] was the beginning of the Mother's work to which was given its first form by Vivekananda, that mighty apostle of resurgent India. It was here that the past spiritual experiences of the race were re-lived and the initial lines of their application chalked out, so that the country by following them might grow in readiness for the new age of the Spirit in the future when that work would be accomplished.

Among the immediate forces that brought about the awakening in modern India one was largely due to the impact upon her of Western pragmatism that urged her, first, to have a clear understanding of the problem and then to find out whatever help the people were yet capable of rendering towards its solution. Religion was certainly an important element in her greatness in the past. And it was then a thing of experience. But being tied to a fixed social system, it could not grow with time so as to be able to satisfy the growing spiritual aspirations of man, and what is worse, faded towards externalism which so dominated in the days of its decline that no enlarging of it or no revival of its true spirit seemed possible.

Religion in India, more than in any other country, tried to take hold of man's parts of life and draw them Godwards, and thereby to reconcile the spiritual Truth with the vital and material existence. But it could not keep to this high aim all through. Instead of making Earth subservient to Heaven, it had the opposite result of making Heaven a sanction for Earth's desires; for, generally the religious idea has been turned into an excuse for the worship and service of the human ego. Thus, cutting itself adrift from its central aim, religion everywhere has got lost in the obscure mass of its self-sanctioned compromises with life. It has even gone so far as to divide the higher expression of man, such as, knowledge, work, art and even life itself, into two opposite categories, spiritual and worldly, religious and mundane, sacred and profane, forgetting thereby the imperative need that is being felt today for a larger opening of the soul into the Light, an open-

---

22. The seat of Shri Ramakrishna's self-discipline and realisation.

ing through which the expanding mind, life and heart of man must be integrated into a harmonious whole where everything that is now condemned as profane will be turned into a divine substance and wear a divine complexion.

This failure of religion to be of any further use to man in his spiritual seeking is today sufficient ground for his not depending on it any longer, and for seeking the guidance elsewhere, in the very depth of his being. And as he grows in his quest, the truth becomes more and more clear to him that his life acquires its intrinsic meaning only when it finds its harmony with the Spirit, and it is in the Spirit alone that lies the secret of a spiritual dynamism that will take into itself everything that life covers and illumine it by the light of the Spirit. There is no gainsaying the fact that this is the dawn-fire of a new age for mankind, an age of subjectivism, whose promise in India was shown by the efforts that began to be made about the close of the last century, indicating that the race is yet capable of giving a good account of its old capacity for inward pursuits which brought to it this much-needed experience. But the far deeper meaning of it is that the integral ideal, the ideal for which India has stood through the ages, has been seen and possessed by the Master of the race who also shows the Path by which man will be led to realise that ideal both in his individual and in his collective life.

VI

What, then, is that vision? It is the vision of a dynamic divine truth which is descending upon the earth to create a new Truth Consciousness and by it to divinise life. The call of the Spirit was responded to in the past by jumping straight from the mind into the Absolute or the immutable Impersonal, regarding all dynamic existence as Ignorance, Illusion or Lila.[23] The fundamental error in it may be traced to the incompleteness of the vision which in the Vedanta was that of the pure Transcendence—a vision from which was derived the partial conception of the colourless Spirit, barren of the creative force of Sachchidananda, and which in the Tantras, was that of the cosmic aspect of the supreme Shakti

---

23. The ecstatic play of the Divine in creation.

effecting a modification of her light and power so that they might be received and assimilated by the inferior nature of mind, life and body.

But these were no solution of the problem. If complete spiritualisation of life is the aim, these instruments also must undergo a total conversion, and for that the plenary power and light of the Para-Prakriti, the Supernature, is necessary. Thus while the Vedantin took his flight up into the regions of the Absolute, the Tantrik brought down whatever he acquired in his ascent and used it to perfect his parts of nature, but the wholeness of the perfection did not come, because his realisation was not of the highest kind which alone could accomplish it. Yet in the Yoga of the Upanishads and to some extent in that of the Tantras, this ascension meant a definite widening of the entire consciousness, an enlarging of it into the higher reaches of truth, light and Ananda.[24] But what was not there was the integration, the unification of all into a whole.

The highest range of consciousness beyond mind, so far attained after the Upanishadic period, is the Overmind in which every power and aspect of the Divine Reality has its own independent push towards the utmost development of all its individual possibilities, so that a complete conception of them as integrally one in the indivisible all-comprehending Unity could not be had there. The splendour of its diffused light dazzled the seekers to such an extent that they took that to be the highest Light and so losing sight of the Oneness they were in quest of, swerved from the path and shot straight towards the sheer Spirit. They, therefore, realised the truth of the One but missed the truth of the Many. Tantrikism and Vaishnavism accepted the Many as the Lila of the Divine, but it was to them the cosmic play and not the manifestation of the one Reality.

The discovery of unity and harmony between these apparent irreconcilables has not therefore been practicable and has remained for ever an object of striving for man throughout his history. The Vedic seers had a glimpse of it, as also the early Upanishadic mystics, but in the later ages when intuition gradually gave way to reason, the vision dimmed, and whatever attempt was made by the mind proved unsuccessful. But the evolutionary Nature has

---

24. Spiritual delight.

all the time been active in preparing man for his ultimate destiny. In India who is to be the leader of human evolution, this work takes a definite form, and an outline of it, traced above, may indicate the inherent trend of her endeavours towards the goal. Her recognition of the sovereignty of the Spirit above everything else has given India much of what she needs for her growth towards the Light. But she needs more. Perfect knowledge or whole knowledge is not possible even in the Overmental consciousness. It has not that integrality which alone can explain creation, and not being in possession of the supreme Conscious-Force, it is beyond it to bring about the perfection of the earthly existence.

What, then, is the solution? Is spiritual perfection of the race always to remain a chimera, a dream? And approaches to it, if ever possible, to be limited to individuals only attaining to particular ranges of consciousness, and the divine destiny of man to continue to remain unrealised as ever? Sri Aurobindo says that there is a solution, and that conditions in life and nature are not only pointing to but also pressing for it. To him has come the vision of that dynamic Truth of Divine Reality, called by him the Supermind, whose descent into the earth-nature is as inevitable, he says, as was the descent of Mind and Life before it. And the ascent too of the earth into this new Power is equally a certainty. If the perfect unfolding of the Spirit is the ultimate fulfilment of man's manhood, then man the mental being, bound to the Ignorance and imperfection, cannot of course be the last term in the evolutionary endeavour of Nature.

Evolution, says Sri Aurobindo, presupposes a process of involution. The Spirit descended into Matter and created in it the urge towards a greater expression. And Life emerged, and then Mind. In man the urge becomes more insistent, taking the form of a definite aspiration for the spiritual living which only can liberate him from his bondage to the Ignorance and imperfection. But no readiness on his part can effect this change in him, though readiness is a basic condition for it. The Supermind alone can do it. The evolution of man into the Supermind, that is to say, into the Light and Truth of this creative power of the Divine would mean its coming down into the earth consciousness and becoming dynamic in it by quickening its own Force already involved in it, even as the powers of Life and Mind became active in the earth through their impact on their own principles involved in it. Evolution is not a mere ascent of a part of our being from one grade to a higher till the highest is reached, in which case the uplift of the whole being would never be possible. It is at once a sublimation and an integration of the whole being.

The spiritual growth of man stops short of its fundamental aim in that the higher light that his upward endeavour brings to him touches and sublimates that particular part of his being by which he makes that effort, as mind in the case of the Vedantin, heart in that of the Vaishnava, and the higher vital and the life-parts of nature in that of the Tantrik; but the *entire being* has never had the benefit of the light. Evolution, according to Sri Aurobindo, is not only an ascent but also a descent making for transformation and integration of the whole nature, and evolution into the highest plane would mean the change and uplift of all the lower stages. The integrating ascent to the Supermind would therefore bring about a total conversion of the *whole being*—the new Truth sending its light into the remotest corners of the being. 'This illumination and change will take up and recreate the whole being, mind, life and body; it will be not only an inner experience of the Divinity, but a remoulding of both the inner and outer existence by its power.' Not only this, but 'it will take form not only in the life of the individual but as a collective life of the gnostic beings established as a highest power and form of the becoming of the Spirit in the earth nature.'

This is the integral vision towards the realisation of which in the life of the race India is to lead mankind, and discharge thereby the mission assigned to her by God. Every endeavour in the past was a preparation for it; and the time has now come for her to reveal this truth to humanity and show the way by which it can be realised. And when this integral evolution is accomplished in the life of man, divinised and new-created by the dynamics of this new Light from heaven, all the highest aspirations of the race, its deepest strivings towards perfection will have been fulfilled; all its golden dreams of the kingdom of God on earth, its sublimest visions of the intrinsic divinity of man will have become a living reality. And the curve of India's adventure becomes the glory of a complete circle, an effulgnt orb radiating the fires of a greater dawn than was glimpsed by the Vedic mystics; for, the Master of the race has seen the Light of the Supermind, seen it in all its vastness, in all its supernal splendours, felt its invincible powers of transformation and of a new creation. Thus is India going to deliver her message—the highest ever possible—for the liberation of the human race, and fulfil thereby the purpose of God in the evolution of terrestrial existence. And the Seer today is also the Leader of the Way. The call therefore goes forth from him re-echoing the ancient *rik*:

'Arise, O Souls arise! Strength has come,
Darkness has passed away—the Light is arriving!'

A full idea of the Supermind and of the consequences of its working in the earth consciousness is not possible mentally to have, far less to express. And for whatever of it is available it is better that one should in the right spirit of seeking go to the Master himself who has given to it a magnificent expression in his *magnum opus, The Life Divine.*

The Supermind is a link between Sachchidananda and the lower hemisphere of creation. A creative consciousness with Unity as its constant basis, it creates, governs and upholds the worlds; and being the nature of Sachchidananda itself, it creates nothing which is not in its own existence. Its truth is inherent in all cosmic force and manifestation. In it the Light is one with the Force; and being, consciousness and will are the three indivisible and harmonious aspects of a single movement. 'To its self-awareness the whole existence is an equable extension, one in oneness and in multiplicity, one in all conditions and everywhere. Here the All and the One are the same existence; the individual being does not and cannot lose the consciousness of its identity with all beings and with the One Being; for that identity is inherent in supramental cognition, a part of the supramental self-evidence.' The truth of Transcendence and the truth of Manifestation are one in it, and therefore also the truths of the Spirit, Life and Matter.

In the supermind there existed the true principles of eternal harmony; and when man is in possession of its Gnosis he will discover that harmony and find in it the permanent solution of all his problems. From his present subjection to the obscure workings of the Ignorance in nature he will then be liberated into the freedom of the Spirit, into the infinite light of the supreme knowledge. He will then live, move and have his being always in the supramental consciousness of the self-existent Truth, of its dynamic and creative power, the Conscious Force, which is the Para-Prakriti, the Supernature, of whose Will his life will be a perfect manifestation, of whose heavenly splendour the whole terrestrial existence will be a luminous revelation.

It is to this Mahashakti, the Divine Mother, that man must open, and consecrate himself wholly and entirely, so that by her Grace he might be made ready for the descent into him of her new Light from above; for the Supermind is her Light, her Force. 'This supramental change is a thing decreed and inevitable in the evolution of the earth consciousness; for its upward ascent is not ended and mind is not its last summit. But that the change may arrive, take form and endure, there is needed the call from below with a will to recognise and not deny the Light when it comes, and there is needed the sanction of the Supreme from above. The power that mediates between the sanction and the call is the presence and power of the Divine Mother. The Mother's power and not any human endeavour and *tapasya* can alone rend the lid and tear the coverings and shape the vessel and bring down into this world of obscurity and falsehood and death and suffering Truth and Light and Life Divine and the immortal's Ananda.'

REFERENCES
For the philosophical and psychological basis of this essay the following books of Sri Aurobindo have been consulted:

Essays on the Gita, Isha Upanishad, Kalidasa, The Ideal of the Karmayogin, The Life Divine, The Mother, The Renaissance in India, The Riddle of This World, The Foundations of Indian Culture, On the Veda, The Synthesis of Yoga. The quotations are all of them from the above books.

For the historical basis the standard works on Indian history and culture by the following authors have been consulted: Ananda Coomaraswamy, K. P. Jayaswal, R. C. Majumdar, R. K. Mookerjee, Sister Nivedita and Vincent Smith.

2

India is One[1]

I

THE LURE of fertile land was the cause of the earliest corporate life of man. The first human unification was effected by *place* from which has developed the idea of a common homeland and through that, in due course, a common nationality. It is the bounties of nature that attracted groups of humanity to settle in river valleys and organise collective existence by taking to agriculture, and gradually to other arts of life that laid the foundation of human civilisation. There is much truth in the idea that a race too, especially in its origin, is the creation of a place which is nurtured by nature into a geographical distinctness. In the chemistry of human intermingling which began with the migration of races, the original types were lost and new ethnic forms were evolved out of the process of admixture which is unceasingly going on in the common life of humanity in more and more subtle ways through the dynamic of social intercourse. It is, therefore, the land, more than the race origins, which binds man to itself and becomes his common object of attachment and adoration. The land where we are born and brought up and which was also the birth-land of our forbears is one of those contributory forces that shape our destiny, the destiny of the nation.

The land is thus the basis on which the growth of a collectivity and also of its culture and institutions depends so much.

---

1. India here is the India of the ages and not the poiltical India of the present day.

If the many races that may happen to people it fail for any reason to realise their unity and solidarity, if even their religions and languages are unable to foster it among them—though religion in India, called the *Sanatana Dharma,* the eternal religion, has throughout the ages been a synthesising factor in the community life of the people—the geographical integrity of the country by itself may and does sometimes help them to grow into a sense of unity, founded in the most vivid fact of their being born in and mothered by a common homeland.

The land of India is endowed by Providence with various features that distinguish her in many ways. This ancient land has its own meaning and mission, its own glory and grandeur, its own distinctive character and interest and culture. Its unity is determined by its definite frontiers, the Himalayas on the north, the Hindukush on the north-west, the seas on the east and west. And this unity has developed into a national consciousness permeating the mind and heart of the people whose love of the land of their birth has been an indissoluble cementing bond of a singularly religio-cultural nature. It is a kind of love which is a sacrament, a worship, and which no language can properly define. It has been growing from within not merely as a patriotic impulse but as an abiding religious feeling, as an almost mystic perception. Indeed the awe and admiration the people feel for the snow-swathed summits of the Himalayas, the menacing hills of the frontiers, the laughing valleys of Kashmere, the rolling downs of the Deccan, the surge and thunder of the seas, the limpid flow of the great rivers of the country, is the proof and measure of its inspiring and formative influence. Says Sri Aurobindo: 'The feeling of almost physical delight in the touch of the mother-soil, of the winds that blow from the Indian seas, of the rivers that stream from Indian hills, in the hearing of Indian speech, music, poetry, in the familiar sights, sounds, habits, dress, manners of Indian life, this is the physical root of that love.'

It is through this appreciation of the romance that India outwardly is that we begin to feel within us a kind of inner relationship not only with her material embodiment but also with her soul; and as this feeling deepens the mere external fact vanishes, and there emerges before our mind's eye, no less vividly, an idea, a dynamic concept, of which the land becomes a symbol, an image, an object as it were, of our love and veneration. Nothing indeed

can more unfailingly develop in us an abiding sense of our fellowship with others, with all, belonging to a common land of birth
than when we are blessed with this exalting experience. And does
not this sense invariably prove real enough as a wholesome and
strengthening factor in our collective life? In fact, it is the very
bedrock of it. The physical loses itself in the ideal, and the ideal
fulfils itself in the real, reconciling the apparent contradictions
into a harmony, a oneness that is built out of the manifoldness of
our country's human and geographical elements. It is a force,
an energy inherent in its soil and pervading in space, that works
this transforming miracle. India is that Force, that spirit which
makes its mystic appeal to the inmost being of her children.
According to the Tantrik conception, the fifty-two sacred centres
of Shakti-worship in India, covering the entire length and breadth
of the country, from Jalamukhi in the Himalayas in the north
to Cape Comorin in the south, from Hinglaj in the west to
Kamrup in Assam in the east, embody and symbolise the fifty-
two aspects of the divine Shakti and represent in the experience
of the Tantrik mystics the integrality of India as the Mother of
the world. Sri Aurobindo once said that India had never been
to him what was merely suggested by her outer vesture, attractive
and gorgeous though they are. She is to him the Mother, the
eternal and infinite Mother, the compassionate Mother of man.
The truth of India is revealed to those who respond to this
appeal and thereby know the secret, the supreme secret of her
motherhood. To this vision of the Mother does the land of India
call her children, whatever their caste, creed or race.

It is interesting to trace the evidences so far available of how
this idea of the oneness of land, all the more defined by its incomparable greatness and magnificence, became a cohesive force in
the evolution of India's culture, whose unity—the land playing its
role in it also—is so unmistakably articulate in her art, literature,
religion and in all her splendid institutions that came into being
as a result of her millenniums of creative striving.

The land-mass that is called India has always been regarded
as one with the human mass that inhabits it, this fusion being effected in the consciousness of the people through its inherent spiritual outlook to which everything is a manifestation of the Spirit.
If the Indian sees God in himself, he sees Him also in others and
even in the phenomenal universe around him. No wonder there-

fore that the land in which he is born should acquire in his conception an inward character, a profound significance compelling
his highest love and admiration. But the land-mass of India is not
an isolated formation. It is a part, however sharply separated, of
a vaster region with which it has always in the past kept up intimate friendly relations. Besides, being bound up with her sister
countries in Asia in a common love of mysticism and spiritual
pursuits, India has had from very early times deep and extensive
cultural intercourse also with almost all of them.

The influence of the pre-Buddhist India on various parts of
Asia and Europe apart, the Buddhist and Hindu communities in
pre-Christian Asia Minor and the Indian missionaries in China
and Japan in the early days of their history represent two extre-
mities of that vast tract of land which together with most of the
south-west Asia and the Islands of the Indian Archipelago does
even today bear witness to the immensity of their indebtedness
to India for much of what forms the texture of their religious and
cultural life. Nevertheless, if India is a living embodiment of the
Spirit, Asia is no less so: and India from that standpoint is an
organic part of it. Though a soul by herself, she in her heart is
as much one with Asia as in her physical setting. And it is not
for nothing that she is called the heart of the Orient. In the
words of Okakura Kakuzo, 'Asia is one. The Himalayas divide,
only to accentuate, two mighty civilisations, the Chinese with its
communism of Confucius, and the Indian with its individualism
of the Vedas. But not even the snowy barriers can interrupt for
one moment the broad expanse of love for the Infinite and Universal, which is the common thought-inheritance of every Asiatic
race, enabling them to produce all the great religions of the world,
and distinguishing them from the maritime peoples of the
Mediterranean and the Baltic, who love to dwell on the Particular, and to search out the means, not the end, of life.'

India, this great country of ours, stands with the parent continent as her grand background. Provided with natural protection
she has lived through the ages to fulfil the mission assigned to
her by the Dispenser of her destiny. Vanished are the splendours
that went by the names of Egypt, Babylon and Greece! The empires that flourished in Europe exist today only in the records
of history. But from times immemorial India has been developing herself not in isolation, as the charge is unjustly made against

her, but in love and friendship with her neighbours, and with everyone who comes to her, be he a foreigner or even an enemy. Yet she has a personality all her own, an individuality, that marks her out as something that has no equal in the annals of the earth.

The geological movement leading to the creation of land in which early human civilisation began in India was the retreat westward of the extensive Euro-Asiatic Ocean called the *Tethys* giving rise to the plains of northern India through a process of formation which must have taken ages. The fertility of this region is due to many factors among which may be mentioned the life-giving waters of a river system that was formed by the linear depressions which remained after the large-scale geological movement was over. The deposits washed down from the northern highlands added no less to the richness of the soil. On these plains, along the banks of the Indus, right down eastward along the banks of the Ganges, streams of humanity flowed in unison with the waters, as it were, and spread out into the interiors till the scene was complete with the drama of the early human migration in India.

The geographical unity of India is indisputable, in spite of the bewildering variety of her physical features; and equally so is the unity of her vast humanity. The uniqueness of her culture is ascribed by some writers to this unity as well as to her natural separation from the rest of the world. It is the conviction of the Hindus that there is an inner meaning behind her physical formation as also a spiritual purpose of her existence as a conscious embodiment of the Shakti that is India. The vision, not once but many times in her history, came to the fathers of the race that India is verily the Mother who has stood through the ages entrusted with the task of 'preserving the Knowledge that preserves the world till Krishna comes back to repossess the Kingdom that is his.' To the Hindus the mother and motherland are greater than heaven itself. Whatever it is, it is clear enough that this vast country, almost a continent, is indivisibly one in the fundamental principle of its individuality which has been developed by the movements racial, social and cultural that have been taking place in India from times prehistoric.

It is not even two decades when the view was held that the story of human culture in India began with the Indo-Aryans. But the excavations in Mohenjo-daro and Harappa have not only pushed back the date by more than a millennium but also revealed evidences of a civilisation superior to many then existing in the world. It is of course the valley of the Indus which was the scene of this great event, proving the remarkable antiquity of Indian culture and the glorious role India played in the early history of human civilisation. The inhabitants who peopled those prosperous cities represent four different ethnic types. It seems racial intermingling began in India even in those days when peoples of various stocks, whether original settlers or emigrants from outside, shared a common land as their home and built a civilisation that was then and is even now a marvel of human creation. The gates of India from west to east were always open; the routes by the sea were so easy; and the inland rivers were mostly navigable. All these offered easy passages for human immigration into India from days unknown to history. The physical types that constitute the present population of India are evolved from the three principal ethnic groups through the continuous process of racial intermingling. The foreign elements absorbed by her are broadly distinguished as Greek, Iranian, Mongolian, Scythian, Hun, Semitic and some even of what constitutes the modern European. All these elements India has assimilated to her being, giving them the stamp of a common nationality. Was it not some magical power of the land that effected this miracle of human unification? And are not always associated with India the beauty that she is, her inexhaustible resources, and a culture that in the past was, and even today is, her greatest contribution to the happiness and progress of mankind?

'This admixture of races,' says C. E. Joad, 'has had important effects on India's past history and present outlook. The first of these is a sense of fundamental unity far more vivid and persistent than can be accounted for by the circumstance of propinquity in the same geographical area. Europeans live together in a geographical area whose size is not very different from that of India. But as the wars which have disgraced European history in the past and the quarrels and rivalries that enfeeble the League of Nations in the present only too clearly show that the inhabitants of Europe are very far from being imbued with the sense of unity which distinguishes the inhabitants of India. We cannot, in short, speak of a "European" with the same appropriateness as we can speak of an "Indian", who, in spite of differences of colour, caste and creed, looks upon all other Indians as his fellow-countrymen and upon India as his home.'

II

The Vedic Aryans were yet in the midst of their victorious campaigns for aryanising the whole of India and bring it under the unifying discipline of a common culture and civilisation when rose the great king Bharata who, as mentioned in the Rig Veda, extended the Aryan supremacy over a vast territory and consolidated different parts of the country into an organic entity knit together by the dynamic influence of the Aryan ideals. It is from him that India derives her ancient name *Bharatavarsha*, just as Rome derives her name from Romulus. To these Aryans came the earliest vision of the oneness of India and they expressed it in the river-hymns of the Rig Veda. Even today the Hindus chant these hymns and recall and worship the image of their mother-country as the land of seven rivers which embrace the whole of India. There is another prayer which conjures up the picture of India as the land of seven sacred cities representing the important regions in the north and the south. There are besides a number of religious practices prevalent among the Hindus from very early times which as well as the prayers, mentioned above, indicate that the religious mind of the Hindus is deeply imbued with a conception of the integrity of India whose sacredness is enhanced by the influence it exerts in shaping the common destiny of the country as visualised by the ancient seers. Pilgrimage also is another sacred institution, most popular among the Hindus, which accentuates this notion and gives it a still more definite shape. Every principal faith or sect of the Hindus has its holy places spread over the length and breadth of the country, Pious Hindus visit these places and meet their fellow pilgrims and feel a sense of comradeship with them fostered by their allegience to the common ideals that are the ideals of their common motherland. Religious fairs contribute no less to the development of this sense in the Hindu mind.

If it is the land of India that has reared up her body of humanity and impressed on it the stamp of its own unity, it is her culture, evolved out of the vision of her seers, which has given the soul of that body its meaning and intention. What that culture is has been discussed by Sri Aurobindo in a series of luminous essays called *A Defence of Indian Culture*,[2] published in the *Arya* from which we shall quote appropriate extracts to show how the life of the Hindus is essentially one in all its varied creative endeavours.

Spirituality, says Sri Aurobindo, is the master-key of the Indian mind. It is this dominant inclination of India which gives character to all the expressions of her culture. In fact, they have grown out of her inborn spiritual tendency of which her religion is a natural outflowering. The truth of the unity of her various religious efforts as well as their synthetic sublimity has been revealed by Sri Aurobindo in the following words: 'The Indian mind has always realised that the Supreme is the Infinite and perceived that to the soul in Nature the Infinite must always present itself in an infinite variety of aspects. The aggressive and quite illogical idea of a single religion for all mankind, a religion universal by the very force of its narrowness, one set of dogmas, one cult, one system of ceremonies, one ecclesiastical ordinance, one array of prohibitions and injunctions which all minds must accept on peril of persecution by men and spiritual rejection or eternal punishment by God, that grotesque creation of human unreason which has been the parent of so much intolerance, cruelty and obscurantism and aggressive fanaticism, has never been able to take firm hold of the Indian mentality. Men everywhere have common human failings; intolerance and narrowness especially in the matter of observances there have been and are in India, violence of theological disputation, querulous bickerings of sects and their pretensions of spiritual superiority sometimes; at one time especially in southern India in a period of acute religious differences, even local outbreaks of active mutual tyranny and cruelty. But these things have never taken the proportions which they assumed in Europe; they have been confined for the most part to the minor forms of polemical attack, intolerance and social obstruction or ostracism and have transgressed very little across the line to the major forms of persecution. Behind these weaknesses of human egoism there has stood always in India the

---

2. Reprinted in book form under the title *The Foundations of Indian Culture*.

saving perception of the higher spiritual mind, which has had its effect on the mass mentality, the living perception that since the minds, the temperaments, the intellectual affinities of men are unlimited in their variety, a perfect liberty of thought and of worship must be allowed to the individual in his approach to the Infinite.... The fundamental idea of Indian religion, the recognition of a one and finite Godhead who can be approached and worshipped through any of his infinite aspects, a supreme and supracosmic Existence which manifests itself in the cosmos and enters into multitudinous relations with the souls in the universe who are one with or part of its own being, gives a many-sided appearance to Indian cult and spiritual experience.... When the Indian mind sees the One without a second, it still admits his duality of Spirit and Nature, his many trinities, his million aspects. When it concentrates on a single limiting aspect of the Divinity and seems to see nothing beyond it, it has still at the back of its consciousness the sense of the All, the idea of the One. When it distributes its worship among many objects, it looks beyond the multitude of godheads to their unity. This synthetic turn is not peculiar to the mystics or the literate or the thinkers nourished on the high sublimities of the Veda and Vedanta, but permeates even the popular mind which is filled with the thoughts, the images, the traditions, the cultural symbols of the Purana and Tantra; for the Puranic and Tantrik ideas, names, forms and symbols are only concrete representations of the combined monism, unitarianism, universalism and synthetism of the Vedic scriptures.... To understand the effect of Indian spiritual culture on the life of the individual and the community, we must recognise its synthetical character and embracing unity. The One Existence, to whom sages give different names, of the Upanishads is the fundamental seeing of Indian spirituality. All comes from, exists in, returns and amounts to that One. To discover, closely approach, enter into whatever unity with this Infinite, this Eternal, is the height of spiritual experience. This is the first idea of the religious mind of India. The second idea is the manifold way of man's approach to the Eternal and Infinite. This infinite is full of many infinities and each of these infinite aspects is the Eternal in his glory. In the limitations of the cosmos God manifests himself to man and fulfils himself in the world in many ways, but each is the way of the Eternal; in each finite we can discover and through all things approach the Infinite. All cosmic powers and manifestations are of the One and behind the workings of Nature are to be seen and adored powers, names, personalities which are the godheads of the one Godhead. The divine Will and Energy are behind all happenings, whether to us fortunate or adverse, and over each way of the universal dealings stands a form of the presiding Deity. He creates and is Brahma, preserves and is Vishnu, destroys or takes to himself and is Rudra or Shiva. His supreme Energy is beneficent in upholding and protection and is the Mother of the worlds, Lakshmi or Durga, or beneficent even in the mask of destruction and is Chandi or Kali, the dark Mother. He manifests himself in form of his qualities; the God of divine love of the Vaishnava, the God of divine power of the Shakta appear as two different godheads but are the one Deity. These things we try to explain now as symbols, which is by the way of an intellectual compromise with modern rationalism; but the Indian religious mentality saw them not only as symbols but as realities, because between the highest spiritual being and material being it is aware of other psychological planes of consciousness and experience and these things are truths of these planes no less real than the outward truths of material universe. Man approaches God at first according to his psychological nature, experience, capacity for this deeper experience, *swabhava, adhikara,* whence comes the variety of religious cult, belief and way of divine union. But also there is a third idea of the strongest consequence, that not only through aspects of the universal spirit and all inner and outer Nature can the Divine be approached but each individual object and being is in its spiritual being intimately one with the one divine Existence. In each individual man is the divinity, Narayana; all corporate or collective being is a form of the divine Narayana. God is in ourselves and in ourselves we have to find him. The supreme truth of all divisions is a secret unity. These three ideas govern the Indian religious mind and the seeing of them is its whole seeing. Indian spiritual culture opens up a hundred ways to arrive at the truth of our religious being, but its consummation is to see God in man and man in God, God in Nature and Nature in God, God in all things and all things in God, and to go beyond them to their origin in the supracosmic Absolute, Eternal and Infinite.'

The words quoted above unravel the hidden meaning of the religious culture of the Hindus and its essential oneness. They explain why one Hindu is a worshipper of Shiva, another of Krishna and the third of Shakti; why it is that there is a multiplicity of gods and goddesses; and yet how all of them are bound by the golden thread of the same soul's aspiration towards the self-same spiritual perfection which to them has always been the ultimate end of human existence.

In ancient India knowledge was transmitted by the oral method. Like the *raconteurs* of ancient Greece who preserved and disseminated the *Iliad* and the *Odyssey,* India also had her reciters and declaimers who carried down from generation to generation and from court to people the great epics, the *Ramayana* and the *Mahabharata.* It was these national minstrels who used to wander about the country, singing the story of the epics and thereby imparting the best popular education to the people. The epics abound in noble examples of sages and saints and kings—men who were the makers of empires and builders of societies—in ideals of human conduct that exalt and inspire, religious and social teachings that guide and give shape; all these have always been the most profound influence in the life of the race forging it, as it were, into a unity of endeavour to live up to the lessons that the characters in the epics so powerfully inculcate. Even today in remote villages in every part of India the epics, whether in Sanskrit or in vernacular versions, are recited by the *kathakas*[3] before gatherings specially organised for the purpose. The art and literature of the Hindus are not a little indebted to these epics for the themes they have always drawn from these almost inexhaustible fountains of sociological knowledge. The *Mahabharata* represents the whole history of the race in one of its most glorious periods. Its authorship goes by the name of a great poet, but it has in it contributions from many sources. A great people speaks through it. Its very name suggests the greatness of India's unity. Says Sri Aurobindo: 'The *Mahabharata* is not only the story of the Bharatas, the epic of an early event which had become a national tradition but on a vast scale the epic of the soul and religious and ethical mind and social and political ideas and culture and life of India. It is said popularly

---

3. Reciters.

of it and with a certain measure of truth that whatever is in India is in the *Mahabharata*. The *Mahabharata* is the creation and expression not of a single individual mind, but of the mind of a nation; it is the poem of itself written by a whole people.' 'The foreign reader of this great epic of India,' wrote Sister Nivedita, 'is at once struck by its two features, in the first place its unity in complexity, and in the second place its constant effort to impress on its hearers the idea of a single centralised India, with a heroic tradition of her own as formative and uniting impulse. Nationhood had crystalised in India long before the birth of Christ.'

To whatever sect he may belong, no Hindu can conceive of spiritual life without its never-failing source of inspiration, the Gita. In the thought of every school of spiritual idealism can be traced the influence of this great scripture. It presents the first synthesis of Hindu thought, and in it lies the secret of a yet greater synthesis of which a revealing exposition has been given by Sri Aurobindo in his *Essays on the Gita*. The Gita moreover contains the very key-word of unity. To see God is not the only ideal set forth in it: to see Him in all and all in Him is the true truth about the oneness of all creation. The influence on the mind of the Hindus all over India of the vast range of literature, both sacred and secular, is no less a unifying factor in the community life of the people.

The earliest evidence of some kind of synthesis in the religious life of India is supplied by the seals of the proto-Indian civilisation of the Indus valley which along with other antiquities of similar nature are believed to indicate a common religious life of the people about whom a more remarkable fact is that they were free from the fear of violence and war, as shown by the absence of war weapons, walls, ramparts or fortifications among the relics that have been so far unearthed of those oldest cities of India. Gerald Heard is of the opinion that this is most likely the earliest form of pacifism in the world.

The influence of the Vedas in shaping the religious life of the Hindus requires no recapitulation. Says Sri Aurobindo: 'The mind of ancient India did not err when it traced back all its philosophy, religion and essential things of its culture to the seer-poets of the Vedas, for all the future spirituality of her people is contained there in seed or in first expression.' There are many hymns in the Rig and the Atharva Vedas which emphasise in a

more subjective sense the need and importance of unity in the
community life. They fervently exhort man to be united with all,
in heart, in aim and in work, to be friendly with all and to pray
so that all may be friendly with him. In the Upanishads the call
goes forth from the Rishis to the whole of mankind to come and
share with them the delight of their spiritual visions. The Upanishads permeate the entire range of Indian thought. They are
also the common source of inspiration to all schools of Indian
mysticism. In a word, Vedanta, as the Upanishads are called, represents the highest spiritual idealism of ancient India. Says Sri
Aurobindo: 'The Upanishads have been the acknowledged source
of numerous profound philosophies and religions that flowed
from it in India like her great rivers from their Himalayan cradle
fertilising the mind and life of the people and kept its soul alive
through the long procession of the centuries, constantly returned
to for light, never failing to give fresh illumination, a fountain
of inexhaustible life-giving waters. Buddhism with all its developments was only a restatement, although from a new standpoint
and with fresh terms of intellectual definition and reasoning, of
one side of its experience and it carried it thus changed in form
but hardly in substance over all Asia and westward towards
Europe.'

The social institutions of the Hindus contributed no less towards strengthening the bonds of social and cultural unity among
the different classes of the people. The essential idea in all their
social thinking is that man is not a machine but a god in the
making born to blossom forth to the best of his potentialities; and
the chief function of the society is to give him every facility so
that he might fulfil his higest destiny both in his individual
and collective life. Says Sri Aurobindo: 'The business of culture
and social organisation in ancient India was to lead man, satisfy
and support him in some harmony of the four aims of life; desire
and enjoyment, material, economic and other aims of the mind
and body, ethical conduct and right law of the individual and
social life and finally spiritual liberation, *kama, artha, dharma,
moksha.* The insistence was always there that except in rare
cases the full satisfaction of the first three of these objects must
precede the last, fullness of human experience and action prepare
for the spiritual liberation; the debt to the family, the community
and the gods could not be scamped.' By fulfilling the first two

of these aims man enriches his mental and physical being, by the third he serves the community, and by the fourth he attains the highest objective of life. But the institution of caste was a more potent force in consolidating the social basis of the Hindu culture. The four grades of culture implicit in the system were integrated into an important factor in the progress of Indian civilisation in the past. The modern idea of a classless society negates the fundamental nature of the human being which generally was divided into the four categories evolved by the psychologists of ancient India. 'The real greatness of the Indian system of the four *varnas*,[1] says Sri Aurobindo, 'did not lie in its well-ordered division; it consisted in the ethical and spiritual contents which the thinkers and builders of the society poured into these forms. They started with the idea of the intellectual, ethical and spiritual growth of the individual as the principal need of humanity, society as its necessary framework and its system of relations. A secure place had to be found for him in the community from which he could serve these relations, maintain and pay all his debt to the society and proceed to his self-development with the best possible help from the communal life. This place they conceived as one provided for him by the indications of his capacity, temperament and nature. Birth was taken in practice as the first test; the heredity was of a high importance; it was taken even in later thought as a sign of the nature and the needed surroundings which the individual had prepared for himself by his past soul-development in former existences. But birth was not considered as the sole test of *varna*. The intellectual capacity, the turn of the temperament, the ethical nature, the spiritual elevation were the important things.' There are many instances of Kshatriya kings excelling in spiritual knowledge. Many of the Upanishads were written by them. Vishvamitra's attaining Brahminhood is not certainly a solitary instance.

A society thrives on the intrinsic worth of its members. And the members can prove their worth only when they are given freedom to grow to the summit of their possibilities. This livingness of social organism is sought to be replaced today by deadening mechanical means with the object of moulding human nature into a single Procrustean type; and to achieve that end, freedom is tabooed lest free-thinking should create conflict, and obedience

4. Castes.

is exacted by forcing man into an artificial existence so that he might conform to the law of the machine. It ought to be clear to those who advocate these views that those who are deprived of their freedom are thereby helped to gather strength to assert their birthright when the time comes for them to rise.

Ancient Indians recognised that true social harmony is possible only when every member in the society has ample opportunities of self-development. The system of caste which was always elastic and flexible was guided by this attitude of the Hindu mind. It is not birth but, as the Gita says, his action and spiritual attainment that determine man's position in society to which every member of any caste, be he a Brahmin or a Shudra, is equally important. It is real worth that matters. In the ancient literature of the Hindus there are examples of great saints and sages born of low and unknown parentage. Even young men of doubtful antecedents were admitted to instruction by great sages simply on the ground of their personal nobility and earnest seeking for knowledge. Satyakama's cannot certainly be a solitary example. The strength and cohesion of the Hindu society lay in this catholic outlook which largely prevented division of the people into hostile factions, as well as any series of internecine wars, which have disgraced many countries. With the advent of foreigners into India, the process of racial chemistry began to be active again and in the first few centuries of the present era we find that the Hunas, Shakas and Pallavas were being absorbed into the Hindu social structure; and for their valour and devotion to Aryan ideals they were accepted by the Brahmins as Kshatriyas and given equal status in the society. Caste did not stand in the way of this notable racial assimilation, but helped it by recognising the intrinsic individual merits of those peoples and their readiness to be naturalised as Indians. In the days of India's decline, the system was exploited by interested people for the satisfaction of their selfish ends and for dominating the society whose downfall they brought about by pursuing a policy of suicidal segmentation and mutual exclusion.

III

The centres of learning in ancient India also made their contribution to the building of the one cultural life of the people. The hermitages of well-known sages were the earliest universities of India where students from far and near used to gather for instruction in various subjects. The *Mahabharata* abounds in descriptions of these hermitages in the Naimisha forest of which the presiding personality was Shaunaka who was honoured with the title of *kulapati,* sometimes defined as the preceptor of ten thousand disciples. There were conferences convened by great kings where representative thinkers were invited to meet and exchange their views. During the sessions of sacrifice the courts and palaces of kings were also the scenes of congregations of learned men who would enter into deliberations over the deepest problems of philosophy in which women also took part. In the age of Buddhism, monasteries were the strongholds and distributing centres of Buddhist culture, which enabled it to maintain its hold upon the country and helped to spread it evenly among the different parts thereof. We may mention the four famous special Buddhist Convocations and many other regular and ordinary ones where religious and philosophical problems were discussed and important decisions taken. In his travels from the north-west across the Punjab along the Jumna-Ganges valley down to Tamluk in Bengal, Fa-Hien in the fifth century noticed almost numberless monasteries full of monks belonging to either of the great Paths of Buddhism. There were no rigid rules for admission to many of these monasteries which accommodated monks of different schools. When Hiuen Tsang visited India in the seventh century there were about five thousand monasteries with a population of more than two hundred thousand monks. The well-known universities of this period, developed out of these monasteries, were Nalanda, Odantapuri and Vikramashila; Taxila, Varanasi, Ujjayini and Amaravati being others which from the beginning flourished as universities even before the former ones.

Taxila, the most ancient known university town in India, was famous as the principal seat of Hindu learning in northern India. In its different schools were taught the Vedas and as many as eighteen other subjects including arts, sciences and a special course in medicine. It attracted students from all over India and across the border. Afghanistan and Central Asia were represented on its rolls as well as Greece and Asia Minor. The Greek Heliodoros and the philosopher Apollonius of Tyana were certainly not solitary instances. In India it was the fashion in those days to send princes and sons of nobles and well-to-do Brahmins to complete their education at Taxila. It was considered an honour and distinction to be a graduate of this University. Panini, the great grammarian of the fifth century B.C., and Jivaka, the court physician of Bimbisara and Ajatashatru, are said to have studied here. Originally a centre of Brahminical culture, Taxila became in later times a seat of Buddhist learning. Its glory however remained undimmed for nearly a thousand years during which it built up a tradition of creative scholarship that was an inspiration to various institutions in India, helping thereby to strengthen the cultural unity of the country.

Varanasi has always been a culture-centre of all-India fame and even in the Buddha's day it was already old. Though not a formal university, it is a place, unique in India, which has throughout the ages provided the most suitable atmosphere for the pursuit of higher studies. The method of instruction as also the curriculum followed there in early times was adopted from Taxila. Varanasi is the only city in India which has in it schools representing every branch of Hindu thought. And there is no spiritual path which has not its centre in Varanasi with resident adherents. Every religious sect of the Hindus has its pilgrimage there. In ancient days Sarnath figured as a recognised seat of Buddhist learning. Rightly, therefore, is this holy city called the very heart of spiritual India.

The most notable of the ancient centres of learning in the North was the international University of Nalanda in Magadha, the largest of its kind in the contemporary world, to which scholars of different castes, creeds and races hailing not only from the farthest ends of India such as Kashmir, Peshawar, Conjeevaram, and Samatata (south-east Bengal) but also from countries far beyond—from China, Japan, Korea, Java, Sumatra, Tibet, Mongolia, and Bokhara—flocked for purposes of advanced studies in the various branches of knowledge as embodied in the culture, both Brahminical and Buddhistic. The Pala kings of Bengal were among its best patrons. Of the 10,000 residents in the University, 8,500 were alumni, and 1,510 were faculty members. Nalanda was famous for the wide catholicity of its method, for the liberal character of its curriculum. Through discussion and debate and conference according to the traditional Indian method it helped to unite its varied elements into a superb intellectual fellowship, and the wide variety of subjects taught provided a veritable feast of reason. The curriculum included all the systems of thought, then prevalent in the country, in spite of the fact that Nalanda was a Mahayanist centre. The Vedas, the Upanishads, the works of different philosophical systems, like Samkhya, Vaisheshika, Nyaya, were studied and taught as also the arts and sciences of the Hindus. The various schools of Buddhism were represented by their reputed exponents and earnest learners. The famous Chinese pilgrim Hiuen Tsang came here to study the Yoga philosophy with the eminent Bengali scholar Shilabhadra who was then its Chancellor. People belonging to almost all the sects and creeds of the time shared a common cultural life in Nalanda, a cosmopolitan university in the true sense of the term. No wonder that it should have fostered a spirit of intellectual brotherhood among the vast number of its members.

The University of Vikramashila on the western frontier of Bengal was founded by the great Pala King Dharmapala and was named after him, for Vikramashila was one of his names or titles. The Tibetan historian Taranath says that Dharmapala founded as many as fifty centres of learning in his empire. Vikramashila was known as a Royal University, its titles being bestowed by kings who presided over its convocations. It had one hundred and fourteen members on its teaching staff and more than three thousand students hailing from all over India and across the border. Its special subjects of study were the Tantras and the Tantrik cults in which Buddhism in Bengal found its new forms. Vikramashila made a great contribution to the exposition of Tantrik thought which helped forward the synthetic fusion of Hinduism and Buddhism. It rose to the height of its fame when that Bengali scholar-saint Srijnan Dipankar was its Chancellor. Dipankar visited many centres of Buddhist learning in India and abroad. He went to Srivijaya—modern Sumatra—and gave a fresh impetus to the study of Buddhism there. At the repeated requests of the king of Tibet, he undertook a perilous journey to that country and founded there a school of Tantrik Buddhism. In many monasteries of Tibet Dipankar is worshipped as next to the Buddha.

When Muslim iconoclasts destroyed these peaceful abodes of culture on the frontiers of Bengal, *tols* or schools of Sanskrit learning, began to flourish in the sequestered villages, far away from the centres of political turmoil. Of these the most famous was Navadwip, for many centuries one of the greatest centres of Sanskrit learning in all India, where scholars from distant parts of the country, from the Punjab and Kanauj in the north and Tamil-Nad in the south, used to congregate for the study among other things, of the Nyaya philosophy of which Raghunath Shiromani was then the highest acknowledged authority. The *Gaudiya riti*—Bengal's own style of Sanskrit composition—was no less an attraction for scholars from outside.

While in the North cultural fellowship grew and developed almost invariably in the Buddhist monasteries, in the South it throve mostly in the temples, those wonderful specimens of massive architecture, surrounded by buildings within big compounds. In fact, each such temple in South India was like a small university town which was the centre of the cultural and religious life of the locality. The temple-colleges maintained free hostels and hospitals and attracted students from different parts of India. Learned Brahmins, in charge of temple worship, were connected with the colleges as their professors. Inscriptions furnish authentic information about these centres of learning, many of which flourished during the ninth and tenth centuries of the present era. A Rashtrakuta minister founded the famous residential college at Salotgi in Bijapur, which had twenty-seven boarding-houses. The Sanskrit College at Ennayiram in the South Arcot district was well-known as a recognised seat of Vedic studies. The rolls of its alumni were strengthened not inconsiderably by learners from the North. The districts of Tanjore, Chingleput, Chitaldrug, Shikarpur and Guntur, had in those glorious days a number of educational institutions where the study of philosophy and grammar, of arts and sciences, was pursued by scholars from all parts of India. Thus the Peninsular plateau and the Gangetic plain were linked up by their culture-centres which privided opportunities for the varied expressions of the Indian mind to build up an intellectual brotherhood that for centuries was a unifying force in the cultural life of the people. Indeed, in the world of learning the whole country was one.

The three principal forms of the visual art of India are united by their common aim to fulfil the spiritual intention of Indian culture. They express not so much the mere exterior of things as their interior profundities, their psychic significance. A

I.V.F.—4

soul state, an inner experience or a light of the Infinite is what
they seek to reveal. In the delicacy of line in painting, in the
suggestiveness of plastic figuration or in the opulent magnificence
of sacred architecture, the one thing that strikes us is a tendency
to achieve that noble aim. In style and technique also there are
many points that are identical in works of art produced in places
at long distances from one another. In painting, whether at Bagh,
Sittannavasal in the South or Sigiriya in Ceylon, the dominating
style is that of the Ajanta masterpieces. The tradition continued,
however indistinctly, in the Rajput and Pahari miniatures; and
not a little has it been a source of inspiration to the neo-Indian
school of painting in modern times. In sculpture the Dhyani
Buddha of the North cannot be distinguished from its southern
figuration and it does not differ much even from its Javanese
adaptation. There are many characteristics common to the
Sarnath and the Mathura schools of sculpture and their widespread influence is clearly discernible, that of the former in the
work of the plastic art in Bengal, that of the latter in the sculpture
of the far-away Sind. The art of ancient India had its heyday
during the Buddhist age when the Buddhist monks made no
sectarian distinction in their choice of subjects. It was not
unoften that they painted and sculptured Hindu themes. And
instances are not rare of Hindu artists working on Buddhist
subjects.

A peculiar tendency of the builders of ancient India was to
make free use of any style or technique, if it would enhance the
beauty of their work. Thus the sacred architecture of India owed
very little of its origin and development to a particular creed or
cult. No definite idea can therefore be conveyed by designating
any type of Indian architecture as specifically Buddhistic, Jaina
or Brahminical. The Vedic sacrificial altars and the *mandapam*
(porch) are common to temples of the North and the South. The
Buddhist *stupas* (mounds) were adapted from the archaic Vedic
mounds. The north Indian *nagara*[5]-shrines of Shiva and Vishnu
influenced enormously the Jaina temples at Khajuraho. The forms
of Chalukya or the later Hoyasala order were indiscriminately
used for Hindu or Jaina shrines. Many Brahminical shrines
adopted the style of the barrel-shaped Vesara temples of

---

5. Curvilinear tower.

early Buddhistic uses. The monolithic temples at Mahavali-
puram are lineal descendants of the earlier Buddhist *viharas*.
Many features of the *shikhara*[6]-temples of the North are
unmistakable in the Mahabodhi temple in Bodh-Gaya. If architecture is the matrix of all arts and crafts, it is more so in India
whose temples and cave-cathedrals with all the decorative beauty
of their sculpture and painting are the very embodiment of the
integral vision of art that came to the builders of ancient India.
Evolved out of spiritual conceptions, they have stood through the
ages as the principal visible and material record of the cultural
evolution of the race, as the symbol of the unity of its godward
aspirations.

IV

The attempt so far has been to make a brief survey of the
cultural unity of India in the early days of her history, which
grew and developed not always as a result of any conscious effort
but largely under the impact of forces that were released by the
creative endeavours of the people, their inborn spirituality
inspiring them all through. It may now be seen what India was
able to achieve towards the political unification of the country.
As in their religious and social thinking, so also in their political
idealism the ancient Indians always showed a tendency to value
freedom above everything else and to so build the political structure that it might provide every member in it with ample freedom
of self-expression. The governing idea was not to strengthen the
framework by imposing rules from outside as was done in periods
of decline, but to allow every man to grow into the fullness of
his creative possibilities by which only is a country's culture
enriched. It was this outlook of the Indians that contributed
largely to the growth and development of their great civilisation.
But individual freedom was not their only aim. The freedom of
the community too was deemed equally necessary for the social
progress of the people.

   To the Indians the collectivity is as much a manifestation
of the Divine as the individual. Their scriptures therefore enjoin

----

6. Tower.

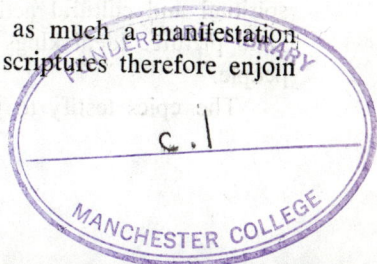

upon the householder certain duties that he must discharge for the well-being of the community. In their idea of the state they wanted the voice of the people to dominate in all its administrative affairs. That was one of the reasons why a central authority could not fully develop in ancient India. When the king came upon the scene he did so more as a protector and servant of the people than as an autocratic ruler.

The life of peace and prosperity led by the Indus Valley people has been already referred to. It is not yet known if they had developed any kind of political organisation. But that they had a form of corporate life is proved by the excavations which show the high order of civic amenities enjoyed by them. The earliest corporate institution of the Indians was the *samiti* or assembly, mentioned in the Rig Veda, which was constituted by representatives from a group of villages under its jurisdiction. Its function was to conduct every work of administration, social, political and religious. This idea of *samiti* is the seed of all the democratic institutions evolved in India in the past. It did not grow into an unwieldy structure. Its smallness sustained its vitality down the ages despite various disrupting forces that swayed over India. The village assemblies of today, the *Panchayats* as they are called in popular parlance, have descended from their prototypes in ancient India.

With the expansion of Aryan civilisation there arose the idea of territory, *janapada,* which gradually developed into a territorial state, *janapadarajya,* and then into a great territorial state, *mahajanpadarajya,* with a king more secure in his position than ever before. These states were most of them of a republican character. But all the time the autonomous forms of local bodies in the villages continued. Social life in the Vedic times was one of happiness and all-round prosperity. It was the splendid youth of humanity in India to which the vision came of the divine destiny of man and of the essential unity of all existence. It is not difficult to visualise from the stirrings of a new intellectual life in the age of the Upanishads that a happy and contented but more organised social life was there to stimulate those spiritual and cultural activities of which the Upanishads give a vivid picture. Ideal kings like Janaka were the protectors of the people.

The epics testify to the existence of many prosperous kingdoms where abundant wealth and continued happiness combined to produce a condition of society that was, as they called it, 'the envy of the gods.' The essential historical significance of the *Ramayana* is that it is a record of the expansion of the Indo-Aryan culture to the south, that was effected by a series of cultural and military campaigns which were perhaps the second of their kind, the first being those of Bharata who had extended the Aryan supremacy and absorbed most of the non-Aryans into the Aryan fold. The sense of territorial unity under the aegis of a single culture which began to grow as a result of the campaigns of King Bharata is found to be more developed in the *Ramayana*. But it had its further flowering in the *Mahabharata* which reflects the evolution of empire, the first of its kind in India, out of a host of petty states fighting for supremacy with one another. Problems of social and political unity are tackled in this epic with consummate mastery. The fusion of clans and tribes, not wholly Aryan, into the social structure of the Hindus is another important event that took place in this period, when the affirmation of the ideals of Dharma, the religious, ethical, social, political, juristic and customary law, organically governing the life of the people served as an effective check on any arbitrary abuse of sovereign power by the king. Any violation of Dharma by the king was severely dealt with. Not to speak of deposition, Manu prescribes even death for the king who would infringe the Law. Thus the majesty of Dharma asserted itself in its own right as greater than that of the sovereign whose sole duty was to administer the Law faithfully and to look to the strict observance of its every injunction both in the individual and the collective life of the people. In this way a common Dharma, a common culture administered by a benevolent king and followed by a dutiful people helped to build up a social and political integrity which gave to the state all its power and vitality.

But the state did not expand beyond certain limits; neither was there any organised attempt at mutual cooperation with others for the formation of a confederacy or a league. Though the ideal of an all-India Empire, *chaturantarajya*,[7] and a feeling of kinship regarding all Aryans or Indians as one people was always there, yet in practice it was a kind of regional patriotism that

---

7. Literally, an empire extending to the four ends of the earth.

remained strong and active. A territorial synthesis, broad-based on a common culture, was all that could and did exist under the conditions prevailing in the period, but a vast empire ruled by a single power or a league of states was far from a reality. Each state valued its own independence as a sacred thing and would resent any interference with it from outside, thereby allowing no neighbouring state to grow into a big power so as to be able to assert its suzerainty and form a strong central government. This love of regional freedom driven to excess made these states selfish and blind to the wider interests of the whole country with the result that by their mutual dissensions and disunity they exposed the country to foreign aggression and could hardly take a united stand against it. There were of course other reasons why India then was not able to build political unity in the strict sense of the term. In the beginning of the sixth century B.C. we find northern India divided into sixteen independent kingdoms. There were also a number of republics and tribal territories. But no strong power was there to combine them, at least against any invasion from outside. Hence, the way was prepared for the Persian conquest and then the campaigns of Alexander. Besides, the kings, emperors and social thinkers of ancient India were well aware that the life-force of a people grows into creative activities better in smaller autonomous groups and communities than under the dead-level uniformity of a too centralised government. As will be seen in Chapter 6, these free smaller collectivities, encouraged directly or indirectly by all concerned, often proved to be a most effective lever of social and cultural progress of the whole country, although their separative regional development did many a time hamper larger political unifications for any practical or especial purpose.

The rise of Buddhism was a notable event in the history of ancient India having important bearings on the then social and political life of the country. Its permanent contribution however was more cultural than religious, although for a long time it figured as a popular form of religious idealism. The abundant creative energy, released largely by the regenerating influence of Buddhism, especially when its Mahayana school arose accepting the Yoga and Bhakti cults of Hinduism, broke into a myriad expressions in art, literature and philosophy; and there emerged a new order of religious communism, conceived after the pattern of the republican institutions of the Hindus. But the yet greater service Buddhism rendered to the cause of Indian unity was that it broke down the racial barriers that still existed in the country and cleared the spiritual atmosphere of all kinds of superstition and priestly obscurantism and bound together in closer ties of sympathy the whole political organisation of the Aryans and by all these helped to lay the foundation of the great empire of the Mauryas.

The Maurya empire constituted the first systematic attempt to unify India politically into a single state with a central government. But the authority of Chandragupta Maurya, whose empire extended over almost the whole of India, does not appear to have been exercised everywhere in the same manner or in the same measure. True to their love of freedom and of fair deal, the Indian conquerors did not for the most part displace the rulers whom they subdue. The empire of Chandragupta included feudatory kingdoms, and there were instances of independent rule too. The old form of local self-government continued in the villages: and all these, despite the injunction, given in his *Arthashastra* by Chandragupta's Prime Minister, Kautilya, that power of all kingdoms or bodies included in the state should be reduced to a minimum. Chandragupta's was an efficient rule though there was an element of autocracy in it. To him however goes the credit of being the first to build a great all-India empire. But no unification as a political necessity was there.

Conditions with regard to this particular problem were no more favourable during the reign of Ashoka who followed neither the Dharma of the Aryans strictly, nor a policy of high statesmanship like Chandragupta's. In all that he did he was no doubt inspired by a large vision of human fellowship, the largest indeed of its kind that has ever come to any monarch in history, but it cannot be said that Ashoka had that political wisdom and that far-sightedness which were necessary for an emperor who aspired to be a universal sovereign, Chakravarti-Raja. The signs of disintegration that were seen in his empire—greater in extent than that of Chandragupta's—were not a little due to his pacific attitude that began to guide the imperial policy after the Kalinga war. His declaration of repentance for the sanguinary massacre he had committed in that war as well as the change of his royal policy of conquest by military force to that by the Dharma of the

Buddha does no doubt raise him in the estimation of the world
as one of the greatest benefactors of mankind, but in the world
of politics they were more or less acts of tactlessness, if not blun-
ders, that led to political stagnation and gradually to the decline
of the empire. If Chandragupta depended more on statecraft than
on Dharma (as defined by the ancient Indo-Aryans), Ashoka
depended more on Dharma (which was a kind of ethical idealism
emphasised in Buddhism) than on statecraft. Neither could he
discharge the duty of a king which according to Hindu polity,
demands a combination of both. Chandragupta did build a
strong central Government but he could not for obvious difficulties gather into it all the threads of its constituent parts; whereas
Ashoka by propagating noble ideals was able to bring about some
kind of unity in his empire founded on justice and righteousness,
but he failed to develop a supreme power at the centre so as to
utilise that unity for the purposes of practical politics. Hence the
Empire of the Mauryas, which indicated great possibilities, began
to be dismembered soon after the death of Ashoka, and its vastness was not possible for any emperor of India to recover for
nearly the next thousand years. Nevertheless the Maurya emperors
did try with all their might to discharge the duties of kingship as
defined by Kautilya in the *Arthashastra* in which a significant
passage runs thus: 'In the happiness of his subjects lies the king's
happiness; in their welfare his welfare; whatever pleases him he
shall not consider as his good, but whatever pleases his subjects
he shall consider as good.'

But if the Mauryas, owing to conditions over which they had
no complete control, were unable to unify effectively their vast
empire, they must however be acknowledged as having helped
not only to keep up, but also to infuse a fresh strength into, the
social and cultural solidarity that had been already there among
the people belonging to various sects and clans and tribes—a
fact which is attested by the vivid picture of the India of the time
left by Megasthenes. 'The Greek Ambassador observed with admiration the absence of slavery in India, the chastity of the women
and the courage of the men. In valour they excelled all other
Asiatics; they required no locks to their doors: above all, no
Indian was ever known to tell a lie. Sober and industrious, good
farmers and skilled artisans, they scarcely ever had recourse to a
law-suit and lived peaceably under their native chiefs. The kingly

government is portrayed almost as described in Manu.' There is
no doubt that this high moral tone of the general character of
the people was an expression of their ingrained spiritual nature
for the development of which necessary facilities were provided
by the administration under the chiefs, which was conducted according to the traditional injunctions of the Dharma Shastras.
Politically, the largeness and extent of the empire did not last
long, but culturally, the reality of its oneness—the oneness of the
whole of India—was a growing phenomenon which seems to have
been accentuated and accelerated rather than disturbed by the
onslaughts that fell upon the country from outside not once but
many times in her history.

With the break-up of the Maurya empire followed a period
when small independent states rose again but they had no friendly
political relations with one another so as to enable them to combine against the irruption of the Central Asian hordes, the Shakas,
the Kushanas, and the Hunas, which began and continued for a
long time. Many of these nomadic tribes settled down in India,
adopted any one of the religions of the land and were later
absorbed into the social life of Hinduism. But these invasions did
not, because they could not, affect the basic cultural unity of
the people, though they made the problem of political unity a
little more difficult of solution. The next great empire was that
of the Kushana king, Kanishka, extending over the whole of northern India in the first century of the present era, but it is not
known how far its oneness as a political entity was achieved.

A few instances of the above-mentioned Indianised foreig-
ners including the Greeks may be cited here. The Greeks who
made India their home embraced either Hinduism or Buddhism.
Among the missionaries of Ashoka there were a number of
Greeks one of whom named Dharmarakshita was sent to Gujarat.
Evidently they were Buddhists and well-versed in Buddhist lore.
Greek kings like Menander and Hermaios became staunch Buddhists and their example was followed by a number of their
countrymen. Menander is immortalised in the celebrated Pali text
Milindapanha or 'Questions of Milinda' (Menander), which is
one of the most notable books in Buddhist literature. Many Greeks
became devout Vaishnavas. Heliodoros, a Greek statesman and
for some time a scholar in the University of Taxila, called himself
a *Parama-bhagavata,* a staunch Vaishnava devotee, in an inscription

on a *Garuda* pillar (the Besnagar column) which he erected in
Vidisha, the Malwa capital, where he came in the second century
B.C. as an ambassador of the then Greek king of Taxila. Among
the immigrants from Central Asia who contributed an important
element to the Indian population in several provinces, the Scythians
were completely Indianised within less than two generations. They
adopted purely Hindu names such as Rudradaman, Jayadaman,
etc. The third king of the Western Kshatrap dynasty was an enthusiastic admirer of Hindu culture and religion. In an official
document he proudly proclaims himself as a pious Hindu and an
ardent patron of Sanskrit language. It is interesting that while his
contemporaries, the Brahmin Shatavahana rulers of the Deccan,
were using Prakrit language for State purposes, Rudradaman
himself was using Sanskrit for the purpose. The second ruler of
the Kushana dynasty bore a foreign name, Wima Kadphises; but
he was a staunch Shaiva. Shiva alone appears on his coins where
the king describes himself as a *Parama-maheshwara,* a great
devotee of Shiva. His successor Kanishka was a well-known Buddhist and a famous patron of Buddhist learning. The Hunas who
invaded northern India during the fifth and sixth centuries
were completely Hinduised. Mihirakula, the second ruler of the
dynasty, was a Shaiva zealot. Inscriptions say that he used never
to bow down his head before any deity other than Shiva. On the
coins of this ruler, we find the Bull of Shiva and the inscription,
'Victory to Shiva.' These facts indicate the dynamic influence of
Indian culture, the catholic outlook and the assimilative power of
the Indian society of the time.

In the fourth and fifth centuries the Gupta emperors appeared
strong enough to consolidate their empire under their paramount
authority. They possessed grit added to a kind of robust optimism
about the success of their mission to revive the traditions of the
Indo-Aryans in every sphere of the national life. Inheritors of a
great past, they conjured up a vision of the glorious days of old
and strove to bring them back by encouraging all kinds of creative activity in the country with the result that India attained
during this period to the highest degree of her excellence in the
realm of arts and letters. Hindu culture was again in the ascen-
dant and took its classical turn, though there was no dearth of
Buddhistic learning. The administration was marked by tolerance
and efficiency. It was conducted according to the laws of the

Smritis which emphasise that a good king should be particularly careful to win the hearts of his subjects by respecting their wishes and promoting their welfare. That the rulers ordinarily lived up to this ideal is testified to by the Chinese pilgrim Fa-Hien who in his account says that the people were virtuous, happy and prosperous, and had no occasion to complain of the autocracy and high-handedness of the government.

A notable feature of the movement ushered in by the Guptas is that it sought to re-assert the Aryan intellectual and political supremacy. The military achievements and wise statesmanship of Samudragupta as also of his son Vikramaditya who succeeded him strengthened the integrity of the empire, a picture of which is given by the great poet Kalidasa in his *Meghadutam* in which he describes the oneness of India in vivid terms. A remnant of this political unity of the Gupta empire even after its destruction by the White Hunas, is seen in the confederacy—perhaps the first of its kind that we come across in the historic period—which was constituted by the rulers of some of the small kingdoms under the leadership of Baladitya, the king of Magadha, to drive away the Huna king Mihirakula.

Harshavardhana, who early in the seventh century became the lord paramount of the North, showed a remarkable combination of the attributes that go to make a true sovereign. By his victorious campaigns and his strong arm of authority Harsha was able to bring about a working compactness of his empire, but it is difficult to agree with some writers that his empire was firmly consolidated. Had it been so, it would not have broken up soon after his death. It must however be said to his credit that after Ashoka he was the only emperor who helped in strengthening his empire on the basis of religion and righteousness by convoking the great Assembly or Congress at Prayag every five years to which all Indians, irrespective of caste, creed or religion, were invited to perform their religious rites, for which every facility was provided by the king. Like Ashoka, Harsha also was generous to a fault. He used to empty the royal treasury every five years by lavishly distributing gifts and alms in the Assembly. Obviously, it was not a wise policy on the part of a king. Huien Tsang testified that during this period all religious communities lived in peace and amity and that the country was everywhere prosperous, and the moral standard of the people high. Harsha's reign witnessed the university of Nalanda at the summit of its glory.

It is true that during the classical age controversies were frequently taking place among ambitious exponents of different schools of thought, but that did not detract from the spirit of toleration and harmony that prevailed among the people belonging to various sects, orthodox and heterodox. A few instances of it may be cited here. The Gupta emperor Samudragupta studied Buddhism in his youth with 'interest and partiality.' He entrusted the education of his son to the famous Buddhist scholar, Vasubandhu. The Buddhist king Damodaravarman of the Ananda dynasty perfomed the Hindu ceremony of Hiranyagarbha. The pious Hindu Nathasharman and his wife, of Bengal, made permanent arrangements for the proper worship of Jaina Arhats. The sister, daughters and daughters-in-law of the Hindu king Shantamula were all Buddhists. The Kadamba kings performed Ashwamedha sacrifice according to the Vedas and made grants to a Jaina establishment. Contemporary Jaina records pay the best tribute to the administration of the Guptas who were orthodox Hindus, and who on their side, extended their utmost patronage to the Buddhist university at Nalanda. The great Pala king of Bengal, Dharmapala, a Buddhist, performed Vedic sacrifices and offered liberal gifts to the Brahmins who conducted the sacrifices on his behalf. His Chief Minister was a Brahmin, members of whose family became for many generations the Chief Ministers of the Buddhist Pala kings after Dharmapala. It is said that Dharmapala granted land for a Narayana temple of the Hindus. There was also complete harmony among the different sects of Hinduism of the time. A staunch Bhagavata like Kumaragupta performed the Ashwamedha sacrifice. Rajamitra concluded his Vedic sacrifice by a donation to a Shaiva temple. A fifth century inscription in Mysore says how people regarded Brahma, Vishnu and Shiva as the different aspects of one and the same God. Later, the eclectic Harshavardhana distributed his devotions among the three deities of the family, Shiva, Surya (the Sun) and the Buddha. Bengal through her Tantrikism made the largest contribution to the movement[8] that led to the absorption of Buddhism into Hinduism, of which the outstanding

---

8. For concrete instances, see Chapter III of the author's book *A Marvel of Cultural Fellowship.*

result was the acceptance of the Buddha in Hinduism as one of the ten incarnations of Vishnu. The earliest literary mention of this is found in the *Gita Govinda* of Jayadeva, one of the greatest poets of medieval Bengal. Buddhist influence can still be traced in many of the religious rites and ceremonies of Bengal, although the Buddhism of Bengal was almost a new creation of her own, different in many respects from the Buddhism of the North, and mainly based on her Tantrik ideas. In the same way Jainism also was absorbed in Hinduism. Shaivism, too, had a part to play in this interfusion of cults in Bengal. These facts undoubtedly reflect the religious tendencies of the times, that indicated the possibilities of a larger synthesis which could not then come about but was certainly to be a reality in the future.

Harsha's death was quickly followed by the disruption of his empire and the rise of numerous independent states always at war with one another. The narrative of their internal dissensions—evidence of political weakness—does not throw much light on the greater problems of Indian history. They however point to the fact that the country was divided against itself and was thrown open to foreign aggression. The Pala and the Rajput kingdoms in northern India deserve mention. In its first century the empire of the Palas of Bengal extended over almost the whole of northern India, from the Punjab to Assam. According to a Monghyr inscription, it included a part of the South too. But Bengal and Magadha only were under their direct rule. The local rulers of the rest of the region submitted to the authority of the Pala emperors, paid tribute to them, and were allowed to continue their rulership. The next three centuries were for this empire a period of ups and downs. The Pala ruler, however, is remarkable in Indian history for more reasons than one. It started with a notable event that indicates how in the eighth century Bengal rose to a sense of her political unity and expressed the democratic tendency of her body politic. For Gopala, the founder of this dynasty, became king by the will and consent of the people. No other dynasty ruled over northern India for four hundred years at a stretch—a period which witnessed among other things a marvellous outburst of the creative genius of Bengal. The Pala kings were all of them ardent patrons of learning, as also the most liberal of the Buddhist emperors of India. The Rajputs were many of them, the Hinduised Hunas, Shakas and Pallavas, merged in the older population. About this period the Chalukyas flourished in the Deccan, and long after them the Cholas ruled over practically the whole of southern India; but it was not exactly a big empire that they were able to build or perhaps it was not their ambition: whereas the definite aim of the emperors in the north, noticed above, had been to extend their suzerainty over vast dominions and be their paramount lords.

Early in the eighth century when the descendants of the Rajputs, called the Gurjara-Pratiharas, were ruling in eastern Rajputana and Malwa, an important event took place in the coming of the Arabs into India and with it began the play of new forces in the social, cultural and political life of the country. The conditions that were indirectly the cause of this foreign invasion proved more favourable then than they had been before when mainly the absence of political unity among the different states was taken advantage of by the aggressors. But on the eve of the Muslim conquest India was not only more weakened than before by disunity and discord among the small states, but also she lacked social cohesion and solidarity.

The rise to power of the Rajputs in the north where Muslim invaders had their first footing gave an impetus to the resurgence of the orthodox forms of Hinduism. The Brahmin came upon the scene, with his hold on the society considerably strengthened by the connivance of the powers that be. The result was that the system of caste, which had been elastic and in places rendered even inoperative under the impact of Buddhism, began to revive and be rigid again and large numbers of people, whose problems the society did not care to solve, were condemned to a life of indignity; and the process which also was started by Buddhism of assimilating to the social organism many tribes and peoples of mixed race-origins could not make any progress owing to deliberate opposition by the so-called custodians of the society. This policy of obscurantism was responsible for a social disintegration and for the creation of a class of people who were in perpetual revolt against the society. It is these disaffected people who supported Muslim invasion. The Jats and the agricultural classes who helped Muhammad bin Qasim in his invasion of Sindh did so not out of any love for the conqueror but to wreak vengeance on the Brahmins, whose tyranny they could not forget, and especially on king Dahir, the Brahmin usurper of the throne of Sindh whose previous king was a Buddhist. The antagonism between the Brahmins and the Buddhists contributed no less to the social demoralisation. Besides, Buddhism by its huge monastic organisation and its widespread influence tended to sap the manhood of India. The conquest of Sindh by the Arabs was made easy by the fact that thousands of the male population had adopted the yellow robe for the sake of the easy life of the monastery. The unity of India in the world of culture was of too subjective a nature to be a safeguard of any practical value against political onslaughts from outside. It was there no doubt, as it is even today, but since the whole country was politically in a state of decline, it could not prove a source of strength, for which a sound external life with an unbreakable solidarity and an invincible morale was the first condition.

There is another reason. The state of decadence into which India began to drift followed not only because she was weak in her political and social life but also because the light of the integral spiritual ideal, which in the days of her glory had illumined every activity of her life was beginning to be dimmed in her consciousness by the rushlight of a mere ethical idealism. Indeed, nothing precipitated the decline of the country so much as the acceptance by it of the anti-pragmatic ideal of monasticism and other-worldliness, which was inculcated in Buddhism. Political changes affect more or less the surface life of the country; they cannot touch its inner life, though under favourable social conditions man can express himself more freely. But there is no worse calamity for a nation than when it deviates from the ideal which it is its destiny to fulfil—its Swadharma.

Shankara may have had a vision of the true spirit of India; but in his effort to rehabilitate what he considered to be the ancient monistic cult, the Brahmavada of the Upanishads, and to counteract the evil effects of the degenerated form of Buddhism, he also stressed the evanescence of life and could not, in spite of the deep spiritual character and fervour of his teachings, reveal to the country its real creative soul. He was not able to discover that harmony between spirit and life by which alone the problem of India, nay, all human problems, can be solved. The Brahminical revival, of which Shankara was the moving spirit, meant no more than a reorientation to the religious consciousness of the Hindus: it had not in it the power to rekindle the ancient lamp which alone could throw light on India's path to her goal. It was a period when the body politic of the country was showing signs of exhaustion and when even the greatest thinker of the time was found unequal to the task of reconstructing her life on the basis of the true truth of the integral ideal for which India has always stood. Nevertheless, whatever its ultimate effects, the *digvijaya*[9] of Shankara brought together the four corners of the country under the surging impulse of a new spiritual awakening, and the artistic and literary activities of the people continued without being very much affected either by the illusionism of Shankara or by the conditions in the external life which were not however wholly favourable to them. It is these creative efforts of the race that kept alive the soul of India, her inner unity, her cultural oneness.

V

The running survey made so far of the development of politico-cultural unity in India reveals an undeniable polarity towards the perfection of a diversified oneness in the self-expression of her soul and life. A manifold aspiration in the national being, an immense diversity of forces striving to realise that aspiration, an equally immense array of forces opposing, and by opposing inevitably helping that realisation, this is the spectacle India presents to the perspicacity of a sympathetic historian. Here is no Egypt or Chaldea or Greece with her harp of being vibrating with marvellous strains of a single melody. Here is a symphony in the making, a rich and grandiose symphony into which, through long centuries, diverse notes, diverse strains, diverse, even contradictory rhythms have entered and combined and clashed and recombined to enrich an ever-swelling volume of music.

The political history of India would have been wholly different had the states of the North united to offer a determined resistance to the invading Persians. If the successors of Chandragupta Maurya had been able to carry on his consolidated sovereignty, India would have been spared the convulsive depre-

9. Triumphal march.

dations of the foreign hordes. Had the orthodox canonists of Hinduism been a little less stringent in their interpretation of the social rules, Indian cultural unity would have easily achieved a more homogeneous self-expression and it would have paved the way for a political unity also.

But these 'ifs' are the speculations of the unthinking historian to whom India is but a tissue of tantalising paradoxes. It takes the placid, probing vision of a wide sympathy and inner affinity to unravel the mystery of India's growth and decline and re-surgence and progress. Indian life has always teemed with pro-blems of all sorts and it has been her constant endeavour to arrive at a triumphant, abiding harmony through a perfect solution of all of them. Now she attempts a movement of expansion, embraces vast spiritual horizons, compels discords into concords, sweeps forward in love and amity and compassion to help and heal the world, lavishes her treasures of wisdom on all who are ready to receive them; now she retires into herself, limits the field of her vision and action, seems absorbed in unravelling some inner skein or slowly, cautiously developing some new strain out of her soul. The threads she drops today she picks up tomorrow; she falls back upon her past and again with a sudden violent start launches forth into the future. But the invariable trend of her genius has always been towards achieving an integral, consummate unity.

The saints of the Middle Ages sang the unity of existence and taught the universality of love. They evinced a remarkable breadth of vision and proclaimed that all religions are essentially one. The lyrical mysticism of Sufism—a delicate blossom of Indo-Saracenic marriage—pulsates in the songs of many of these medieval min-strels of the Spirit. It is interesting to note that most of them were of low origin and that they had as their disciples men and women of all denominations. The lives and the mystical trend in the teach-ings of these inspired saints gave a new orientation to the spiritual endeavour of India; their wide popularity indicated possibilities of a larger synthesis in the social and religious life of the people. In Bengal there was evolving a new kind of synthesis[10] out of an interfusion of cults derived from Buddhism, Tantrikism and Vaish-navism, Islam also playing its part in this diapason. In fact, a

---

10. See Chapters III and IV of the author's book *A Marvel of Cultural Fellowship.*

time came when Hindus and Muslims in Bengal were very near opening into a common cultural consciousness.

After Ashoka it was Akbar who as an emperor felt in himself the deep urge of India's soul towards the oneness of her national being. He built up and consolidated a vast empire and cherished dreams of a compact cultural and political unity. But it was destined to be a fugitive dream and whatever solidarity had been achieved began to slacken and disintegrate in the inefficient hands of his short-sighted successors. India gave up for the moment the expansive movement and plunged into intense regional whirlpools. Yet the salient elements of Saracenic culture had already been woven into the texture of the country's life. Shivaji rose and with him arose again the idea of unity. His short career was a meteoric blaze of astute statesmanship and burning patriotism. A thrill passed through the nation, its limp body became tense with the energy of expectancy and fervour. But the wave soon spent itself and an ominous hush fell upon the country. Nevertheless, Shivaji, inspired by the Ancient Vision, was a brilliant source of the nation's resurgence towards its high destiny. The next notable attempt, a daring and dazzling one, was made by Guru Govind Singh. His Khalsa was a startling feat of militant nationalism wedded to religious ardour, and there was in it an echo of the democratic spirit of Islam. It was a 'fellowship of equals' to which the people impetuously dedicated themselves, fired by a new-found sense of their strength and solidarity. The result was magnificent and thrilling but unavoidably short-lived in its burst of splendour. And the country sank again into a politico-cultural apathy and gloom.

Last came the assault of Europe and the yoke of England. A few earthquake shocks, to be precise, a few slight tremors, and the whole of the land lay at the feet of the alien adventurers, supine, but—mark the mystery—united in stunned subjection. A unity was achieved, a many-sided unity that had never been possible before, though it had yet to be fuller and more abiding for the growth of India towards her goal. The problems that faced the country at this stage of her evolution were the rousing of the people, the discovery of the true truth of her ancient culture, the affirmation of her spiritual ideal. The bondage of a foreign rule accentuated by a relentless exploitation of her proverbial wealth created discontent in the country. Discontent broke into struggle,

struggle meant an awakening of the Leviathan. Besides, the impact of Western civilisation and progressive thought made India sceptical and curious. For a time she rejected her past as outworn and dead, and blindly imitated everything foreign. But as she grew in her curiosity she wanted to know and master the truths not only of Europe but also of her own cultural heritage. There were then born that radiant band of dynamic personalities, the spiritual architects of the nation's later glory. The signs of a general stirring of life began to be visible in the land and it was unity that loomed large and clear on the distant horizon.

Rammohun Roy with his unerring intuition perceived that the soul of India responds only to the truth of the spirit and he called upon the people to unite in the indivisible oneness of the Brahman. His was a mighty call, a great rallying cry, that rang from one end of the country to the other. Many an invidious distinction of society was swept away by the flood of his reforming zeal. India learnt anew to look within, to return to her own self and find in it her own line of development, also assimilating what she received from the West. Then came Keshab Chandra Sen, a more magnetic but less Olympian spiritual genius, driving Rammohun's work deeper into the consciousness of the people. Dayananda, a towering and dynamic figure, attempted a revival of the Vedic past in the changing present. 'A soldier of Light,' he shook the superstitious sluggishness of the people and turned them round to the glory of ancient India. He did great spade work and left the field considerably prepared for the next sowing. His principle achievement was the unsealing of the Vedic lore, the perennial well-spring of Indian spirituality and culture which none of his predecessors had ever dreamt of doing.

The source of unity was now glimpsed, but rather dimly and from a distance, and the way had yet to be discovered to reach that unity and bring it down and out even into the external active life of the nation. To help effectuate that, came Shri Ramakrishna with his gospel of the unity of all religions in the spiritual life of every individual. A colossal synthesis silhouetted itself against the background of a growing clarity and catholicity, and the jangling discords of the sects seemed for a moment to be dissolving in an all-embracing diapason of the oneness of all existence and all creatures, above all, in the inalienable oneness of India. And to vindicate the dynamic reality of this unity, Shri

Ramakrishna gave to the world that heaven-born awakener of souls who spoke in the accents of a god and worked with the force of fire—it was Swami Vivekananda. The Master thundered to the Disciple: 'Fie upon thee, thou avid of personal salvation! I thought thou wouldst be like a great banyan tree giving shade and shelter to thousands of weak and weary souls wallowing in ignorance! Thou hast come to do the Mother's work and do it thou must. Here, I keep the key of Samadhi with me, thou wilt not have it again till the Mother's work is accomplished.' Astounding words these in the mouth of one who had himself realised the Nirvikalpa Samadhi of the Vedantins! They ushered in a new dawn of awakening and action in the land which was still ridden and heavy with the negation of the ascetic. The door was thus slammed for ever upon the escapist tendency of the sannyasin and an unbanked immensity appeared in the front—a rich field for the harvesting of an integral perfection of man here upon earth, *ihaiva*. The essential unity of the Vendantic realisation was wedded to the unity in diversity of the Tantrik vision. A stupendous synthesis was achieved that would prepare the country for a larger and deeper unity—its goal and future destiny.

What then is that unity—the integral unity India has been dreaming of and developing throughout the ages? It is the unity of the Spirit fully expressed in the unity of Life. All men are one, nay, all creation is one; not yet, it is true, in the outer structure and facts of Life, but eternally in the Spirit. Man has, therefore, first to travel beyond the apparent divisions and distinctions that delude him, and attain that in which all differences meet and merge for ever. That is the eternal essence and substratum of all this diversity of the universe. That attained, man will feel himself existing in all and all in him; he will become the universe and yet remain transcendent of the universe. He will become one with the one all-pervading Reality. He has next to translate this unity in terms of his mind, life and body. A perfect expression and enjoyment of its blissful unity in the manifoldness of the universal existence is what the Spirit seeks in creation. It is this integral unity—unity in the Supreme Light and unity in the splendid play of Life—which India has been evolving variously through countless vicissitudes in her inner and outer existence. This is the truth that gives meaning and purpose to all her age-long endeavours.

There is also a truth in the physical unity of India's form.

India was hailed and hymned by the Rishis of yore as the one land on earth which is destined to lead mankind to the realisation of its intrinsic oneness in the Spirit. She was visioned as the beating heart of the world, the creative centre from which one day would go forth not only the message of the unity of all existence but also the supreme force to make that oneness a reality in the life of mankind. It is, therefore, not unreasonable to believe that if India has the Light which will one day illumine the darkness of the world, she has also the potentiality to develop a physical body that will be a veritable powerhouse, a radiating centre of that Light. It is this integral oneness—physical, cultural and spiritual—which will be the glory of the India of tomorrow. All the ferment and turmoil of the past and the present, however disconcerting and discouraging, are but the churning of the ocean of Force, the travail of the soul of India for the birth of a divine humanity.

It is surely not a mere freak or a phantasy of a blind chance that has produced such a glorious constellation of spiritual luminaries, one coming after another in an unbroken succession—Rammohan Roy, Keshab Chandra Sen, Dayananda Saraswati, Shri Ramakrishna, Swami Vivekananda, Sri Aurobindo, not to mention the many giants in various walks of life—in Art, in Literature, in Science, in Politics, in Philosophy, in Education. They cannot indeed be a gratuitous gift of an inconscient Nature. The country that can give birth to such creative souls even in her hour of decline or incipient reawakening is no hapless forlorn mother doomed to perish in an eclipse of her ancient glory, her high honour unretrieved, her message of love and harmony undelivered. The Conscious-Force who works from above and behind the frontal flux of appearances, the divine Shakti, the creative, preservative and destructive Mother-Power whom the whole world has ever worshipped in one form or another, manifests herself in India today—yes, in spite of her present life of distress and discord, and is working out her puissant Will right through a phalanx of opposing forces. The first streaks of the golden dawn have already appeared on the horizon. Led by the Mother and strengthened by her Grace, India advances towards and apocalypse of Light and Harmony that will bring into birth a new heaven and a new earth and make of the life of man a glowing epic of divine perfection.

This is the vision of the Future, the vision of man fufilling his divine destiny in a richly diversified unity of the Spirit. It is for this that India, one and indivisible in her soul and body in the Divine Shakti, has lived and suffered and laboured on throughout the centuries of her chequered existence. India is not for herself but for God and, as the chosen instrument of God, for the whole world.

REFERENCES

Cambridge History of India, Vol. I, and other standard works on Indian history and culture by A. K. Coomaraswamy, A. S. Altekar, E. B. Havell, E. J. Rapson, H. C. Roychoudhury, K. P. Jayaswal, O. C. Gangoly, Rhys Davids, R. C. Majumdar, R. D. Banerji, R. K. Mookerji, S. K. Aiyangar, Sister Nivedita, Sri Aurobindo, V. A. Smith. The quota-tions in Section II are all from Sri Aurobindo's *The Foundations of Indian Culture.*

3

A Great Unifier

I

AKBAR represents the acme of the political endeavours of the Muslims in India; and the success that attended his sincere and earnest efforts to build a happy and united India was largely due to the kingly virtues he possessed and brought to bear on the ways in which he tried to accomplish his great work. Rarely had a king a lofty and comprehensive vision such as inspired Akbar; and never was a king so eminently capable of translating his vision into such a splendid series of radical acts.

A unique personality, Akbar stands out as 'one of the wisest, most humane and most cultured of all the kings known to history.' It is not for us to crab and carp at his political career or merely to single out his defects and shortcomings in order to pass a summary verdict of failure on him, as is sometimes done by narrow historical criticism; nor is it our aim to study him with a mind biased by considerations which are outside the scope of impartial history. No doubt accuracy demands a searching enquiry into all the facts and problems associated with his rule, and even a dissecting analysis of the motives that actuated his policies and measures, but what is of paramount importance is that the attention of the historian must be focussed not upon the side-issues and stray events but upon the central drift and significance of his life and work, the cardinal conception and creation of his administrative genius—the political and cultural unification of India. Akbar stands or falls upon this single bed-rock fact of his reign.

Akbar in the outer expression of his nature was first and foremost an empire-builder: but in the inmost core of his being he was a seeker, and his seeking deepened with age and persisted through life, possibly because he never reached the end of it. It cannot be gainsaid that he was the architect of a vast empire, a tireless promoter of human fellowship, the inaugurator of an area of remarkable cultural activity; but history says very little about the 'inner man' in Akbar, his characteristic cast and insistent creative impulse. The religious reforms that he tried to introduce are generally interpreted either as expressions of his earnest desire to bring about a religious synthesis or as his deliberate intention to shake into sense the orthodox canonists of Islam who felt very much scandalised and shamed by Akbar's open-hearted acceptance of truth from whatever source it came to him. But these do not take us deep enough into the inner working of Akbar's nature, a revealing glimpse of which, however, we get in the following incident. When he was a mere boy of fourteen, one day he suddenly left the splendours of the Imperial Camp and, unnoticed by anybody, rode out all alone into a vast wilderness. After a while, when his entourage missed him, search parties went out in all directions. One of these noticed the boy-emperor's favourite horse, Hamid, quietly grazing on a plot of grass at a distance. The daylight was failing. The party searched all around and at last found the boy-emperor on his knees, gazing at the vast open space in front of him with tears streaming down his cheeks. They could obtain no explanation from the emperor as to why he had strayed away from the Camp, but only succeeded somehow in persuading him to return to his anxious family and bewildered guardians.

This was not the only instance of Akbar's love of solitude and devout contemplation of God and Nature. Abul Fazl says that Akbar used often to pass the morning alone in meditation, 'sitting on a large flat stone of an old building which lay near the palace in a lonely spot, with his head bent over his chest and gathering the bliss of the early hours.' When he reached his twentieth year Akbar confessed that his soul was filled with exceeding sorrow from the consciousness that he 'lacked spiritual provision for the journey of life.' 'Although I am the master of so vast a kingdom and all the appliances of government are in my hands, yet, since true greatness consists in doing the will of God, my mind is not at ease in this diversity of sects and creeds; and apart from this outward pomp of circumstance, with what satisfaction in my despondency can I undertake the sway of the empire? I await the coming of some wise man of principle who will resolve the difficulties of my conscience.' It is obvious that Akbar was in search of a spiritual guide. He met many philosophers, thinkers, scholars, Hindu, Muslim, Jain and Christian; but none of them, it seems, could give him the light, the spiritual pabulum his soul was hungering for.

Perhaps Akbar was aiming at something which he was not ready to receive, preoccupied that he was by various interests of a mundane and distracting nature. Nevertheless, his hours of meditation, his contemplative turn of mind and his thirst for truth enabled him to a large extent to control the adverse circumstances in which he found himself. Akbar was not free from the influence of the rationalism which was breaking all over the world in the sixteenth century. But in him very much more than in his great contemporaries, Peter of Russia, Elizabeth of England, and Henry IV of France, it was the religious urge that guided the trend of his action. And it was this again that helped him to transcend the bigotry that reigned rampant all over Europe in the wars of religion and in the burning of saints. On the whole, Akbar's signal successes overshadowed his failures; and it is always the calm, noble and grand monarch in Akbar that appears to our vision prominently. It was an era of great monarchs in which Akbar lived, and our minds naturally turn to a comparison between him and the maker of Russia or between him and the founder of Protestant England. This comparison is justifiable from an international point of view, but for a proper understanding of the philosophy of Indian history it is necessary that the student should dive below the surface and appraise the inner man in Akbar.

Like so many other great figures in history, Akbar was moulded less by his heritage and environments than by the native fire of his royal soul. And yet heredity and environments had not an inconsiderable formative influence upon his life and character. A descendant of the lion-hearted Babar was bound to be a great soldier; the ward of the astute Bairam Khan to be a noted statesman; the son of the broad-minded Humayun— the Rakhi-brother of a Rajput princess—to be an uncompromis-

ing cosmopolitan; and the beloved grandchild of the wise Gul-
badan Banu an expert reader of human nature. The son of a
Shia mother, the friend of Abul Fazl and Faizi, the beloved master of such widely differing personalities as Birbal, Man Singh and
Todar Mall, the patron of Tansen, could hardly be a bigoted
Sunni. All these influences worked in Akbar and led him to
formulate a policy of expansion and conciliation by marriage
or otherwise, which was at least as successful as a similar policy
of the contemporary house of the Hapsburgs. But Akbar was
greater than any of the Hapsburgs; for the Hapsburgs' conciliation
and alliance was strictly limited to the Catholic world while
Akbar's undoubted toleration was founded on an integral view
of humanity, however vague it might be.

II

Indeed Akbar owed much to these facts about his life and heritage; and his impartial attitude towards all was not a little the
outcome of their cumulative effect on his character. In matters
of religion this sovereign virtue of the emperor rose to its supreme height. He issued a standing order that there should be
no interference with anyone's religious convictions, and that in
the matter of worship utmost freedom should be allowed to non-
Muslims. Thus while Catholics were murdering Protestants in
France, and Protestants under Elizabeth were murdering Catholics in England, and the Inquisition was killing and robbing
Jews in Spain, and Bruno was being burnt at the stake in Italy,
Akbar invited the representatives of all the religions in his empire to a conference, had their honour pledged to peace, and
issued edicts of toleration for every cult and creed, and as an
evidence of his own equality, himself took part in the religious
festivities of the Hindus as well as in those of the Muslims. His
greatest pleasure was in a free discussion of religious beliefs,
and to this may be traced 'his unwillingness from the outset,
to accept the theory that because he, the conqueror, the ruler,
happened to be born a Muhammadan, therefore Muhammada-
nism was true for all mankind. Gradually his thoughts found
words in the utterance: "Why should I claim to guide men be-

fore I myself am guided?" and as he listened to other doctrines and other creeds, his honest doubts became confirmed, and noting daily the bitter narrowness of sectarianism, no matter of what form of religion, he became more and more wedded to the principle of toleration for all.'

In the debates organised under the auspices of Akbar's court, the representatives of various religious sects, each trying to prove the superiority of his own faith, exhibited their own passion in wordy outbursts, the emptiness of which was too shocking for the emperor to bear. He felt within his heart that with such differences bordering on mutual animosity there could be no collective progress among his people, no real peace. He knew that all religions have their own core of truth, but what he could not understand was the dry, dogmatic intellectualism and polemical perversions into which they had lapsed in his days. Religious at heart, he was pained by the bitter wrangles of their orthodox exponents. It was a new, wide and impartial outlook, the emperor thought, that alone could liberate man from the cramping bonds of narrow sectarianism. A common path for all must therefore be explored which would lead man to the truth that unity and solidarity are indispensable to the growth of a vigorous national life. While he was immersed in these thoughts there came to the vision of Akbar a light that, he thought, would chase away the darkness by which he was surrounded. He perceived that it was the king who could really be the symbol of national unity, the living and focussing centre of all the co-ordinated interests and activities of a nation's life. Loyalty to the king, he felt, would prepare and perfect the people's loyalty to harmony and unity and a concordant mutuality in the country.

It was this conception that took shape in his mind in what the emperor promulgated as *Din-i-Ilahi* or the Divine Faith. It was like an order whose members were required to be always ready to sacrifice all they had and all they were for the Padshah who was regarded as their sole protector. Thus the Divine Faith, which included the truths of various religions, assured that honour should be rendered to God, peace be given to the people and security to the empire. The conception was indeed grand and whatever its practical application, it cannot be said that it proved a complete failure. Unity, which was Akbar's aim, could come only when, as he believed, allegiance to a great ideal was rendered in common by the people. And he tried to incarnate this ideal in himself by assuming the leadership of the people. The idea was that the people, irrespective of their creed or race, should, by dedicating themselves to the Order and through that to its supreme head, the emperor, feel united by the same community of interests, the same ideals and aspirations, the same principles for the guidance of their inner and outer life. But Akbar did not use his royal power to force this on his subjects. There were conscientious objectors and he respected them. In fact, the emperor gave full liberty of thought to his subjects. And for the acceptance of his views he would always appeal to their conscience with all the ardour of his soul.

III

Unity is one of the central teachings of Islam, and there is no doubt that Akbar was an apostle of it. And the very way in which he tried to give form to it was by itself a marvel demonstration of human fellowship. The cultural unity which Akbar saw among his Hindu subjects helped to strengthen his conviction, born of his essentially religious nature, that a great nation would in future evolve in India taking its stand on a larger unity; and it was the truth of this unity that the emperor sought to emphasise in all that he did politically and culturally. The very fact that he persistently endeavoured to unite India even in the teeth of a tough opposition is an eloquent testimony to the ruling passion, the lifelong dream, the master-idea of this great personality. To Akbar's intuition this vast country was one and indivisible, one people and even one race; and he was daring enough to encourage racial intermingling, so that a new type of humanity might be produced by this fusion.

Akbar could see far into the future. He was verily a practical idealist who commanded a vision of the greatness of India in future, broad-based on her fundamental oneness. And if he did not live to see the realisation of his noble vision, he was of course happy to feel and find that his subjects—Hindus, Muslims and various sects and communities—were tending to grow into a common national consciousness through the recognition of the incontestable fact that the land of India was their common home and that the king was a benevolent organizer and promoter of their collective well-being.

While it is true that the membership of *Din-i-Ilahi* was confined to a sincere few of the Hindu and Muslim aristocracy, it is also true that the desire to serve the common good, which was the basic aim of the Order, made a profound and lasting impression on the masses. Thousands used to flock to the polo ground of Fatehpur to receive the bounty which Akbar lavished upon the poor without any distinction of race or creed. When the Padshah appeared at the *Jharokha* window of the palace every morning to say his prayers and to show himself to his subjects, crowds of Hindus assembled below in the hope of being able to begin their day with a sight of 'Vishnu's viceregent on earth,' *Dillishwaro va Jagadishwaro va* (The Lord of Delhi is the Lord of the earth).

Thus did the Hindus find in Akbar an emperor whose magnanimity and saintliness revived in them their age-old virtue of unstinted loyalty to the king, which was one of their racial traits lying dormant for a long time. It was this spontaneous loyalty from all communities of his subjects, specially from the Hindus, which was one of the most valuable of the legacies that Akbar left to his descendants. Indeed many an achievement of the later Moghul emperors was possible only because of what Akbar had done in a spirit of broad-minded statesmanship and politico-religious equity.

Akbar would not allow the Ulemas to interfere with the affairs of the State. He disdained the idea that the religious creeds of one community, especially those of its orthodox section, should dominate the political life of a country in which there are many other influential communities forming the major population and belonging to different faiths. He abolished social evils like *sati*[1] and early marriage among the Hindus, since he thought that life could not fully grow in a society demoralised by preposterous customs. He revoked iniquitous laws and taxes imposed on the Hindus by the previous Muslim rulers for the simple reason that religion should not be made a ground for any special impost, far less for those which stand self-condemned in

---

1. Voluntary self-immolation of the widow in the funeral pyre of her dead husband.

the eye of God. In the midst of the jubilation of victory when spirits naturally run high and the brute impulse to sack and pillage acquire an unchallenged traditional legitimacy, Akbar showed a remarkable magnanimity towards the conquered by forbidding all exhibition of cruelty and vandalism on the part of his troops. This was no less an act of humanity and large hearted ness than a fine stroke of statesmanship which won the hearts as well as the bodies of the conquered and made for peace, security and stability in his kingdom.

The builder of an empire, Akbar felt the need of political unity in it, and his constant concern was to consolidate his whole dominion into an inviolable integrity that would render it safe from all forces of disruption, and make it possible for the people to progress smoothly in all directions. Akbar appropriated all *jagirs*[2] and converted them into Crown lands as a step, among others, towards centralising his authority which was politically indispensable. But his success in bringing about the unity that existed in his empire came largely as a result of the way in which he gave form to his conviction that peace and goodwill form the strongest foundation of an empire. Babar and Sher Shah had tried to base their administration on this idea; but it was left to Akbar to make it the very guiding principle of his rule. His declaraion of *Sulh-i-kul* (universal peace) at a time when in Europe the principle enforced was *cujus regio ejus religio* (as is the religion, such is the region), sprang from a soul that knew and lived the noblest ideals of kingship. The emperor proclaimed: 'A monarch is a pre-eminent representative of God. Upon his conduct depends the efficiency of any course of action. His gratitude to his Lord, therefore, should be shown in just government and due recognition of merit; that of his people in obedience and praise. Tyranny is unlawful in everyone, especially in a sovereign who is the guardian of the world.' Every word of it rings with sincerity, reminding us of similar edicts of another emperor of India who, nearly two thousand years before Akbar, had tried to conduct his administration according to the tenets of Dharma. Akbar made the best use of all his extraordinary qualities to discharge this self-imposed responsibility; and history testifies to the success of his efforts, of which the most glowing proof is

---

2. Fief.

furnished by the spontaneous fealty that the Padshah received from all communities.

Akbar had as his Revenue Minister, Todar Mall, a Hindu who introduced many beneficial measures which improved the financial position of the State; and the highest offices were thrown open to Hindus and Muslims alike, appointments being made on the merits of the candidates. Man Singh, who has been characterised by a Muslim historian as a Hindu wielding the sword of Islam, was one of the most trusted of Akbar's generals. There are instances, too numerous to mention, of Hindus having been placed in position of trust and responsibility. The administration of the State was based mainly on the principles of Hindu polity enunciated in Kautilya's *Arthashastra*. More than half of Akbar's army was Hindu, the Rajputs being an important element in it. The winning of the Rajputs' loyalty was undoubtedly a triumph of Akbar's equitable statesmanship. It is because of them that millions in northern India looked with favour on Akbar's government and had always its welfare at heart. And greater, indeed, was their contribution to the synthesis of religions and cultures which was the most cherished dream of the emperor's life. Neither is it to be overlooked that by their acceptance of the democratic Muslim ideas of political and social organisation, the Rajputs helped in the fusion of the Hindus and the Muslims in many spheres of their corporate life. No impartial historian can fail to give credit to these pioneers of Indo-Muhammadan culture which is the greatest gift of the Moghuls to this country.

Akbar's insatiable thirst for knowledge brought him into intimate contact with many saints and scholars of different schools of thought. The renowned Muslim saint Shaikh Salim, the famous mystic Dadu with whom Akbar had discussions for forty days, the Sufi free-thinker Mubarak who was well-known for his knowledge of the literature and philosophy of Greece, the Brahmin Pandit Purushotam, the Jain scholar Hiravijaya, the Parsi theologian Dastur Meherji, the Jesuit Father Rodolfo were only a few out of a large number of thinkers and saintly personalities of the time, with whom Akbar used to have free exchange of views regarding philosophies and cultures of which they were then the recognised exponents.

The emperor was also keenly interested in science and history. 'Among the books of renown,' says Abul Fazl, 'there are few that are not read in His Majesty's assembly hall; and there are no historical facts of the past ages, or curiosities of science. or interesting points of philosophy, with which His Majesty, a leader of impartial sages, is unacquainted.'

Thus sumptuously fed and nurtured upon the treasures of wisdom, Akbar's mind developed a large synthesis in its essential cast and outlook, and a love of culture and refinement. We find the former expressing itself in the new idealism propounded by him out of the fundamental truths of all religions, and the latter in the wonderful forms of arts and letters that grew under Akbar's fostering care and gave to the Moghuls all their greatness and glory. Indeed, the Emperor was an enthusiastic patron of every kind of cultural activity and the creative energies of the Hindus and Muslims broke into a combined endeavour to produce what may be called a new and composite expression of Indian culture.

Akbar dreamt of an all-India empire. Evidently, such a dream could not be realised but by the suppression of local independence and the welding of the provincial principalities into a systematic central control. But as it was not the dream of a politically ambitious ruler like Alexander but that of an idealist lover of India and her people and culture, it entailed little bitterness and disorder, provoked little resistance or revolt except in a very few cases where regional patriotism sought tenaciously to cleave to its own soil. An all-India empire was a mighty dream and it can only be the faint-hearted who will fling criticism at Akbar for this. The establishment of an empire undoubtedly requires diplomacy as well as statesmanship of a high order, but, as we have emphasised above, Akbar the man was far greater than Akbar the diplomat or Akbar the statesman. For, no other ruler of men in history could even have imagined the activities of an *Ibadatkhana* in which were held the philosophical conferences under Akbar's own direction. Some critics have characterised Akbar's *Din-i-Ilahi* as an attempt at his own deification; but an impartial study of the history of the age will convince all that Akbar never sought to deify himself. The utmost that can be said was that the great emperor was aiming at the establishment of a unified and cosmopolitan theocracy in India with a benevolent monarch at its head, and there was nothing improper or unjust in it. For, theocracy has been the character of all States in the East, even from the days of Egypt and Assyria. It was the Hindu ideal, and it was the ideal of Islam too. All that Akbar sought to do was to modernise it and bring it into line with the political ideals of the sixteenth century, and the special needs of a country like India—a land of many creeds and many peoples as she then was.

But the greatness of Akbar lay in this that he did not believe in bringing about a seeming homogeneity by the application of external pressure; he wanted to change the very hearts of the people, fire them with a wide national idealism and provide them with a new politico-social outlook, a new framework of corporate self-expression. This was the earnest effort of a sincere soul to realise the integral unity of national thought and culture. But alas! the task was too great and complex for even an emperor, however gifted and inspired he might be. A spiritual genius of the highest order was needed, a perfect combination of the unclouded vision of knowledge and the infallibly effective power of knowledge to actualise this colossal dream of a united India—united in faith and culture, in aspiration and achievement, in all the teeming diversity of a richly flowering national life.

IV

Yet in appraising the work of Akbar the historian must acknowledge that in all that he did for the political advancement of India he was guided by a vision of her oneness and integrity. But this vision opens into a greater truth, a deeper meaning, a higher purpose. It is not for nothing that the seers and sages of ancient India worshipped this holy land as the Mother—the Mother who holds in her bosom infinite bounties not only for the physical nourishment of man but also for his spiritual sustenance and growth. Even what she externally is was regarded by them as a conscious formation of the Mahashakti, the supreme Mother, who will manifest here and liberate humanity and lead it to its divine goal. 'One India' is not a mere glowing dream, wrought out of the fire and fantasy of a perfervid patriotism. It is a preordained fact, a spiritual reality waiting for materialisation when the children of this country, transcending the bounds of their caste, creed or race, will awaken to a deeper and larger vision of the Mother and discover in it their oneness. The cultural unity necessary for such a consummation has always been there as an unfailing foundation. Attempts have been made through the ages both by Hindu and Muslim emperors from Chandragupta Maurya to Akbar to build on it the structure of a strong political unit; but the structure took its definite form under the British rule—a device of Nature to bring about that eventuality after so many previous means had been found wanting. The political unity of India is a requisite condition for that real and permanent unity which it is the destiny of India to achieve. And the time for that is approaching, despite the reactionary forces that stand in her way. For, the Shakti of India must fulfil her Will. And no power on earth can stop that.

What Akbar foresaw and began is being progressively developed and perfected by a complexus of politico-cultural forces of prodigious magnitude. Akbar's was the greatness of the vision, the largeness and nobility of the conception, the intrepidity of the first decisive formation. The kingliest of political dreamers, the mightiest of political architects, the most humane of legislators and administrators, Akbar stands unique in history. Neither Alexander nor Caesar, nor Napoleon was endowed with such an amplitude and depth of humanity combined with such a quiet strength and far-seeing constructive genius. Akbar was no power-hunter, no fanatic of a religious or political idea, no reckless gambler with the fortunes of a nation. Chandragupta, Ashoka and Akbar—these are the three great names that shine out with a striking lustre from the galaxy of Indian monarchs. The first two were the pure product of ancient Hindu culture and the last, a fine flower of that Indo-Saracenic fusion which bids fair to play an important part in the creative life of the united India of tomorrow. It is time we tried to reassess the greatness of this royal unifier of our motherland.

REFERENCES

Ishwari Prasad, *A Short History of Mughal Rule in India;* Tara Chand, *A Short History of the Indian People;* Laurence Binyon, *Akbar;* V. A. Smith, *Akbar the Great Mogul;* Abul Fazl (Tr. Blockmann and Jarret),

Ain-i-Akbari; Cambridge History of India, Vol. IV; M. Roychoudhury, *Din-i-Ilahi;* E. B. Havell, *History of Aryan Rule in India;* J. H. Robinson, *Medieval and Modern Times;* J. N. Sarkar, *Mughal Administration;* Badaoni, *Surat-ul-baqarah* (Lowe's translation).

4

Cultural Fellowship in Medieval India

I

OF THE TWO tendencies that mainly characterise medieval India, its builders and movements, one is towards the establishment of a State, and the other towards the creation of a composite culture, both having their value and significance for the future of the country. In what follows an attempt is made to study these latter tendencies and how they are reflected in the cultural and social movements in medieval India.

Not that Hindu-Muslim relations were all through smooth sailing. Conflicts of ideals were there with their consequent repercussions on the life of both the communities and these were anything but happy. Maybe, the conflicts brought them nearer in their hearts and minds and helped their mutual understanding.

An idea of the life of the people of both the communities during the medieval times as also of the efforts on their parts towards mutual cooperation and understanding may be had from their cultural and social activities. Thus while a settled, centralised government or a condition of peace could not be there as a cohesive factor in the collective life of the people, an Arab scholar was committing to memory the rules of Sanskrit grammar; a Hindu king was hearing the Quran read to him; an Amir Khusru was giving poetical expression to the love-episode between a Muslim prince and a Hindu princess, and evolving new styles of music out of the Persian and Hindu ones; an Iz-ud-din Khalid Khani was translating into Persian a work on Hindu philosophy; a Hindu architect was drawing designs for a mosque or supervising the construction of one; a Nizam-ud-din

Aulia was preaching the Sufi doctrine of love; a **Kabir** was singing impassioned lyrics on the glory and oneness of God, proclaiming that God is above all religions and that to Him Hindus and Muslims are one; and a philologist was busy devising a technique with which to systematise the new and common language that had already been growing up partly as a matter of course, partly under the stress of necessity.

The story is indeed a romantic one of how this fellowship was taking shape almost in every sphere of Indian life.

The Hindu converts did not completely give up their old habits and usages, and their contact with the Muslims produced a syncretisation of the two faiths and rounded off many angularities on both sides. The Hindus took part in Muslim festivities, and were entering the world of Islamic ideas through more and more acquaintance with the Persian and Arabic languages and literatures. The Muslims on their part had begun to show interest in Indian culture long before they started to hold political sway over India. Mention may be made of the Abbasid court's patronage of Hindu scholars, the Buddhist inclinations of the Baramikis of Baghdad, and of the glowing terms in which the culture and religions of the Hindus were praised by Arabic and Persian scholars, studied in Chapter Nine.

The study of Sanskrit by the Muslims may be said to have begun almost immediately they came into contact with India. Many Muslim scholars visited the country after the invasion of Sind by Muhammad bin-Kasim in the eighth century. One of them wrote the first history of Sindh, and another its first geography. In order to know the country and its culture more thoroughly, they learnt Sanskrit through which alone could such knowledge be had. They translated into Arabic a number of Sanskrit works including the astronomical treatise *Brihaspati Siddhanta* and the scientific writings of Arya Bhatta. On the other hand, Mirza Raja Sawai Jai Singh, himself a keen student in astronomy, had a number of Arabic works on astronomy rendered into Sanskrit. The Arabic version of *Panchatantra* is attributed to the Sanskrit-knowing Arab scholars. In India some of the Muslim scholars got many Sanskrit texts translated into Persian, and later Akbar was the greatest among these patrons of learning.

Muslim inscriptions written in Sanskrit have been discovered in Gujarat. They are written in a manner which reveals the profound admiration of the Muslims for Hindu culture. The Somnath Patan inscription (13th century) recording the building of a mosque is a celebrated instance. It begins with the following peculiar invocation according to the Hindu fashion: 'Om, Adoration to holy Visvanath. Adoration to Thee who art the Lord of the Universe, adoration to Thee whose form is the universe.' The inscription mentions the then ruling Hindu king of Gujarat with all his titles, and pays a reverent tribute to the chief Hindu priest of Somnath. It also says that the Muslims in one of the holiest places of the Hindus, Somnath Patan, received warm support from the local Hindus in building a mosque and endowing a property for its maintenance. Thus Mahmud's brutal depredations on the temple of Somnath two hundred years ago did not affect the Hindu spirit of toleration and generosity towards the Muslims. And the Muslims also did not hesitate to write such an important inscription in nothing but purely Sanskrit terms.

Sandesa Rasaka is a work of the Muslim poet Abdul Rahaman of the twelfth century. It is written in Apabhramsa, the current popular speech of western India, derived from Sanskrit. In *Rasaka* the celebrated Muslim poet shows his deep understanding of and respect for Hindu life and culture then prevalent in Mulasthana (modern Multan). Its poetical excellence attracted two Jain monk-scholars and inspired them to write commentaries on it in Sanskrit. Zain-ul Abdin (15th century), the king of Kashmir, who looked equally to the welfare of his Hindu and Muslim subjects, extended his patronage to the poets and writers of both the communities. He was as much interested in the study of Sanskrit as he was in Persian. He commissioned the Hindu pundit Jona Raja and the Muslim scholar Mullah Admad to bring down to his day the famous *Rajatarangini* of Kalhana; the former did it in the original Sanskrit and the latter in Persian. The saintly character of Abdin led to a popular belief among the Hindus that he was the reincarnation of a Hindu ascetic.

II

The interest of Hindu scholars in Arabic and Persian is no less remarkable. It is possible that this started in Bengal and the

Punjab earlier than in other parts of northern India, in Bengal because the Pathan and the Afghan rulers there did not take long to adjust themselves to the country. Rupa and Sanatan, before they became the companions of Shri Chaitanya, belonging to his inner circle, held responsible offices in the courts of Sultan Hussain Shah of Bengal. The former was in charge of the literary department and the latter was the Chief Minister of the Sultan. Both of them were erudite scholars in Arabic and Persian as well as in Sanskrit. They had an intimate knowledge of the teachings of the Prophet and composed notable works in Persian. In the North, particularly during the Moghul rule, when Persian had already established itself as the language of the court, it was more and more widely cultivated. In Western India, Nandalal Munshi, Bhagavandas, Ranchhodi Amarji are some of the noted Hindu writers in Persian. Lalla Ded, the well-known literary celebrity of Kashmir, combined in herself both Sanskrit and Persian cultures. She was regarded as a link between the classical Sanskrit traditions of the past and the Persian poetic patterns of the more recent times. Munshi Bhawani Das Kachru, the eminent Hindu poet of Kashmir, evolved the new style of the Bahari-Tavil in Persian poetry. Teba Ram (Betab) is still remembered for his *Jang Namah* which is considered by some to stand on a par with the *Shah Namah* of Firdausi.

The early Sufi teachers in India proved a great unifying force in the common collective life of both the communities. Theirs was the Path of Love which would lead the seeker to the All-Pervading One, the centre and source of all existence. Large numbers, Hindus and Muslims, followed their teachings. Al-Jullaqi (11th century) was the first preceptor of Sufism in India. His tomb in Lahore is a place of pilgrimage for Hindus and Muslims. Muinuddin Chisti (12th century) had his seat in Delhi and later in Pushkar in Ajmer. His *dargah* attracts a constant stream of Hindu and Muslim pilgrims from various parts of the surrounding country. Music and dancing as in Hindu temples are a remarkable feature of this Sufi shrine. The Husaini Brahmins of Pushkar are descendants of his disciples. They are neither orthodox Hindus nor orthodox Muslims. They say, 'We are Brahmins, our scripture is the Atharva Veda in which Hindu and Muhamedan doctrines have been synthesised.' Priests or *kakas* of the Imamshahi sect are something like the Husaini Brahmins. Members of the Shahadulla sect also invoke the authority of the Atharva Veda. Bin-Sir or the beheaded saint was no other than Shah Inayat who, because of his sympathies for the Hindus, was killed by the fanatical Muslim princes of Sindh. The Muslim devotee Baba Fattur of Kangra owned his spiritual life to the Hindu saint Gulab Sing. The followers of the *Piran Panth* of Gujarat have Hindu names, observe all Hindu customs except that their dead are buried with Islamic rites and that they are disciples of a Muslim guru. The inspired saints of medieval India, like Kabir, Nanak, Dadu, Ravidas and Rajjab, had immense influence over members of both the communities. Indeed, there was no difficulty in the way of a Muslim to be a member of Dadu's Brahma Society. It is these mystics that built up a new kind of religious fellowship during medieval times, and their work must be given the highest place in the cultural history of the period.

In other spheres also the intercourse between Hindus and Muslims was taking its own shape. Sikander Lodi had a Sanskrit text on medicine translated into Persian. Once when a pious Muslim protested against an order of his that no Hindu should be allowed to use the bathing ghats of Mathura opposite to which he had erected mosques, the Sultan drawing his sword in rage cried, 'Wretch, do you maintain the truth of Hindu religion?' 'By no means,' replied the brave man, 'I speak according to the law. Kings should not persecute their subjects on any account.' This answer, says Ferishta, pacified the Sultan. During his reign, according to the same authority, the Hindus began to learn Persian and study Islamic literature. Besides, there was then beginning to grow a common political consciousness among Hindus and Muslims, as is evident from the instances of both the communities fighting together a common enemy.

Ratan Singh of Chitor and Bahadur Shah of Gujarat assisted the Rajputs of Malwa against the Afghan Sultan Mahmud. When the fort of Batmir, a Rajput stronghold, was laid siege to by Timur, Hindus and Muslims fought side by side and perished together in the *jauhar* which terminated the struggle. Mahmud II, the last Sultan of Malwa, was under a deep obligation to the Rajput nobleman, Medini Rao, for his invaluable assistance in securing his succession to the throne when many muslim nobles had espoused the cause of Mahmud's elder brother. In recognition of his services, Mahmud appointed Medini Rao to the office of a minister with the result that Rajput influence became predominant in his court. It was due to the gallant defence of his Rajput bodyguard under the command of the Raja of Dhankulia that Ahmad Shah of Gujarat was able to escape when Hushang of Malwa made a sudden night attack on him and surrounded the royal pavilion. Rana Sanga of Mewar had many Muslims allies when he fought Babar in the famous battle of Khanwah.

III

The story of how cultural fellowships developed in medieval India is not confined to her northern regions only. Ample and striking evidences are available of the forms it took in her eastern and southern parts. In Bengal there was a perceptibely growing tendency between both the Hindu and Muslim communities to come closer to each other almost in every walk of life. The Muslim rulers were keen on having Hindu ministers; and marriages between Hindus and Muslims were not rare. Sultan Shamsuddin's *nika* (widow remarriage in Islam) with the Hindu widow Fulmati who exercised great influence in administrative matters, and the marriage of the two sons of the highly respectable Brahmin Raja of Ektakia with the daughters of Sultan Hussain Shah are not surely solitary cases of the Hindu-Muslim intermingling of blood.

There are abundant instances of Hindu or Muslim saints having followers in both the communities, and of Hindus fighting for Muslim rulers. There were sects which included both Hindu and Muslim members. Sahajiya Vaishnavism had in its fold Hindus, Muslims and, later, even Christians. Pagal Nathi and Gobra sects also recognise no difference between races and castes and had, besides Hindus of all castes, hundreds of Muslims as their members; and occasions were not rare when they were led and guided by Muslims or Hindus of low birth. So also were the other sects like Khusi Viswasi, Ramaballabhi, Jagamohini, Balarani, Neda or the shaven, Aul-Baul-Darbes-Sain, Samayogi, in each of which Hindus and Muslims were regarded

as members of a common spiritual fellowship. They did not believe in castes or sects, temples or images, and were, to a certain
extent, influenced by Islam, though originally they were derived
from the esoteric schools of Buddhism, Tantrikism, or the Vaishnavic scholars of Hinduism. Of these sects the most influential
was the Sahajiya one founded by Baba Aul. The followers of
it lived in couples practising the delicate and restrained art of
esoteric love. Men and women were comrades in spiritual discipline believing that the greatest self-control attained that way
would lead them to *Mahasukha,* 'the great Bliss,' the aim of their
sadhana, one of the most daring spiritual ventures ever undertaken by man.

Thus was evolving in medieval Bengal a spiritual synthesis
of a unique kind which was not without its bearing on the future
of the country. Many of these sects exist even to this day. There
were folk-forms of religious worship, such as, *Satya-Pir, Manik-
Pir, Kalu-Ghazi, Olai-Chandi, Tinlakh-Pir, Neda-Pir,* which
were equally popular among both the communities. *Satya* is a
Sanskrit word for truth and *Pir* is an Arabic equivalent for the
Hindu conception of *Guru,* the Master. The consecrated food at
this religious ceremony is called not by the Hindu name *prasad*
but by the Muslim name of *sinni* which is derived from the Persian word *sireen* meaning sweet. Satya-Pir, with which Husain
Shah's name is associated as the originator, has the largest number of worshippers almost in every part of Bengal. Even today this
is a common deity of both Hindus and Muslims. The feeling of
fellowship between the two communities so deepened that 'many
a Mohamedan offered puja at Hindu temples, as Hindus offered
sinni at Mohamedan mosques.' And this they continued up to
about two decades ago.

The contribution of Muslim rulers and, under their patronage, the contribution of Hindus and Muslims generally towards
the development of Bengali literature has been acknowleded as
immense and inestimable. The Afghan rulers of Bengal had the
Hindu epics and Puranas translated into Bengali. Many Vaishnava lyrics were composed by Muslim poets such as Garib Khan,
Shah Akbar, Aliraj. Recorded instances are there of Muslim
writers starting their works with an invocation to Hindu gods and
goddesses for their blessings. An attempt to identify Hindu gods

and saints with Islamic ones is noticed in the writings of Muslims like Aliraj and Saiyad Muhammad Akbar.

It is well known that the Afghan and Pathan rulers had their armies mainly formed by the natives who fought the Moghuls when they invaded Bengal. Sanatan Goswami was the Chief Minister of Sultan Hussain Shah. Later, Nawab Sarfaraj Khan of Dacca had in Yasawanta Rao of the same place a trusted friend and adviser. Nawab Alivardi's Chief Minister was the Hindu Durlabhram who revolted against Sirajuddowala when the latter began to ignore him and preferred in important matters of State the advice of Mohanlal, a Hindu young man well-versed in the arts of peace and war. History will never forget the exemplary courage and devotion to duty with which Mohanlal fought for Siraj, for his country, in the battle of Plassey.

In the architecture of medieval Bengal, as in that of other parts of northern India, Hindu and Buddhist styles combined with the Saracenic to produce a new form of the building art. The craftsmen of the mosques and tombs of Gauda, Pandua and Malda were most of them Hindus who almost invariably adapted their own technique to the needs of their Muslim masters. The designs on the brick-built *liwan* of the famous Sona Masjid (15th century) at Gauda, its door-ways, arches and their frames of curved architraves, are adaptations from Hindu shrines. Its stone pillars are distinctly Hindu, and its curved cornices and the vaulted side aisles are imitative of the ancient bamboo roofing of Bengal. The domes of the Jami Masjid (14 century) retain their Hindu finials. The Saracenic influence on them is the ex-quiste calligraphic work done by the Arabic and Persian artists. The beautiful *mihrab* of the Adina mosque (14th century) at Gauda is too obviously Hindu in design to require any comment. The outer arch of it looks like the trefoil arched canopy of the image of Vishnu, found in the Manbhum district, but the inscriptions and arabesque ornament in it are contributions of Saracenic art. These Muslim buildings influenced the construction of many Hindu temples, an example of which is the temple (18th century) at Kantanagar in the Dinajpur district.

The number was not small of the Muslims in medieval Bengal who erected temples for Hindu deities, made liberal grants for their maintenance and the celebration of necessary festivities, and of Hindus who spent money lavishly on the construction of

mosques and tombs of the Muslims. Hussain Shah restored
many Hindu temples of Navadwip. The Shahshuja Mosque in
Comilla, built by the Hindu Maharaja Govinda Manikya of Tri-
pura, and the temples of Kali in Narayanpur, erected by Mirza
Hosen Ali, are by no means solitary instances.

In the building up of this cultural fellowship in Bengal the
cult of Sahajiya and the neo-Vaishnavism of Shri Chaitanya
played a very important part. Shri Chaitanya in his ecstatic sense
of oneness of all, made no distinction of race and religion and
freely admitted Muslims into the loving arms of Vaishnavism.
Haridas, a Muslim, belonged to his inner circle.

Shri Chaitanya's influence, however, was not confined to
Bengal alone. His victorious campaigns in the west as far as
Gujarat and in the south as far as Rameshwaram wrote a glorious chapter in the history of cultural fellowship in India. Fired
with a heavenly zeal which only the God-possessed can feel,
Chaitanya set out on his holy mission of disseminating the sacred
name of Shri Krishna, and conquered by his consummate wisdom
and matchless devotion the heart of Prakashananda Saraswati of
Kashi, the then greatest authority on Vedanta and head of the
Dandi Sannyasins; of Prataprudra, the king of Orissa; of Vasu-
deva Sarvabhauma of Puri, the foremost scholar of the Deccan;
of Rudrapati, the king of Travancore. The Vaishnava communities in Deragazi Khan, Sindh, Gujarat, Vrindaban, Orissa and
the Deccan, proclaimed the widespread influence of Shri Chaitanya, through which was built up a unique spiritual fellowship
in India. Nor was this fellowship a one-way movement. Shri
Chaitanya would never fail to appreciate what was of devotional
value in the culture of the places he visited. Mention may be
made of two instances. In the temple of Tiruvattar in South
India he heard the recital of a portion of the *Brahma Samhita,* a
Sanskrit treatise on Bhakti, and was so much impressed that he
prostrated himself before the book. He was filled with ecstatic
joy. He had the book copied out and popularised it wherever he
went. Another book of a great sage of South India (probably
Kerala) the *Krishna-Karamrita* of Bilvamangala was also introduced into Bengal by Chaitanya who regarded these two books
as the most valuable of the treasures he secured in his wanderings
in South India.

IV

In the South which was less disturbed by the political turmoils of the North, this bhakti movement, though slow, showed signs of steady progress as was evident from its results in a later period when happy relations between the two communities were almost an established fact. The Vijayanagara kings had a large number of Muslim cavalrymen and archers in their armies. The kings showed scrupulous regard for their religious feelings and, according to Hindu custom, rewarded them with grants of land. These Muslims lived in a quarter of the city, where the State erected a splendid mosque for them. The Quran was brought into the royal court when Muslim officers came to swear loyalty to the king. The king Ramaraja of Vijayanagar had many Muslims even in the royal bodyguard.

Compelled by defeat in a battle with the Bahmani Sultan Tajuddin Firoz, the Vijayanagara king Deva Raya (early 15th century) gave his daughter in marriage to Firoz. This is the first matrimonial relationship between a Muslim Sultan and a Hindu princess in the Deccan, with which, it is said, began a new era of friendship between the two kingdoms. The Sultan also married his eldest son, Hasan Khan, to Parthal, the pretty daughter of a Hindu goldsmith. These two marriages as also his appointment of Narsingh of Kherla as an Amir of his kingdom were really instances of the policy the Sultan set before himself, that of befriending the Hindu elements of the population. Brahmins who were then probably the only learned men among the Hindus were taken into the services of the State in large numbers and rose to positions of power and responsibility. The Sultan also maintained friendly relations with Hindu chiefs of Telingana, some of whom like the Velamas of Nalgunda actually allied themselves with Firoz against their enemies, the Vemas of Rajamundry. Firoz was a linguist and he knew the languages of the country so well that he could speak them fluently. The conciliatory attitude of the Bahmani Sultans towards the Hindus reflected itself in the architecture of the period. Thus the Perso-Bahmani arch of the great tomb of Firoz himself at Gulbarga rests gracefully on purely Hindu jambs; and the brackets supporting the Chhajja of the fine tomb of Gesu Daraz, the patron saint of the Deccan, remind one of the brackets in some of the well-known Hindu temples of the Deccan.

When Ibrahim became the Sultan of Bijapur, he introduced certain changes into the administration, one of which was to keep the revenue accounts in Marathi instead of in Persian, in consequence of which the Brahmin accountants began to acquire considerable influence in the government of Bijapur. Ibrahim was truly a great king. He took upon himself the title of *Jagatguru* (world-teacher), and brought into being a new language. We find several State documents of his time beginning with an invocation to Saraswati, the Hindu goddess of learning. In one of the palaces of Bijapur there is a temple dedicated to the Hindu saint Narasimhasaraswati by a Sultan who is said to have received spiritual boons from the saint. The Muslim court of Ahmadnagar had a Brahmin minister who even acted as a confidential adviser to Amir Berid, a professed champion of the Sunni sect.

In the thirteenth century Syed Jamaluddin, an Arab refugee, who got many favours from the Pandya king Sundara Pandya Thevan, became the latter's Prime Minister and ultimately, on his death, the ruler of the land. The golden image of a Muslim princess under the feet of the idol of God Cheluvaraya Pillai in Melkote, a famous Vaishnavite centre of South India, reminds one of the story of Ramanuja's quest for the same idol taken away by a Muslim king of the North, the father of the same princess. Ramanuja got back the idol through the miracle of its walking straight to him when, after reaching the palace of the emperor, he was earnestly pleading for its return. The princess who had been most devoutly worshipping the idol followed it to Melkote all alone, and when on her arrival found Cheluvaraya in the shrine, she was seen no more, having been absorbed into the god whom she loved with the love of a perfect devotee. The image of such an ideal devotee has thus come to be installed along with the god of her heart.

The munificence of the Muslims for Hindu temples in the South deserves mention. Gulam Ali Khan Saheb, a Viceroy of Bijapur, made a grant to the Venkataramanaswami temple at Alamgiri. This grant, it is said, was continued during the Moghul rule. Mention may be made here of a letter from another general of Bijapur named Ranadulla Khan, to the Guru of the Sringeri Math, in which he prayed for the latter's blessings. There is also documentary evidence that Ranadulla made a grant of some villages to the monastery of Shankaracharya at Sankeshwar. He was on very friendly terms with the Sardesai of Vantmuri in the Belgaum district. The many ways in which Hyder Ali and his son Tippu Sultan showed their interest in the Sringeri Math are proof of the great influence the Guru of this Math exercised over these Muslim rulers. Tippu actually sought the help of its Guru when he was hemmed in with danger.

In several states in he Deccan, participation by Hindus in Muslim festivals and by Muslims in Hindu ones have from early medieval times been a common feature. And this mutual participation has always been encouraged by the Hindu rulers of these States. The Muharrum is one such festival in which the Hindus used freely to take part, and the Ganapati is another which the Muslims used to attend in large numbers. Occasions were not rare when Hindus and Muslims carried shoulder to shoulder the *tazia,* the model tomb of Hasan and Husain in Muharrum processions. It is believed that in early days when the Hindus forgot their feuds with the Muslims they used to associate themselves with the Muslim religious festivals out of a genuine religious feeling.

There are in the South shrines and tombs of Muslim saints which are visited as places of pilgrimage both by Hindus and Muslims. The *dargah* of a Muslim saint known as Sayyasaheb at Mudhol in the Deccan, attracts Muslims and Hindus including orthodox Brahmins. Many Hindu families named their children after the saint. The Raja of Mudhol used to pay his homage to the saint on the eve of any important function in the family. The tombs of the Muslim saint Miran Saheb in Nagore and of another in Mysore city are visited by large numbers of Hindu worshippers. On a little hill in Madura there is a temple dedicated to God Subrahmanya and a shrine of Fakir Sikandar, a Muslim saint. Devotees of both the communities, whenever they visit the hill, pray at both the places of worship and it is a common sight to see a Hindu in the Sikander shrine and a Muslim in the Subrahmanya temple.

These are only a few instances of how in different parts of medieval India Hindus and Muslims were cooperating in common corporate endeavours and how through them they were beginning to understand each other, reconcile their differences and grow towards a common cultural outlook. These efforts bore abundant fruit during the heydey of the Moghuls whose amazing success was principally due to three factors. The first was the pioneer work, but very valuable from a political standpoint, done by the Turks; the second was that the Moghuls had a clearer vision of an empire in India than the Turks; and the third, but the most important of all, was the new spiritual outlook of the people created by the lives and teachings of the saints who opened up, and to a considerable extent fulfilled, the possibilities of a wonderful religious synthesis broadbased on direct spiritual experiences and thereby enlivened the innate spirituality of the race and sought to rouse it for its larger fulfilment in a greater Future which will transcend all credal religions by a direct vision of God, God in all, as the inspired medieval mystics proclaimed.

In the One World of Tomorrow it is this vision, the Ancient Vision of India, that would guide all affairs of man, all his relations and activities.

REFERENCES

Atulananda Chakravarty, *Cultural Fellowship in India;* C. S. Srinivasachari, *The Vijayanagara Empire;* Dineshchandra Sen, *Brihat Banga* (Bengali); E. B. Havell, *Indian Architecture, History of Aryan Rule in India;* Ishwaru Prashad, *History of Medieval India, History of Muslim Rule in India, Society and Culture in Medieval India;* Kshitimohan Sen, *Mystics of Medieval India, Medieval Mystics* (in *Cultural Heritage of India,* Vol. III, First edition); K. Sherwani, *The Bahmani Kingdom;* Sisirkumar Mitra, *A Marvel of Cultural Fellowship; Cambridge History of India,* Vol. IV; A. Krishnaswamy Iyengar, series of articles in *The Hindu* on Hindu-Muslim Relations in the South.

5

A Mighty Nation-Builder

I

AFTER THE last Moghul Emperor, Aurangzeb, the important power of note in India for almost a century was the Maratha confederacy. But the Marathas were not the only people to throw off the thraldom of Delhi. There were many others, at least three of whom were Muslim. The fact was that the Moghul Empire had never really consolidated itself. Its whole history was one of struggle between a greedy and powerful central authority and a host of champions of local independence scattered all over the country. These latter were both Hindu and Muslim, whose courage and patriotism rank them high with heroic soldiers of liberty like Bruce and Hannibal, Wallace and Washington. In the eye of history a hero is a hero whether he fights for an empire or for a fortress. The life of a champion of local freedom becomes doubly important to a student of history when he succeeds in establishing a new power in the land. It is from this point of view that we have to study the career of Shivaji. It was on the firm foundation of his achievements that Baji Rao and others raised the edifice of Maratha supremacy. And we must not lose sight of the fact that this great king was as great a soldier as a statesman, as great an idealist as a practical organizer.

These few aspects do not exhaust the achievements of Shivaji's many-sided genius. He was indeed greater than any of them, greater in a way than any of the great conquerors of history from Alexander to Napoleon. These latter had, every one of them, at least some ready material to build on, but Shivaji had none. He reared a powerful army of heroes out of common clay; he created a people, a nation, once observed Sri Aurobindo. This was possible because there was in him a power of God at work.

In order to view Shivaji's work in its proper light we must have a glance at the past history of the Deccan and at the conditions in which he was born and brought up. About the time when Mahmud of Ghazni was leading his plundering hordes into northern India there flourished in the extreme south the powerful and extensive empire of the Cholas. This Chola empire broke up in the course of time but despite the lure of its fabulous wealth, the Afghans had never ventured to that part of India, possibly due to its being far too away from the Afghan base. Islam did ultimately cross the Vindhyas but that was much later. Even then it did not extend very far south. Hence the integrity of Chola culture remained unaffected.

The history of the conquest of Devagiri, the establishment of the Bahmani empire, its disintegration and the rise of the five Musalman kingdoms of the Deccan are too well known to require more than a passing notice. While the Bahmanis were consolidating their power north of the Krishna, there arose south of that river and of the Tungabhadra, the powerful Hindu kingdom of Vijayanagara. Founded for a definite purpose by the famous Minister-General Madhavacharya, comparable only with his prototype of the great Minister of the Mauryas in ancient history, it never quite lost its original character and continued to function for well-nigh two centuries not only as an invulnerable bulwark against the oncoming tide of Muslim conquest but as an ardent champion of the cultural traditions of the country.

In the sixteenth century, only a few decades after Babar's victory at Panipat, the Vijayanagara kingdom succumbed to a concerted attack by the five Sultans of the South. But the days of these five kingdoms also were numbered. Vijayanagara no doubt fell a prey to her own vices but not before she had successfully stemmed the onrush of the Pathan conquest. To the Moghul emperors, from Akbar to Aurangzeb, the conquest of the five southern kingdoms was the pivot of their military ambition. Aurangzeb's very attempt to realise this ambition brought about the end of the Moghul empire. To understand it one has to understand the significance of Maratha Swarajya under Shivaji.

II

Shivaji was the famous son of a famous father, Shahaji Bhonsle, known as the king-maker of Ahmadnagar. This noted soldier and far-sighted statesman played a most important part during the final stages of the struggle between the Moghul empire and the Nizam Shahi of Ahmadnagar. In the wide field of Deccan politics he was constantly playing one Muslim power against another in the interest of his Sultan of Ahmadnagar. When his last effort failed and his puppet king was taken prisoner by the Moghuls, he took service with Bijapur and became in time one of the most powerful personages in that Sultanate. There is reason to think that this statesman foresaw a great future for the Hindus in the history of the Deccan. Whether he actually intended to establish a kingdom of his own or not is a matter of doubt. But the fact is there that he did establish in the extreme south a powerful *jaigir* (fief), which, like other Maratha *jaigirs* in the South, was nominally under the control of the Sultan.

Shahaji, however, was the only Hindu statesman of the time with a clear vison of the day, not far off, when the Hindu power would preponderate in the Deccan. And this vision, as every historian knows, would have come true but for the almost accidental circumstances through which Nature brought about the ascendancy of the British power in India. Even such a shrewd statesman as Warren Hastings did not visualise any power but the Maratha to be supreme in India. For, when Emperor Shah Alam's son came to Calcutta to solicit British protection for his poor father, did not Hastings reply that the only man who could give that protection was Mahadaji Sindhia?

There was in the Bhonsle family a tradition that by the special grace of Shiva, a scion of that family would one day free Maharashtra from the alien grip. That this tradition existed is beyond doubt. Whether Shahaji believed in it or not is another matter. But the manner in which he had Shivaji brought up and educated would seem to indicate that he believed in a brilliant

future for this rather wayward boy of his. Shahaji kept with
himself his elder son, a sedate youth, as a sort of general assis-
tant in the management of his southern *jaigir*. But he posted his
younger son at Poona, a strategic position of great importance,
under the careful tutelage of his mother Jijabai and a trusted and
able Brahmin officer Dadaji Konddeva.

During his early years at least, Shivaji never received any
encouragement from his father or from his tutor, Dadaji, to em-
bark on a career of reckless adventure, but different was the case
with his great mother. Born a princess of the ancient Jadav
family of Ahmadnagar, full of the traditions and aspirations of
that house, she dreamt golden dreams of her beloved son, and
kindled in his tender breast a fiery zeal for his religion and an
ardent faith in the future of his people. And she was no idle
dreamer. Her efficient administration of the Poona-Supa *jaigirs*
on behalf of her son marked her out as a woman of high practical
abilities. In saying this we do not wish to belittle the services of
Dadaji, but in all such things the inspiration came from Jijabai
till her son was old enough to know his own mind, and even then
through subtle ways—known only to a loving mother of her type
—she exercised about Shivaji's noble ambition till almost his last
few days, but Jijabai was always fully aware of her son's inmost
aspirations and was in complete sympathy with them: In fact,
she sustained him through all the trials and tribulations of his
eventful career. We have a suspicion that even the plan of his
earliest exploit, the capture of Torna, was known to his mother
beforehand.

Here is a contemporary account of Shivaji's appearance and
the impression he made on others: 'At sight Shivaji's body
looks lean and short. His appearance is wonderfully fair in complexion, and even without finding out who he is, one does feel
instinctively that he is a ruler of men. His spirit and manliness
are apparent. He is a very brave high-souled man and wears a
beard.'

As a Kshatriya boy, Shivaji was put through a complete course
of military training, and was moreover fully trained in the work
of developing and administering his father's *jaigir* of Poona and
Supa. In his early youth, during his several months' stay with
his father at Bijapur he had first-hand knowledge of practical
statecraft of a higher order, and studied under the direct guidance

of his father the details of administration of a large kingdom like Bijapur. On the other hand, Dadaji had not omitted to equip the mind of his pupil with the rich contents of the Hindu epics and the history of his own people. There are some who deny that Shivaji had a scholastic training such as was given to all Sardars of position in those days.

But the salient feature of Shivaji's character, the spiritual, was undeniable and was nobody's gift. He was born with a vision vouchsafed to a rare few in this world. From his early youth right up to the last he sought and enjoyed the company of godly men, both Hindu and Muslim. In this connection it may be stated that regard for Muslim saints was a tradition in the Bhonsle family; both Shahaji and his brother Sharifji were born under the blessings of a *fakir* of the name of Shah Sharif. Shivaji's spiritual urge had nothing in it of the Hinduism of narrow-minded bigotry and knew no distinction between race and race. Instances are many of his having employed Muslims in positions of great trust in the State, and it is worthy of note that he had a mosque built within the walls of Raigarh itself. He was out to create a great national kingdom in which he would leave no room for petty sectarianism. Never once did Shivaji show the slightest disrespect to the Muslims' holy book. Even Khafi Khan, his greatest detractor, admits that whenever a copy of the Quran came into the king's hands he had it conveyed with reverence to the nearest Muslim of position. It would be cynical to describe Shivaji's consistent fairness towards his antagonists as a matter of policy. It was part of the character of the man, a man moulded by Jijabai, powerfully influenced by Tukaram and perfected by the great Saint Ramdas.

Ramdas was an ascetic but he never failed to impress the fact on Shivaji that he had been born a king and a king of the highest type he should remain to the last. When on one occasion, as the famous ballad recites, Shivaji made a gift of his kingdom to his preceptor and expressed a desire to spend the rest of his life in ascetic meditation, the latter returned the gift to his disciple and enjoined him to hold it thenceforth as a special trust from God. Giving his ochre-coloured scarf to Shivaji, Ramdas said: 'Let this be the symbol that you are the viceregent of the Great King of kings.' The fact stands recorded in a State document bearing Shivaji's own seal.

Long afterwards, Shivaji, then of ripe years, was about to
give up his life in a temple of Bhavani when, it is said, the Deity
herself appeared and asked him to desist, calling upon him to live
and administer her kingdom which he held only as her trustee.
Such was Shivaji, such his selflessness. Primarily his aim was to
free his own people and to establish a state where they could pur-
sue their own faith in peace. Whether there was behind it an
idea of an all-India empire or not is not clear.

III

An enemy to none, Shivaji was actuated, in all his deeds, by
high ideals of kingship the keynote of which, in the words of his
preceptor was *Maharashtra Dharma,* 'the religion of Maharashtra,' religion being understood in its highest and broadest sense
of the Sanskrit term *Dharma,* the rule of ideal living. In fact,
his policy during the last eight years of his life was one of con-
solidation rather than of expansion. He foresaw that to be prosperous his people would have to be kept secure on the defensive
in the near future, and so with that end in view, he constructed
the great line of fortresses in the south. And his foresight was
justified by subsequent events. After the death of Aurangzeb
the Marathas burst forth from behind the line and built up a
mighty power on the basis of Shivaji's Swarajya, 'national kingdom.' It was the example of this great king that inspired Baji
Rao's dream of an all-India empire.

Shivaji can be best studied in the context of India's historic
evolution. The key-word *Maharashtra Dharma* means the great
religion of nationalism, or the religion of a great nation. Shivaji's
life-work has left its impress, as much as Akbar's, if not more,
upon the evolution of political consciousness in India. Shivaji
set the ideal for all time that India's nationalism must be comprehensive enough to embrace all groups, ethnic or communal.

Of late years short-sighted historians have tried to represent
the great Maratha king as a champion of blind fanaticism and
narrow communalism. But the facts cited above give the lie
straight to such statements. Perhaps a few more facts and reasons
will suffice to clinch the issue. Khafi Khan's encomiums, already

referred to, coming as it did from an avowed enemy, is the strongest refutation. This great antagonist of Shivaji, in two letters, still extant, addressed him as *Muti-ul-Islam*. No astute diplomatist would call his Hindu enemy 'Friend of Islam' without good reason. That among Shivaji's officers in the Army and Navy a goodly number were Muslims is a fact of history. That he had a whole corps of Afghan body-guards is also an undisputed fact. One of Shivaji's secretaries, Kazi Haider, was a Muslim of such eminence that after Shivaji's time he rose to be a chief judge at Delhi.

History itself justifies the esteem in which Shivaji was held even in the Muslim world. The queen mother of Bijapur, hard pressed by the Moghuls, appealed to Shivaji for help: 'You know our condition. We have neither friends, nor wealth, nor troops. The enemy surround us on all sides. We are unable to save ourselves without your help. Kindly turn your face towards us. We shall do exactly as you want us to do.' On receipt of this letter, without a moment's hesitation, Shivaji sent his troops and chased away the Moghul general from the neighbourhood of the capital. He then visited Bijapur as a friend and a well-wisher. The young Sultan, his mother, and his subjects gave the Maratha king a whole-hearted welcome. We could also cite the well-known fact of how kindly and respectfully Shivaji treated the captive daughter of a Moghul Governor. No wonder Khafi Khan had to admit that any Muslim ladies found among his captives Shivaji would immediately hand over to a respectable Muslim family. Maulvi Basiruddin Ahmed in his history of Bijapur bestows high praise on Shivaji both as a man and as a king, and adds that the name of this hero would for ever be written in letters of gold in the history of India. Mr. Abdul Ali of Calcutta said a number of years ago in a speech at Poona that if Shivaji had succeeded in establishing an Indian empire, Hindus and Muslims would have lived therein in peace and friendship and in enjoyment of equal rights. No need multiplying instances. The bright figure of the great Maratha has his place in the heart of the nation for all time and will shine in its history as the ideal of a brave, true, chivalrous and selfless life nobly lived for men and God.

Shivaji undoubtedly ranks high as the first statesman in medieval and modern India having a practical grasp of the Nation-State idea, though perhaps his nation was not so much

Indian as Maratha. The point becomes quite clear when we compare his Swarajya, national kingdom, with the other two almost contemporary States in the Deccan-Mysore of Haider Ali and Hyderabad of Nizam-ud-daula. These latter were remarkably well-knit and powerful kingdoms, but it can never be said of their rulers that they represented their people. There was no question of caste and creed in Shivaji's Swarajya, for he was a representative not only of his Hindu subjects but of the Muslims and Jews and Christians as well, not only of his Kshatriya castemen but of his Mavli and Pathan soldiers and his Abyssinian sailors as well. This was certainly not the case in regard to Mysore and Hyderabad. Later India, it appears, realised this fact. For, we find that the revolutionary nationalists of the early years of this century, both in Maharashtra and in Bengal, accepted Shivaji and his ideals as the principal source of their inspiration. To them, the great Maratha was the beau-ideal of patriotism and the name Bhavani—the name both of Shivaji's deity and of his sword—stirred their hearts so objectively as nothing else did.

IV

As a man, Shivaji typified in his person the complete Indian ideal of culture; he was a synthesis of the Brahmin, the Kshatriya and the Sudra. By birth and training a royal Kshatriya, he combined in himself, as the flowering of his culture, the Sudra's spirit of humility and service and the Brahmin's spirit of detachment and of devotion to God with the natural courage and generosity of the Kshatriya.

Another fact which constitutes his outstanding importance in history is that at a time when the whole of Aurangzeb's organised might was out to crush anything that was not Islam or Islamic, when the morale of the country had sunk to a very low ebb, when unity and solidarity, whatever of it was there at the time, had gone by the board, in short, when the darkness of decline and decay had almost covered the fair face of India, Shivaji rose in her firmament, a lone star, but a star of the first magnitude, of hope and confidence. And to the formidable odds against him he opposed his indomitable determination, boundless courage, consummate skill, keen intelligence, and above all, a serene outlook on things, all betokening a divinely inspired soul.

Shivaji created a new State which was in no way inferior to any that had existed in Hindu India. His idealism was noble, his organisation was sound, and everything that he did was the concrete expression of Maharashtra Dharma, of which he was a glorious incarnation and an inspired champion. 'Shivaji's political ideals,' says an authority on Maratha history, 'were such that we might accept them today without any change. He aimed at giving his subjects peace, universal toleration, equal opportunities for all castes and creeds, a beneficent, active and pure system of administration, a navy for promoting trade and a trained militia for guarding the homeland.... The activities of Shivaji's government spread in many directions, and this enabled his people to attain to a full and varied development such as all modern civilised States aim at.'

In proportion to the greatness of his capacities, Shivaji's achievements were no doubt small. But the way he formed and lived his ideals and gave them shape in the administration of the State that he set up, possibly as a nucleus to one of all-India dimensions—for his conception was not a Rashtra 'State' but a Maharashtra, 'great State'—compels our admiration, takes our mind back into the far ages, reminds us of his Western compeers on the one hand, and on the other, puts him in the wake of a Janaka, a Ramachandra, an Ashoka whose mantle seems to have fallen on their worthy spiritual descendant.

Shivaji has been called a 'grand rebel.' An unjust epithet. In the perspective of truth he was a mighty revolutionary. For he did far more than a rebel could even think of. He revolutionised the whole tone and tenor of the life of the people. He proved the unique vitality of his country's culture, vindicated its supremacy and gave promise of the day when it would again burst forth in all the wealth and splendour of its Spirit and bring in the dawn of a truly new age. His minister, Ramachandra Pant, utters a great truth when he says that Shivaji created wholly a New Order of things.

That Shivaji did not succeed in establishing a permanent empire is due more to external circumstances than to any defect in his policy or personal character. History shows that the few decades in Maratha life after Shivaji's death were a period of concentrated work behind the veil on the scheme of an all-India empire under the leadership of Baji Rao the Great. That the Peshwas also failed in their time to give India peace and unity is also due to circumstances beyond their control. The Providence that watched over India's destiny so ordained that the country should, before its renaissance, pass through a phase of abject humiliation and, being chastened by it, prepare for its great destiny—to conquer the mind and heart of humanity and become the leader of its evolution into a higher, a diviner perfection.

REFERENCES

Charuchandra Datta, *Ramdas O. Shivaji* (Bengali); D. V. Potdar, *The Marathas—A Historical Sketch;* Dennis Kincaid, *The Grand Rebel;* H. W. Rawlinson, *Shivaji the Maratha;* Jadunath Sarkar, *Shivaji and His Times;* M. G. Ranade, *Rise of the Maratha Power;* S. R. Sharma, *Shivaji; Cambridge History of India,* Vol. IV.

6

Sri Aurobindo and Indian Polity[1]

I

IT IS impossible by any stretch of imagination fully to measure, or by any critical acumen, to justly evaluate, the literary output of Sri Aurobindo, so stupendous it is in its variety and content. It includes poems without number, plays, essays, literary and historical, philosophical disquisitions, expositions of spiritual ideas and ideals, letters—a vast literature by themselves on a wide range of subjects varying from those of ordinary interest to the Yogic, but all of them from his own peculiar spiritual standpoint. Indeed his published writings have brought home to the intellectual élite of humanity the consummate wisdom, the transcendent truths about the fundamental problems of human existence, most of which he revealed through the pages of his monthly philosophical review the *Arya,* from 1914 to 1921. And has he not said, as an eminent Indian thinker observed, the last word on these problems? The *Arya* is in a sense an epitome of Aurobindonian thought in many of its aspects.

In one of the sequences in that journal the Master delineated the various expressions of India's creative soul, primarily as a counterblast—and what a powerful and devastating one at that! —to the vile aspersions cast on Indian culture by the author of *India and the Future,* Sir William Archer. The reading public in India, far less in other countries, did not perhaps know how this English vilifier of India compelled Sri Aurobindo to take

1. Some views from historical standpoint, mainly based on Sri Aurobindo's book *The Spirit and Form of Indian Polity.* The quotations in this article are all from this book.

up the challenge and give a smashing reply whose negative and the then importance stands today far outweighed by the positive light it throws on the cultural achievements of India in the past. Indeed, it leaves the reader wondering if there were any similar writings with which to compare the excellence of this revealing exposition of the secret of India's soul, the essential aim and intention of her historic development, the inner, and therefore, the real significance of the ways in which her children have tried through the ages to give form to their aspirations and strivings.

The first thing that strikes the reader of Sri Aurobindo's book on Indian Polity—a section of his above-mentioned exposition in the *Arya,* called *A Defence of Indian Culture*—is that almost all the works, the so-called standard ones too, on the history of India are utter misnomers, entirely lacking in the correct perspective of India's cultural evolution. An integral vision, a coherent picture, embracing all the manifold aspects of the creative life of the people is rarely found in what passes for the history of India. Unending narrations of political events may tell us much but not everything about a people, since these events as they outwardly are, do not, because they cannot, indicate the real intention of Nature in them, without an understanding of which we know next to nothing of the true history of a country, far less of the forces that have shaped its destiny. The story of India's political development will be not only inaccurate and incomplete but a fundamentally poor and wrong representation, if it is not told with reference to the true nature and tendency of her racial being, and the psychology that impelled that tendency to fulfil itself in the endeavour of the people to build up a strong collective life based on the ideals set forth in the Dharmashastras.

The work of the foreign Indologists for the reconstruction of India's history must always be gratefully acknowledged. But it must also be said that the writings of most of them as well as of Indian scholars who have followed these Western pioneers, betray defects which greatly detract from their value as a faithful record of India's historic development through centuries. Besides, the ulterior motives of many of these European writers and their attitude of superiority towards the Indians, because of their long—fortunately now past—political subjection, are not a little responsible for the deliberate attempts they have so often made to belittle ancient India and her greatness and to prove to the world her incapacity to manage her own affairs. But what is more deplorable is that few Indian historians have so far cared to understand the 'inwardness' of their country's history, the central purpose of its existence. And this understanding they can have only through an insight into the true character of India's culture and civilisation, into the spirit that has inspired and moulded the various expressions of her soul. Their exclusive attachment to the scientific method of the West, confined to the obvious and superficial view of things, has blinded these historians to the deep and subtle truths of the dynamic and all-embracing spirituality of India.

There must therefore be an intuitive seeing into the very depth of things so that ideas and forces that actualise themselves in the outer actions and movements may be comprehended in their proper implications, and facts appear in their true bearing on the dominant tendency and the characteristic genius of the race.

The history of India must be a true mirror of all the inner and outer activities of her people, showing at the same time what part her soul played in every one of them. It must therefore be rescued from its subservience to ends that are anything but genuinely historical.

Trained in a system of education which is a poor and perverted imitation of what the West had long ago rejected, we have never learnt how to study and appreciate our own past, and no wonder that we should so often exhibit our colossal ignorance of it in all that we are doing today to rebuild our country on the true basis of our national life, as we conceive it. The impact of an alien culture has dulled in us the power to feel what we really are as a race, with a magnificent past whose meaning and purpose have been rediscovered and reaffirmed and shown to us in their proper light by a seer like Sri Aurobindo.

II

As we glance through the pages of Sri Aurobindo's book on Indian polity, mentioned above, a book small but closely packed

with the thoughts and ideas and visions of a seer, we feel trans-
ported back to those splendid days of our past when India showed her incomparable political genius in the building up of powerful republics and vast empires and in administering them with
superb efficiency and in accordance with the spiritual bent of her
mind, enabling the free individuals in them to live up to the
highest ideals of the race, so that there might grow up a collectivity comprising such individuals, and moving towards a perfect form through the perfection of its human constituents. Where
is the text-book that has dealt with this deeper truth underlying
India's political endeavours? Foreign writers have distorted facts
and desecrated the pages of Indian history with fabrications in
order to prove to the world the weakness of our ancient corporate organisations, and our incapacity to govern and build up
any homogenous and progressive body politic. Even some of our
own scholars are not free from such false notions. Moreover, these
ideas find support in another wrong view, also widely held, that
India had her attention always fixed on the contemplation of
the Spirit to the total exclusion of the things of life. Sri Aurobindo's luminous essay is a flat contradiction of such myths. It
exposes and nails to the counter once for all the utter absurdity
of such statements. If India was great in her spiritual achievements, she was no less great in her material pursuits, for she regarded them, according to *Arthashastra,* as the basic condition
of her spiritual endeavours. India would not have been able to
live the rich and colourful life that she has done through the
ages, had her people rejected life as a mere illusion. But, on the
contrary, life had no meaning for her if it was denied the scope
for the fulfilment of its spiritual possibilities.

How has India managed to have such a long and chequered
existence in history and what is the future it points to? There is
in every people a common soul, mind and body. And like the individual man, a people also passes through the cycle of birth,
growth and decline. And if at the last stage the soul or the life-
force of a people becomes incapable of a recovery or a renewal,
the people dwindles and slowly makes its final exit from the
world. In this way have passed away many of the ancient peoples
who are only remembered in history as the builders of great
civilisations. It is a soul idea or a life idea that really governs and
inspires the activities of a people. In the history of the world

China and India are the only countries with a more or less unbroken record of ceaseless creative strivings. It is these two ancient peoples alone that have retained their old strength and
energy and are able to make ever-new endeavours not unworthy
of the greatness of their heritage. In the case of the Chinese this
is so because of the indomitable power of life that sustains and
guides them towards their high destiny in the future, and in the
case of India, because the immortal spirit of her collective being
and her inexhaustible creative energy have never failed her whenever after a spell of inactivity or lassitude, she has made an
attempt to ascend to a new and higher summit of glory. An attempt is made here to present from Sri Aurobindo's vision the
more significant among the aspects of India's political striving in
the past along with those facts and movements which reflect the
peculiar bent of her mind and which are not generally found in
books on Indian history.

India's ancient seers envisaged in her the Mother, the Infinite
and Compassionate Mother of man, a conscious formation of the
Supreme Shakti. And her history shows how true this vision has
been. The spiritual mind of India, says Sri Aurobindo, regarded
life as a manifestation of the Self, the people as a life-body of
Brahman in the *samasti*, the collectivity, the collective Narayana;[2]
the individual as Brahman is the *vyasti*, the separate Jiva, the individual Narayana. If the physical form of India embodies the
Shakti, her human content incarnates Brahman. But to the Tantriks, everything that exists is a form of the Shakti, and to the
Vedantin, Brahman pervades everything. And these two ideas
find their identity in the transcendent vision of that creative
power of Sachchidananda which is ever behind every endeavour
of evolutionary Nature to prepare man for a divine existence
upon earth. In the acceleration of this all-important preparation
India has already taken a hand. It is a goal towards which she is
destined to lead mankind by her already acquired spiritual power.
That is why after a brief slumber she is again having a new resurgence of her soul. That is why her greatest Poet and Priest of
the Spirit is proclaiming today the highest truth of human existence, the truth of a perfect form of man's social living in which
the individual soul rising into a higher consciousness will live in

---

2. The indwelling Godhead in man.

complete harmony with the collective soul of humanity and follow that 'sunlit' path of free participation by all in the service and adoration of the One in the Many. This will be the spiritual foundation of the World-State of the future, as envisaged by Sri Aurobindo.

Spirituality is indeed the key-note of the Indian mind. 'The master-idea,' says Sri Aurobindo, 'that has governed the life, culture, social ideas of the Indian people has been the seeking of man for his true spiritual self and the use of life as a frame and means for that discovery and for man's ascent from the ignorant and natural into the spiritual existence.' As it was thought, and rightly, that for the attainment of this end, the one prerequisite is full freedom and utmost opportunities of self-development for the individual, so also it was believed that man's collective living could grow into its perfect form only when it was smaller in size, having an individuality of its own, and was therefore better able to achieve its purpose and serve more effectively the larger collectivity of the country to which it belonged.

Every step in the forward march of man is first taken by the individual, the individual who is always the pioneer and the precursor. It is the labour of the individual that fructifies into what we call the progress of the race, for it is to him that the vision first comes as also the urge to give shape and form to it. And what is true of the individual may also be true of the collectivity, but the latter cannot so easily move forward if it is larger in size and lacks compactness and inter-communion, as it happened in ancient times when communications were extremely inadequate to the purpose. Hence the existence then of smaller forms of corporate living.

Every individual is more or less a particular type, and the more creative these individuals, the more markedly do they vary, one from the other. These very individuals having developed on the distinctive lines of their *swabhava*,[3] constitute the greatness and glory of the community to which they belong, and by the variety of their achievements immensely enrich and exalt its cultural life. This is how they aid the general progress of the community, and therefore, its integration into a compact whole with the individuality of its own composed of racial, cultural,

---

3. Self-nature.

linguistic and geographical factors peculiar to the region inhabited by the community. In the same way can such groups become free participants in the collective existence of a larger whole, having spiritual, cultural and political ideals which in their fundamentals are common to all the constituent groups, each of which by its distinctive characteristics contributes to the progress and well-being of the larger whole. The central State in ancient India emerged out of this larger collective life both as a necessity and as a natural development. It was strengthened, among other factors, by the formation of representative assemblies for the deliberation of matters of common interest to the whole empire. And its growth had always been inspired by the great ideal of the race, the ideal of unity in diversity and diversity in unity. Indeed there can be no effective unity unless it evolves out of multiplicity. The many is the strength and contents of the one, even as the one is the truth and essence of the many. The autonomous and progressive units were thus the sustaining limbs of the body-politic or the central State, which stood for the oneness of the collective life of the race.

The beginnings of the State in India may be traced to the Vedic times when the unit of corporate existence starting with the family (*griha* or *kula*) enlarged itself through the village (*grama*), the clan (vis), the people (*jana*) till it embraced the whole country (*rashtra*). A region inhabited by a community was called a *janapada* which gradually developed into *janapadarajya*, a territorial State, and then into *mahajanapadarajya*, a larger territorial State, with the central authority vested either in a king or in a popular assembly, the *sabha* and the *samiti* of the Vedic age, or in both, the latter always limiting the powers and prerogatives of the former. It was this system which formed the framework and the mainspring of the mechanism of the State that evolved later in ancient India. And what is important about it is that notwithstanding the changes made at different epochs in the shape and character of these political structures, the village-unit ever remained the constant and vital factor as the very foundation for their growth and progress, thus showing the individualistic tendency of India's political being. It is with this village-unit that the Indian idea of democracy is always associated, since all its affairs, secular and religious, used to be looked after by the people's assembly. The *panchayat* system prevalent almost everywhere in India today, has derived from this. Will Durant, the eminent American thinker and historian, believes that the village community of ancient India is the proto-type of all forms of self-government and democracy that have ever been evolved in various parts of the world. The Greek Agora, Roman Comitia or German folk-moot, to which may be traced the democratic institutions of modern Europe, are said to be echoes of the Vedic Samiti; but whereas no discussion was permitted in the former assemblies of Europe, the Vedic Samiti, a sovereign assembly of the whole people (*vis*), was a delibera-tive body where speeches were delivered and debates took place. In his evidence before a Select Committee of the House of Commons in 1832, Sir Charles Metcalfe, the well-known British administrator, said that these little village democracies of India which saved her culture and soul against the disintegrating forces of political revolution retained their full municipal vigour even up to the eighteenth century until they were swept away by the onrush of British imperialism and over-centralised administration.

The aim of the Vedic Aryans in their units of community life was to bring together the various parts of the country under the exalting influence of the Aryan culture. That they had a vision of India's oneness is evident from the river-hymns of the Rig Veda; and their political endeavours indicate that they visualised a vast State representing the collective life of the people and seeking to establish the Aryan ideals as the ideals of the race. The sovereignty of the Dharma as a guiding force in the life of the individual and the collectivity was a later and higher phase, when the social ideals of India had been already defined and systematised, and the units of community life had acquired a more definite shape. These units, as already seen, were formed and sustained by the village democracies and were linked up with the larger territorial units that existed at the time.

What really existed and was liberally encouraged was, says Sri Aurobindo, 'a kind of complex communal freedom and self-determined and self-governing communal body, having its own natural existence and administering its own proper life and busi-ness, but always joining with others in the discussion and regula-tion of matters of mutual or common interest in the general assemblies of the kingdom and empire.' Many of these small States were of a republican character—another proof of their distinctive individuality—which gave them much of their strength and stability.

There is abundant evidence to show that monarchy was not the only form of government India knew in her past, that she was equally familiar with democratic ideas to which she gave form in her own way. The Vedic ritual of *Anumati* (permission from Mother Earth) which the head of the state had to perform, the constitutional and democratic nature of the checks and remedies in the early Vedic political institutions, are clear indications of the democratic tendencies of the times. According to Aitereya Brahmana, among the Uttara Kurus and the Uttara Madras— two powerful peoples— 'the whole community was consecrated to rulership.' The Shantiparva of the *Mahabharata* is full of references to the republican form of government. It mentions five republican peoples who formed themselves into a confederation under Shri Krishna as their federal president. And this government had also its Opposition with its leader. Panini, the famous grammarian of the eighth century B.C., speaks of as many as eighty different republics of the time, a number of which had federal constitutions, and a number were under confederations, all having laws and institutions comparable with those of the most progressive of modern states. Many of these republics continued during the Buddhist age and in later times, existing side by side with monarchies and empires. As a Sakya the Buddha himself was a born democrat. The Sakya parliament consisted of five hundred members. Its President was called a Raja, a king. The Buddha's father was a Raja of this type. The Parliament met in its hall called *Samasthagara,* the assembly hall. The Buddha opened a new Parliament House and gave a series of lectures.

The Buddha once said that if the republican character could be maintained in its purity and vigour, the state would remain ever invincible even against the attack of such a powerful emperor as Ajatasatru of Magadha. During the Buddha's time ten such republics of northern India were at the height of their power and glory; and of these the Lichchhavis of Vaisali were the most famous. There is evidence to show that the real strength of these republics lay not so much in their government as in the character of their people. Did not Plato say, 'Like man, like state.' 'Governments vary as the characters of man vary.' Mention may be made here that many republican states had existed in northern and central India till the fifth century of the present era.

III

It is normal to Indian nature to regard as inviolable the right of the individual as well as of the collectivity—the smaller the collectivity, we may repeat, the stronger and more progressive it is likely to be—to grow into the fullness of its being by following its own particular line of development. There can indeed be no higher conception of democracy. And its modern advocates have yet to realise that the democratic ideal enshrines, however inchoately, the truth of a higher perfection which men, both in his individual and collective life, is destined to attain. That is why there is so much insistence on the necessity of utmost freedom for man, so that he may be able to express all that is latent in him, and the best and highest that is latent in him is his eternal and immaculate divinity whose uncurbed manifestation is the goal towards which he is moving. Freedom and democracy are but its necessary aids.

It is a remarkable fact—singular and unique in the history of the world—that the wide prevalence of popular freedom in ancient India hardly found itself in conflict with the system of monarchy that existed, the reason being that the latter served only to augment the collective well-being of the people. The king was the servant of the people, the upholder of the Dharma, and his power was so hedged in as to prevent the growth of any personal despotism or any tendency towards absolutism or autocracy. Manu prescribes and justifies dethronement and even capital punishment for a king if he defy the law and develop into a tyrant. The land, says the same authority, belongs to the people, to those who cultivate it, the king being only its custodian. Not any temporal power but the ideal rule of living, the Dharma, enunciated, fostered and enjoined upon the kings by the Rishis, was the real and greater sovereign. The king as a person, his ancestry, his family traditions, his personal and family prestige were matters of no moment from the point of view of this Dharma. His chief function was to see to the proper observance of the

Dharma by the people, and to prevent crimes, serious disorders and breaches of the peace. He himself was bound to obey the Dharma as also the rigorous rules and restrictions it imposed on his personal life and conduct and on the province, powers and duties and even on the prerogatives of his regal authority and office. The *Ramayana,* the *Mahabharata* and the Puranas—these and other yet unexplored sources of much historical information —abound in such examples of dutiful kings and equally dutiful subjects. Besides, the monarch almost always reflected the dignity of a stable civilisation and represented a free living people. He was the symbol of the country's greatness and glory even as the representative assembly of his kingdom or empire mirrored the mind and will of his people.

The theory of the divinity of the king does not seem to have found much favour in the Vedic age. Several *mantras*,[4] however, composed during the period of the Smritis, speak of the entry of deities into the king's person at the time of his coronation. In certain sacrifices kings were compared with gods, and declared as the visible symbol of Prajapati, the Lord of creation. But, barring a very few of the law-makers, almost all of them were against placing the king above the Law. To them the majesty of the Law was higher than the majesty of the king. The view of Gregory the Great that even bad kings are divine was not only foreign but repugnant to Indian thinking. We know Manu's dictum on this point. Sukracharya calls a vicious and oppressive king not divine (*divya*) but demoniac (*rakshomsa*). The king Vena who claimed exemption from punishment on the plea of his divinity was killed by the sages who did not care to examine the validity of his stand. The *Mahabharata* declares that if a king is unable to protect his subjects and administer his kingdom righteously, the subjects should kill him like a mad dog.

It is therefore clear that the idea of the divinity of the king was not accepted in India in its literal sense. It stood for virtues, great, noble and godly, which the king must possess that he might be fit to discharge the sacred and onerous duties of his high office. That is why so much stress was laid in ancient India on the training of the princes, for which the best teachers of

---

4. Mystic gospel.

the time were appointed. The Smritis assert that the king is the
trustee of the peoples' interests, the State an instrument through
which he is to guard those interests and provide scope for their
full satisfaction, and that his supreme function lies in dealing
out even-handed justice to all. *Arthashastra* says that 'the ruler
is created by Brahma as servant of the people.' In order, therefore, to be equal to this delicate, difficult and sacred task, the
king must have in him divine qualities. This is the true meaning
of the divinity that was attached to royalty in ancient India.

IV

The State in ancient India, whether republican or monarchical,
was not, as Sri Aurobindo points out, a mere mechanical structure as the States in the world are today. It was a natural
growth out of the extraordinarily complex social organisation of
the people. And its real character can be understood when studied
as a part of, or in relation to, the organic totality of the social
existence of the people. The laws, the customs and the institutions of ancient India were a natural organic development, and
the State embodied them as a co-ordinating centre which for its
sustenance and growth depended on the vitality of the parts
comprising it. These parts were the social orders elaborated by
the makers of the law. These law-makers or law-givers were the
Rishis whose treatment of human nature was based on their
knowledge of the inner laws and forces that operate in the life
of man and guide his evolution stage by stage. Their clear perception of what man is in his nature enabled these unerring
psychologists of ancient India to evolve a socio-religious system
in which every individual nature would fulfil itself by following
its own *swadharma*,[5] and this fulfilment meant for every man his
fitness for the next stage.

Thus, the people's adherence to common ideals, their observance of common rules, and above all, their loyalty to Dharma,
brought about a cohesive society consisting of diverse orders
and institutions helping the people to feel at every stage and in
every activity of their life the quickening and directing influences

---

5. Self-law of the being.

of a common social existence. This was how there developed a common social consciousness which became a most unifying factor in the community life of the people. It was this consciousness again which largely promoted the growth and expansion of the State representing the people's will to build and strengthen corporate organisations based on the sovereignty of the Dharma, the religious, ethical, social, political, juridic and customary law organically governing the life of the people.

The State was thus a natural and realistic expression of the social inclinations of its human constituents freely and flexibly following, each according to his nature, the rules of a comprehensive scheme of life. It was never a rigid mechanical contrivance but a supple and spontaneous creation of the will of the people's social being, a marvelous creation indeed, which, if ever viewed in the right perspective, will furnish the most conclusive proof of the socio-political genius of the race. We wonder how the society, and for the matter of that, the State could weld into its body-politic so many diverse elements, giving scope to each one for contributing its share to the growth and expansion of the whole. Yet it was a fact borne out by a mass of indisputable evidence. A correct presentation of the early history of India must include this unique achievement of the race. It is because of this power of theirs to create unity out of apparent diversity that the ancient fathers of the race were able to build up a superb political system which lasted not for centuries but for millenniums. And this they were able to do because of their intuitive perception of the inner springs of the actions and interests of man as a social being. Manu has said: 'Great is the majesty of sovereign authority which cannot be held by the rulers without a knowledge of the spiritual laws.'

The Western approach to polity is too superficial to be of any real and lasting benefit to the collective well-being of man. It creates problems but does not—because it cannot—offer any solution to them. It is tied to the blundering ways of the mind and constructs precarious external patterns in which the deeper urges of life find no scope for self-fulfilment. Sri Aurobindo points out its basic defect when he says: 'The sophisticating, labouring, constructing, efficient, mechanising reason loses hold of the simple principles of a people's vitality; it cuts it away from the secret roots of life. The result is an exaggerated dependence on system and institution, on legislation and administration and the deadly tendency to develop in place of a living people, a mechanical state.'

V

In spite, however, of its being founded on the intrinsic truths of human nature, the socio-political system of India succumbed to the shock of the Muhammedan onslaught. Even a cursory view of the social and political conditions of the time would show how she was taken at a disadvantage and hit upon the most vulnerable point of her socio-political structure. The cultural and spiritual unity remained almost intact, no doubt, but the country had little political integrity worth the name, mainly because the society—always in ancient India the basis of her political structure—had ceased to be a cohesive force in the communal consciousness of the people. The conservative mind of India took the continued irruptions of the barbarians during the earlier centuries of the present era as a threat to the life and culture of the country. Although most of these foreigners were gradually incorporated or assimilated with the collective being of the people, the custodians of the ancient traditions did their utmost to preserve their sanctity. They thought that the best way of doing that would be to reinterpret the social laws to meet the exigencies of the time. Unfortunately, however, in their efforts to do so, they followed the letter and forgot the spirit, placing restrictions upon the application of the laws, erecting new caste-barriers and curtailing the social rights of the non-Brahmin communities, so much so that the society became more and more rigid in its organic movements and showed signs of decadence and disintegration. This was of course a long protracted process but it took a worse form during the Muslim invasion. The effect of this on the already enfeebled national consciousness surviving in the states and kingdoms was a progressive decay and an eventual incapacity to coalesce with the various political units and present a solid and united front against a foreign aggression.

A unification of the whole country under one central authority, forming an impregnable bulwark of defence, could not be fully achieved in ancient India, owing, among other causes, to insufficient communications and the lack in the powers that be of any will to crush out of existence the smaller states and principalities. Many of these states whose compactness and individuality were largely responsible for much of their social and cultural progress, tended almost for the same reason to be more and more exclusive and self-centred and therefore unwilling to stand any imperial authority at the centre, with the result that an integration of the whole country which in historic times was possible on several occasions through the impact of such an authority, could not grow into a cohesive force in the political life of ancient India. Moreover, the indifference of these states to the larger interest of the country and the lack of an effective solidarity among them exposed India to foreign aggressions. Nevertheless, the attempt was always there to synthetise these states as well as peoples and nations by bringing about their unity while maintaining their respective autonomies in a larger free-and-living organism. The institutions of the royal sacrifices, such as *rajasuya*[6] and *aswamedha,*[7] the ideals of universal kingship, such as *sarvabhauma* (*dominus omnium*), *chaturanta, chakravarti,* point to the constant efforts of the kings and emperors of ancient India to extend the territorial boundaries of their empires to the utmost limits, and to consolidate their integrity under one imperial authority. The epics and Puranas give vivid descriptions of the vastness and splendour of these early *maharajyas*[8] of India.

The royal sacrifices, however, had a deep political significance in that they fostered the growth of a kind of federation of the various states and kingdoms in early India. And this federation, like everything Indian, had a spiritual basis too. For, though the emperor was there to whom due allegiance was professed by all the attending kings and potentates from different parts of India, the inner consecration of the heart was always made to the Lord of the Sacrifice, the King of Kings, the Supreme. To these rulers

---

6. The consecration of an emperor symbolising his conquests in all directions.
7. The royal horse-sacrifice in which a king would let loose a white horse, duly consecrated and protected by an army, to move about at its free will as a challenge to other kings. It would be brought back after a year when the king would be consecrated as an emperor of the regions in which the horse moved unchallenged.
8. Vast empires.

as to every Indian Bharatavarsha was the *devabhumi,* the holy
land of God, and it was God alone whom they worshipped as
the real Dispenser of their country's destiny. And was it not this
spontaneous adoration by which they were united into a fellowship of service to their common motherland whose welfare, greatness and glory they regarded as their sole concern and which
they knew they could best promote by furthering the cause of
progress in their own autonomous kingdoms? A remarkable endeavour, indeed, of that heroic age of India! It may be noted
that the kings who participated in these sacrifices did so not as
vassals or subordinates but as free comrades pledged to the common ideals of the race, dedication to which they used to reaffirm
in these royal functions. The Satapatha Brahmana and the Aitereya Brahmana contain references to a number of such gigantic
royal ceremonials. Of great historical importance however is the
rajasuya sacrifice described in the *Mahabharata.* It was responsible for the creation of a federation, a Federal Union, so to say,
comprising most of the states and kingdoms of the India of the
time following the Kurukshetra War. The institution, especially
of *aswamedha,* has for centuries been celebrated by the monarchs
of India not only as a symbol of their prowess and victory but
as a sign of their effort to strengthen the integrity of the whole
country under the sovereignty of an *ekrat,* the Lord-Paramount,
the highest of whose duties it was to uphold the Dharma and to
see to its proper observance by the people, on which, they believed, depended the progress of the race. But in later times—
and it continued to be performed almost throughout the whole
period of Hindu kingship in ancient India—the institution lost
much of its pristine grandeur, owing, among other reasons, to
the largeness of vision which had inspired it in the early days
having begun to diminish in the consciousness of the monarchs
concerned. But these Unions were more or less of a loose nature
and could not grow into compact ones, lasting, as they did,
only for a time. Nevertheless they are proof of how India tried
to build political unity in those dim days of her past.

'... spiritual unity is a large and flexible thing and does not
insist like the political and external on centralisation and uniformity; rather it lives diffused in the system and permits readily
a great diversity and freedom of life. Here we touch on the
secret of the difficulty in the problem of unifying ancient India.

It could not be done by the ordinary means of a centralised uniform imperial State crushing out all that made for free divergence, local autonomies, established communal liberties, and each time that an attempt was made in this direction, it has failed after a long term of apparent success, and we might even say that the guardians of India's destiny widely compelled it to fail that her inner spirit might not perish and her soul barter for an engine of temporary security the deep sources of its life. The ancient mind of India had the intuition of its need; its idea of empire was a uniting rule that respected every existing regional and communal liberty, that unnecessarily crushed out no living autonomy, that effected a synthesis of her life and not a mechanical oneness.'

In historical times the largest all-India empire was that of the Mauryas, but it also had within it a number of independent kingdoms which were left to develop on their autonomous lines. The empire of the Satavahanas of Andhra had in it a number of self-governing feudatories. The famous Gupta Emperor Samudra-gupta allowed certain states in Gujarat, which he had conquered, to continue their own rule under his hegemony. The Palas of Bengal showed similar magnanimity to some of the smaller states within their big empire which extended far to the north and the south. But these are only a few among many instances of the far-sighted and large-hearted statesmanship of the emperors of ancient India, who knew well enough that the vitality of a people flourishes better in the freedom of small autonomous groups and communities than under a dead-level uniformity of a too complex centralised government. When therefore these emperors found any group strongly individualistic in its self-expression, far from viewing with disfavour or attempting to suppress, they used often to respect and recognise its liberty.

VI

That India, till the Muhammedan conquest, never showed her incapacity to absorb many foreign peoples and their cultures was largely due to the free play of her life-force conserved in the various units of her collective life as a result of the freedom

of growth and development either voluntarily granted by the
central power or wrested out of its unwilling hands. Even during her days of decline when conditions were not at all favourable to such a phenomenon, India witnessed an outburst of militant patriotism among the Marathas and the Sikhs who proved
that the race was yet capable of giving a good account of itself
by summoning up whatever vitality it still had in it when a right
leader, a heroic and selfless soul, came forth to carry out the
will of the Mother as her chosen instrument.

The coming of the British to India is an event of outstanding
importance in her modern history. It was responsible for many
things that were good but also a lot that proved positively disastrous for her. British imperialism destroyed, among other things,
the natural divisions of the country and erected artificial boundaries to suit their administrative convenience. A unity came
into being, no doubt, but it was not the perfectly natural and
flawless unity of a living organism, every part of which could
freely function and contribute to the well-being of the parent
body. It was a mechanical superimposition, a levelling but fetter-
ing regimentation, devised to serve the interests not of the people
but of their alien rulers. And yet, as things went, it did bring
about a sort of political unification of the country. The time has
now come for these artificial divisions to give place to the natural
that alone can guarantee ample scope for the free development
of its regional peoples. There must, therefore, be a State which
would recognise the need and importance of diversity playing
its part in the building up of that larger, livelier, richer unity to
which the genius and destiny of the race are insistently pointing.
If India is to be one and great—and in the Divine Dispensation
that is what she is going to be—she must before long be so
spiritually, culturally, politically and geographically at one and
the same time. There must therefore be an integration of all
her powers and potentialities into the wholeness of a composite
national life, founded on and fortified by the full deployment of
her inherent spiritual power.

How can this consummation be achieved? It will be, says
Sri Aurobindo, 'when man in the collectivity begins to live more
deeply and to govern his collective life neither primarily by the
needs, instincts, intuitions welling up out of the vital self, nor
secondarily by the constructions of the reasoning mind, but first,

foremost and always by the power of unity, sympathy, spontaneous liberty, supple and living order of his discovered greater self and spirit in which the individual and the communal existences have their law of freedom, perfection and oneness.'

The hour is propitious today for India to prepare herself for this great fulfilment of her collective existence; and this achieved, she will be able to set an example to mankind and lead it to the self-same goal, the new World-Order of the future. She must therefore awake to the truth of her soul, and enlighten and enlarge herself with a more comprehensive experience from within and without, a more certain knowledge that shall effect a reconciliation between life and the Spirit, and be that way able 'to found the status and action of the collective being of man on the realisation of the deeper spiritual truth, the yet unrealised spiritual potentialities of our existence and so ensoul the life of her people as to make it the Lila of the greater Self in humanity, a conscious communal soul and body of Virat, the universal spirit.'

7

The Vision of Ajanta[1]

I

A LITTLE over three centuries before the Christian era, when
Buddhism was beginning to give a fresh impetus to the creative
genius of India, a certain king—most probably Ashoka whose
highest of all virtues was to proclaim the message of Lord Buddha
—took upon himself the sacred task of helping a group of Buddhist monks to undertake the excavation of a series of cave-
temples in that part of the mountain-chains known as the Western
Ghats, which marks the boundary of the Deccan tableland and
separates it from that of Khandesh, along the valley of the river
Tapti. The valley, just where it tends to a convex crowned with
a number of cliffs, offers a peculiar position and was chosen by
the ancient monks for cutting out those caves and carving and
decorating them with a most beautiful composition of plastic
and graphic arts. Begun about the third century B.C., the excavations had continued under the patronage of kings and nobles
for a period of about one thousand years, with occasional breaks
at times, till the close of the seventh century of the present era
when the latest of the caves were finished. The caves, twenty-nine
in number, are rich with the most wonderful art-relics of India
that have survived the ravages of time, escaping somehow the
vandalism of religious iconoclasts.

An outstanding feature of Ajanta art is that it combines,
in its variety of expression, the three vivid art-forms that were

1. Based on a lecture delivered at the Kala Bhavan of Rabindranath
   Tagore's Viswa-Bharati, Santiniketan.

so wonderfully, and at the same time so usefully, cultivated in ancient India for the elevation of the human soul in its eternal quest for Truth. Indeed the cutting out of the rugged mountain cliffs into beautiful *chaityas* (cathedrals) and *viharas* (monasteries), some of which are considered 'the most perfect specimens of Buddhistic art of India' and are admired for their beauty and completeness of architectonic details, required the most consummate knowledge of constructional science; the carving in them of rhythmic figures of Buddhas and Bodhisattvas, and of various other gods and goddesses, all immensely suggestive of the deepest spiritual moods, expressing religious conceptions and carrying intimations of divinity—the two prominent characteristics of Indian sculpture—necessitated a perfect employment of sculptural technique; and the decorating of these caves by paintings frescoed on their walls and ceilings, treating of religious and secular subjects in mystic touches of lines harmonised with certain simple colours, would never have been possible without a complete mastery of the brush. Although each of these art-forms is by itself a typical example of the best creation of Indian art, what gives Ajanta its character as a centre of art culture is the splendid blending of those art-forms into a unity of artistic conception, the spirit of which pervades the whole atmosphere of the shrines and strikes even the most uninstructed visitor with a wondering admiration.

The selection of the site is peculiar in more ways than one. The situation is romantic, like that of the majority of the Buddhist shrines in India. For, an artistic appreciation of natural scenery is particularly noticeable in Buddhist paintings, more prominently in the Ajanta ones: that the monks as a body were alive to the inspiring influence of beautiful surroundings is evident from their invariable selection of picturesque sites. Nature appears to have most lavishly poured out the wealth of her soul in robing the environs of Ajanta in poetry and beauty. Leaving aside the fact of its being on a series of mountains (which is ascribed to the belief cherished by the monks that the greater the exertion needed for excavating the caves, the greater the merit), we have to consider the no less important question as to why they chose this isolated hill-cleft which is difficult of access, and, being confronted with massive slopes of rocky scrap opposite, is shut out from a direct view of the open country below.

The oldest of the caves, Cave IX, appears to have been excavated in about 300 B.C. when the earlier phase of Buddhism known as the Hinayana school was the dominating creed in Buddhistic theology; and the monks who were directly or indirectly connected with the excavation must have been strict observers of the rigid discipline prescribed by the exponents of that particular school. As such, they felt inclined to select this inaccessible spot excluded from even a view of the outside world so as to be able to carry on their spiritual practices, safe from all distractions of mundane life. But the figures of the Buddhist gods and goddesses in the caves, made in the sixth and seventh centuries, the most glorious period of Ajanta art, show the influence of the Mahayana school which was then a popular cult in various parts of northern India. The artists of these shrines were no doubt Buddhist monks but they were imbued with the new creative spirit of the age which gave India her classical expression.

By its insistence on freedom and universal brotherhood Buddhism liberated the social life of the country from many of its cramping evils. The disciplines of Yoga and Bhakti, adapted to the Mahayana Path from Hinduism, opened up new channels of spiritual activity among the Buddhists. And they started to worship their Lord and his previous incarnations through beautiful figures which they themselves created out of the fervour and intensity of their hearts' devotion. By Yoga they were led into those illuminations in the depth of their soul in which they discovered the oneness of the physical and the supra-physical. The outer is indeed the vesture of the inner. The body is verily the temple of the Spirit, an image of the Divine and it never ceases to be so, whatever the condition in which it may find itself. To reveal this truth is the highest function of art. The art of Ajanta fulfilled this function by its opulent representation of the manifold phases of life against the background of their essential unity.

Another event that contributed to the growth of the creative spirit of the age was the revival of Hindu culture under the Guptas during whose time Ajanta had already produced many of its best works. The Gupta emperors showed Vaishnavite inclinations and extended the utmost possible patronage to the monk-artists of Ajanta, among whom there were Hindus who worked on Buddhist subjects, and Buddhists who worked on Hindu sub-

1

Standing Buddha. Mathura. Gupta period, 5th century A.D.

(Courtesy, National Museum, New Delhi)

2
Mother and Child.
Wall-painting, Cave
No. XVII, Ajanta.
Late 5th century A.D.

3
Bodhisattva Padmapani. Wall-painting, Cave No. 1,
Ajanta. Second half of 6th century A.D.
(Copyright, Archaeological Survey of India)

4

Facade. Chaitya Cave No. XIX. Early 6th century A.D.
(Copyright, Archaeological Survey of India)

5

Nagaraja and consort. From facade of Cave No. XIX, Ajanta.
Early 6th century A.D.
(Copyright, Archaeological Survey of India)

6
(*Previous plate*)
Buddha. From facade,
Cave No. XIX, Ajanta.
Early 6th century A.D.

7
**Standing Buddha and pillars in interior. Cave
No. XIX, Ajanta. Early 6th century A.D.**

(Copyright, Archaeological Survey of India)

8

Wall-painting. Sigiriya, Sri Lanka. Late 5th century A.D.

jects. But almost always the artists were spiritual seekers or monks. They are, therefore, remarkable instances of the religious fellowship of the age in which Buddhism began to be absorbed by Hinduism.

II

The pragmatic mind of today finds it difficult to reconcile this cultivation of art by monks with the austere life of discipline they were required to live in that centre of spiritual culture. The fact is that apart from the favourable conditions that the social and religious outlook of the time provided for the renewal of India's artistic genius, there is indeed a yoga in art too, and by practising it in the right spirit the artist-seeker grows in his spiritual stature. That is why the artists in ancient India were called *shilpiyogins*.[2] Not only that, in a *Shilpa-shastra,* the artist is strictly enjoined to undergo a course of ceremonial purification and perform in a solitary place the 'sevenfold office' beginning with the invocation of the hosts of Buddhas and Bodhisattvas, and the offering to them of real and imaginary flowers. Sukracharya, a celebrated aesthete of the period, says: 'The artist should attain to the images of the gods by means of spiritual contemplation only. The spiritual vision is the best and truest standard for him. He should depend upon it, and not at all upon the visible objects perceived by the senses.'

It is, therefore, quite possible that the monks took to art not for any personal pleasure or, as has been commonly supposed, for any express purpose of educating the pilgrims, but primarily for the sake of their own sadhana, as a course of art, they thought, would help them in attaining to higher stages of spiritual unfoldment. Theirs was 'not art for art's sake, but art for the Divine's sake.' Had it been their concern that those beautiful works of their art should please their own tastes or instruct pilgrims visiting the caves, they would have chosen a less inaccessible site and carved or painted the figures of gods and goddesses only. But what did they do instead? They gave free vent to their aesthetic impulses and translated them into the

2. Mystic artists.

rhythmic forms of their craft. Their daring romanticism in depicting various scenes, of the royal courts, processional demons-
trations, racial types, and so many other secular incidents of life,
all throbbing with vitality and action, is indeed remarkable if
we judge the merit of their art not by its exterior motif but by
the light of the inspiration which created and developed them.
Their choice of secular subjects may be attributed to the desire
of the monk-artists to sublimate their vision of life into the intensity of symbolic spiritual expression so that, divested of its
earthly grossness, life might appear resplendent in the native
glory of the Spirit.

The origin of Ajanta art should, therefore, be traced not
merely to what it outwardly is, but more surely to the vision of
the seeker-artists, and to the way they tried to render that vision
articulate on the walls and screens of those holy cave-cathedrals
which still bear eloquent testimony to their ardent striving to
discover for man the eternal verities of life. The soul in the
artist, awakened to a consciousness of its own power of self-
expression, found its vehicle in the simplicities of line and colour,
in the rhythms of plastic figurations, and broke out in the immensity of its overflowing joy to reveal its vision of the all-pervading beauty and harmony that underline the varied manifestations of life. The art of Ajanta unfolds the secret of the unity
of all existence.

The archaeologist has racked his brains to trace in the motif
and technique of Ajanta art influences of foreign countries such
as Persia and Greece (this myth has since been exploded), and
the utmost he has said in appreciation is a few dry words in
praise of the assimilative power of the artists. The historian
has been at great pains to read into the inscriptions so far deciphered at Ajanta some meaning relating to facts or events
bearing on the contemporary periods of ancient Indian history,
the works of art there having struck him only as materials for
studying the social and political life of the country and for describing that glorious heritage of India. The thinker has discovered there the true atmosphere and setting for 'a live university of creative culture' where, away from the distractions of
the work-a-day world, the monks carried on their researches to
solve the problem of spiritual science; he revisions with his
mind's eye the surging waves of a new faith fertilising the mind

of India with the potentiality of an inevitable renewal of her cultural destiny.

But crowning all these different standpoints from which Ajanta has been viewed or studied are the passionate weal and the worshipful spirit with which the artist full of the optimism of the archaeologist, the historian and thinker, has described his pilgrimage to these still-today-the-most-wonderful art-shrines of India. He has heard the music, read the poetry and felt upon his soul the subtle and sweet touches of the Unseen Beauty which gleams through these superb creations of Indian art. The charm of Ajanta art lies not only in the perfection of its convention and perspective but also in the vital and vigorous spontaneity with which it has rendered into the universal language of art the pulse and passion of the artists' longing for communion with the Soul of Eternal Life. The unsophisticated artist or art-critic visiting Ajanta will, doubtless, through his deep and sympathetic study of the cave-temples, be able to fathom the spiritual vision that was the well-spring of the living art of Ajanta, to enjoy the dulcet harmonies of this musical choir beating to the measure of the music of the spheres.

'All Indian art,' says Sri Aurobindo, 'is a throwing out of a certain profound self-vision formed by a going within to find out the secret significance of form and appearance, a discovery of the subject in one's deeper self, the giving of soul form to that vision and a remoulding of the material and natural shape to express the psychic truth of it with the greatest possible purity and power of outline and the greatest possible concentrated rhythmic unity of significance in all the parts of an indivisible artistic whole.' This is yoga in art, a creative union of the being of the artist with the self-manifesting Spirit of the universe, and its practice in ancient India flowered forth into those wonderful works which characteristically fulfil the spiritual and, therefore, the real intention of Indian culture. The mural paintings of Ajanta are among the best of them. The only surviving as also the most beautiful examples of the pictorial art of ancient India, these frescoes are in every respect true to and typical of the artistic genius of the race. Their peculiar appeal springs from the presence of a remarkably spiritual and psychic aroma and atmosphere, imparted to the artistic conception and method by the contemplative turn of the Indian mind. The beauty and power of the idea, the subtlety and flexibility of the line, the vibrant depth and richness of the tone, and the dreamy inflexions of the music of this painting are too obvious and enchanting to be missed by the sense of the soul: the psychical appeal usually carries something in it which evokes a ready response in every cultivated and sensitive human being. The whole creative force comes here from an inner vision of the artist, a deeper intuition of his soul. To him the outer is but a garment of the inner. And if he makes the garment glow and glitter, it is only to convey a bare hint, shoot a single ray of the infinite effulgence within, which is the glory of his vision. An impeccable sense of symmetry and unity guides his brush, and even in unstinted profusion, he invariably ends by creating not a grotesque exuberance but a veritable dance of the stars. A high discerning austerity in technique, *tapas,* saves him from introducing into his conception and execution anything that is likely to detract from the unity and harmony of his creation. He goes deep within, looks into the soul of the thing he is inspired to express or interpret in his own soul, catches the native form and rhythm and colour of that soul and lets them reveal themselves through his trained but sensitive and plastic medium. The expression, therefore, is not a replica or a faithful reproduction of the line, colour and design of the physical nature, but a psychical transmutation of the natural figure. The shapes he paints are the forms of things he has seen in the psychical and other planes of experience. 'They are the soul figure of which physical things are a gross representation and their purity and subtlety reveal at once what the physical masks by the thickness of its casings. The lines and colours sought here are the psychic lines and the psychic hues proper to the vision which the artist has gone into himself to discover.'

III

The famous group of the mother and child before the Buddha (Pl. 2), frescoed on a beautifully designed panel in Cave XVII, is a remarkable example of the highest that Ajanta achieved in painting. Here is a revealing study of it by Sri Aurobindo. He says: 'If we look long at the adoration group of the mother and child before the Buddha, one of the most profound, tender and noble of the Ajanta masterpieces, we shall find that the impression of intense religious feeling of adoration there is only the most outward general touch in the ensemble of the emotion. That which it deepens to is the turning of the soul of humanity in love to the benignant and calm Ineffable which has made itself sensible and human to us in the universal compassion of the Buddha, and the motive of the soul moment the painting interprets is the dedication of the awakening mind of the child, the coming younger humanity, to that in which already the soul of the mother has learned to find and fix its spiritual joy. The eyes, brows, lips, face, pose of the head of the woman are filled with this spiritual emotion which is a continued memory and possession of the psychical release, the steady settled calm of the heart's experience filled with an ineffable tenderness, the familiar depths which are yet moved with the wonder and always farther appeal of something that is infinite, the body and other limbs are grave masses of this emotion and in their poise a basic embodiment of it, while the hands prolong it in the dedicative putting forward of her child to meet the Eternal. This contact of the human and Eternal is repeated in the smaller figure with a subtly and strongly indicated variation, the glad and childlike smile of awakening which promises but not yet possesses the depths that are to come, the hands disposed to receive and keep, the body in its looser curves and waves harmonising with that significance. The two have forgotten themselves and seem almost to forget or confound each other in that which they adore and contemplate, and yet the dedicating hands unite mother and child in the common act and feeling by their simultaneous gesture of material possession and spiritual giving. The two figures have at each point the same rhythm, but with a significant difference. The simplicity in the greatness and power, the fullness of expression gained by reserve and suppression and concentration which we find here is the perfect method of the classical art of India. And by this perfection Buddhist art became not merely an illustration of the religion and an expression of its thought and its religious feeling, history and legend, but a revealing interpretation of the spiritual sense of Buddhism and its profounder meaning to the soul of India.'

The secular paintings of Ajanta have also their soul mean-

ings. They represent the manifold expressions of life. But the
acme of artistic excellence is reached in those among them that
appeal not so much for their force and vividness as for their
suggestions of the Spirit's adventure in Life. The artist pours out
his whole soul in colour, he articulates in line a beauty that is
not of this earth, a grace that is supernatural, and all this to
such a high degree that even pictures of ordinary human
activity become a mystic revelation of the life of the soul.[3]

The sculpture of India also springs from spiritual visions,
and what it creates and expresses at its greatest is the spirit in
form, the soul in body, this or that aspect of living soul power in
the divine or human. His immobile medium does not of course give
to the sculptor that liquidity and fluency which colour and line give
to the painter. Nevertheless, he is equally able to embody in
stone a soul state or experience or any deeper soul quality. A
typical example of this is the figure of the Buddha,[4] evolved
during this age. We have in Ajanta this figure as well as those
of the Bodhisattvas, all done in the characteristic style of the
plastic art of India. The sculptured group by the entrance of
the most splendid of the Chaitya halls in Cave XIX is one of the
best creations of Ajanta sculpture. A Nagaraja is seated with
his queen who holds in her hand a lotus and on her head the
crown of a coiled cobra. Both of them, the Nagaraja more visibly,
are in a mood of contemplation, almost in a state of trance, into
which they have been plunged by the invocations chanted by
the monks in that Chaitya hall, a fact which shows the artist's
sense of harmony between his subject and his surroundings. An
atmosphere of other-worldliness pervades the whole group even
in its minutest details. The sitting posture, particularly the loose
setting of the legs of the king as also of the queen indicate their
deep absorption in what they are hearing—an absorption that
has made them forget to compose their legs. Thus does the group
combine naturalness with soul suggestion.

Ajanta is no less famous for its architectural excellence.
Indeed it represents the perfection of form to which cave architecture attained in India. The exquisite facade of Cave XIX is
evidence enough of the fact that the Ajanta artists were no less
great in their mastery of constructional science than in the arts

---

3. Example studied in Section III of Chapter 1.
4. Studied in Section III of Chapter 1.

of painting and sculpture. This facade is undoubtedly an improvement on the Nasik type. The Chaitya-window stands over the double-corniced flat roof of the doorway supporting the roof by its four pillars. To the right and left of the facade and on the wall of the excavated court in front of the Cave are carved in bold relief many figures of the Buddha. Inside the Cave there are a number of aisle pillars which are richly ornamented fluted columns with pot and foliage capitals, and massive, decorated rounded brackets supporting an elaborate frieze of niches with Buddha figures. The innumerable figures of the Buddha suggest the exuberance of the artists' devotion, and their eagerness to show the onnipresence of that divine personality. The vastness of their vision of the Master can certainly not be circumscribed in a single figure. The whole atmosphere of the Cave—a marvellous combination of sculpture and architecture—is resonant with the raptures of worship expressed in syllables of silence through which the monks poured out the prayers of their soul. That art to them was a part of their sadhana goes without saying. Indeed what a strenuous labour they must have undergone for centuries to transform these rugged hills into beautiful temples! Nowhere in Ajanta do we find the names of those who created these wonders, which affords another proof of their self-effacement in their endeavour to give artistic interpretation to the psychic and the spiritual.

IV

The history of Indian art, so far as its graphic elaboration in colour and line is concerned, is in the most part an attempt to study the psychology and expansion of a distinctly peculiar tradition that grew and developed at Ajanta in that creative epoch of Indian history. Indeed Ajanta offers the most living and powerful of art-traditions of ancient India. Yet while it tends to assert its distinctiveness, it had the special quality of being absorbed in the technical execution of the works of any contemporary or subsequent school of painting which it inspired or influenced; and where regional characteristics have not been so dominant, Ajanta tradition, instead of outshining whatever there remained of local peculiarities, has helped to evolve newer forms possible within the environs of their growth.

The frescoes at Sigiriya in Ceylon, executed during the reign of Kashyapa I in the last quarter of the fifth century A.D. bears striking resemblance to some scenes of Caves XVI and XVII of Ajanta. Though the subjects of the paintings as a whole do not breathe the spiritual fervour and show the extraordinary technical standard of Ajanta, yet they are regarded as typical examples of the Buddhist school of painting in Ceylon in which is unmistakable the influence of the tradition that was built round the marvels at Ajanta. Next in order but contemporaneous with Ajanta are the paintings of the friezes in a series of caves excavated at Bagh in Gwalior State, about a hundred and fifty miles from Ajanta. In craftmanship they are closely similar to those at Ajanta, and maintain the same solemn poses, differing only in the themes executed, which, however, are all of them human. They depict scenes from the social life of the times; yet even the most casual observer will not miss in them the sweetness and grace of Ajanta frescoes. The discovery, in 1920, of fresco paintings in a temple at Sittannavasal in the ancient Pallava country in the Madras State, attributed to Mahendravarman I in the first quarter of the seventh century, records a distinct continuation of Ajanta technique. In the opinion of James H. Cousins, there are obvious in the Sittannavasal frescoes the same high mood of solemn serenity, the same rhythmical graciousness as are discernible in the frescoes at Ajanta.

The importance of Ajanta tradition is to be judged not merely from the standpoint of its local and contemporary influence. There is another and more convincing proof of its power and influence in that even after the lapse of as many as eight centuries since the latest of the Ajanta caves was excavated, it is found to stimulate the growth of newer styles, however primitive. Witness the miniature paintings of the Rajput and Pahari schools which flourished, the former in Rajasthan (Rajputana), and the latter in the Punjab and the foot-hills of the Himalayas. And its original vigour had not a little to do with the growth of the neo-Indian school of painting in modern India.

So far in the realm of its birth. In the art relics of Central Asia, China, Japan, Java and Cambodia—those distant outposts of Indian culture—unmistakable proofs are found of the far-reaching influence of the art of Ajanta. Inspiration from Ajanta can be traced in the Buddhist grottos, sculptures and paintings discovered in Bamiyan, Bactria, Khotan, Miran, Kuchar, Turfan and Tun-huang. The influence of Ajanta's cave architecture is particularly distinct in the grottos in the hills surrounding the valley of Bamiyan. Many of the frescoes in them, too, owe their origin to Ajanta. The fresco representation of the *Kinnaras*[5] swimming in the sky is clearly Ajantan. Ajanta's contribution to the making of Indonesian art cannot be overestimated. It was Ajanta which gave to China the idea of excavating caves and of decorating them, as are best exemplified by the well-known sculptured caves of Yun Kang near Ta-Tangfu, exacavated under the patronage of the Northern Wei dynasty at the close of the fourth century A.D. Japan shows strong traces of Ajanta influence in the painting of the Nara period in the seventh century A.D. Edward Dillon, in his book called *The Art of Japan,* says that some famous ancient paintings of Japan owe much to the technique of Ajanta frescoes. The recent discovery of Ajanta influence in the work of a Japanese artist who presents Shiva and Parvati in Japanese style deserves mention. Again, in connection with the famous fresco in the temple of Horiyuji, presumed to date from the first part of the eighth century, Laurence Binyon states that 'this is quite Indian in character, recalling the frescoes of the cave-temples of Ajanta, in its grand strongly outlined figures and in the feeling for character and life which it reveals. There seems no doubt that it is modelled upon the Ajanta frescoes, and the fact is an eloquent and significant testimony to the freedom of intercourse then existing between India and Japan.' German authorities like Stutterheim and Juynboll are of opinion that the style of the figure of a woman with a child drawn on a central Javanese engraved copper-plate is essentially Ajantan. Fergusson held that the builders of the world-famous Boro-Budur monument in Java migrated from Western India. According to him, 'the character of the sculpture and the details of the ornamentation in caves at Ajanta, Nasik and other places are so nearly identical with what is found in the Javan monument, that the identity of the workmanship is unmistakable.' The French orientalist Goslier opines that the Buddha

---

5. Heavenly singers.

figures from Romlok, Ta Teo, in Cambodia, are closely related to the rock-cut Buddhas in the precincts of Cave XIX of Ajanta.

Further study and closer examination will reveal newer truths about the expansion of the distinctive characteristics that grew up and developed in the art of these peculiarly cut cave-cathedrals of ancient India. This celebrated epic of Indian art has attracted art connoisseurs from distant parts of the world, who have recorded in inspired language their rapturous appreciation of the unparalleled merit of the art-forms inclosed in it. Sister Nivedita saw in these caves magnificent temples that are still vibrant with the fervour of devotion with which the monk-artists worshipped the Lord of their heart. Christiana J. Herring-ham, a reputed English artist, who came all the way from England to study the paintings of Ajanta, called them amazing and unique in the history of art. The delicate curves on the sur-face on a ceiling of one of the caves appeared to John Griffiths 'to be nothing less than miraculous.' Says Sir William Rothens-tein, the distinguished British artist and art-critic: 'On the hund-red walls and pillars of the rock-cut temples of Ajanta, vast drama moves before our eyes, a drama played by princes and sages and heroes, by men and women of every condition, against a marvellously varied scene, among forests and gardens, in courts and cities, on plains and deep jungles: while the messengers of heaven move swiftly across the skies. From all these emanates a great joy in the surpassing radiance of the face of the world, in physical ability of men and women, in the strength and grace of animals and the loveliness of men and flowers and woven into this fabric of material beauty we see the ordered pattern of the spiritual realities of the universe. It is this perfect combination of material and spiritual energy which marks the art of Ajanta.' A Danish artist, who has published a valuable professional cri-ticism on Ajanta, declares that the paintings there represent the climax to which genuine Indian art has ever attained; and that everything in them, from the composition as a whole to the smallest pearl or flower, testifies to the depth of insight coupled with the greatest technical skill. E. B. Havell, the foremost of all foreign admirers of Indian art, asserts that these paintings cons-titute India's claim to the respect and gratitude of humanity.

What is that in Ajanta which has won for itself such praise

from the whole world? Why does it make such a universal appeal? and how in the past could it influence the art of almost the whole of Asia? Apart from the charm and magic of its beauty, its classical excellence, which without doubt strengthen its hold on the aesthetic sense of mankind compelling its spontaneous homage, there is in that appeal a deeper force, a diviner power, which touch the very soul of man and awaken it to an inner truth than what the works outwardly suggest. A light from above dawned on the vision of the artists. It was the light of the world of eternal beauty and bliss, whose glimpses the artists had; and having created out of the very stuff of that vision, they were able to enliven their work with some ray of that infinite Splendour, some portion of that immortal Ananda. It is this in Ajanta that endows it with the supreme virtue of captivating the soul of man, opening to his intuition the greatness and grandeur of that perfect world into which the present is destined to be reborn. The discerning spectator perceives in Ajanta this supernal glory and breaks into words that shoot straight from the inmost core of his heart.

The monk-artists in their moments of inspiration rose far above the boundaries of their theology and saw and created in the vastness of the realms that are eternally immune from the invasion of mind-made distinctions. Consecrated in thought and feeling to the Most High, contemplative and self-controlled, these Fra Angelicos of Ajanta have woven in the dim solitude of their rocky retreat such mystic marvels of beauty and sublimity that mirror the profundities of the abiding truth of existence and point to a brighter future not only for the art of India but also for the race that has produced them.

REFERENCES

Sri Aurobindo, *The Foundations of Indian Culture* (the quotations in this Chapter are all from its chapters on Indian Art); G. Yazdani, *Ajanta;* Asitkumar Haldar, *Ajanta and Bagh Caves* (Bengali); Lady Herringham, *Ajanta Frescoes;* K. H. Vakil, *At Ajanta;* A. Cunningham, *Archaeological Survey of India,* Report X; J. Fergusson and J. Burgess, *Cave Temples of India;* James H. Cousins, *Cultural Unity of Asia;* Sister Nivedita, *Footfalls of Indian History;* V. Smith, *History of Fine Art in India and Ceylon;* Ananda Coomaraswamy, *History of Indian and Indonesian Art;* Probodhchandra Bagchi, *India and China,* and *India and*

Central Asia (Bengali); E. B. Havell, *Indian Sculpture and Painting;* J. Griffiths, *Paintings in the Buddhist Cave Temples of Ajanta;* Edward Dillon, *The Art of Japan;* Laurence Binyon, *The Spirit of Man in Asian Art.*

8

India's Cultural Empire[1]

'Hearken unto me, ye children of immortality, all ye who once dwelt in abodes divine, I have known the Supreme Person, the One whose light shines forth from beyond the darkness.'

IN THESE solemn, sublime and prophetic words the Rishi in the Upanishad voices the call from India's soul. It is a call upon all humanity to arise and awake to that heavenly vision without which life has no meaning. It is this vision which has ever been a source of inspiration to India for all the creative endeavours that she has made and made continuously for ages. It is this again which has always motived her desire to share with others the fruits of all her cultural enterprises.

The thought of India has always regarded life as a movement of the Eternal in time, of the Universal in the individual, of the Infinite in the finite, of the Divine in man. Her seers declared that man can become not only conscious of the Eternal and the Infinite, but can live in the power of that Consciousness and universalise, spiritualise, divinise himself by that Force. They held that the aim of man's life was to grow by an inner and outer experience till he could live in God, realise his spirit, become divine in knowledge, in will and in the joy of his being. This is the deeper intention, the dominant motive of all the creative

---

1. Revised and enlarged version of a paper delivered before a meeting held under the joint auspices of the Greater India Society and the National Council of Education, Calcutta.

strivings of India. A divine perfection has always been her ultimate objective. And it was this ideal which India has ever endeavoured to fulfil in the life of the race and in the life as well
of the entire humanity. That is why our ancient fathers have
voiced forth, ringing through the ages, their solemn call: *krin-
vantu vishvan aryam,* 'Aryanise the whole world,' meaning not
anything racial or ethnic but the supreme culture of self-perfec-
tion which is to be the basis of the world-culture of the future.
That is why there has been throughout history the expansive
movement of its ideas which took their birth in India and spread
beyond her borders so that the foundation may be laid for the
future culture of the world, the spiritual civilisation of Tomorrow.

Almost from the dawn of her history it has been the sole
privilege of India to carry the torch of her unique ideals to distant lands and inspire them to noble adventures both in the inner and outer fields of human activity. Her matchless wisdom,
her splendid art have left their indelible stamp on the civilisations of almost all the great peoples of history.

The culture of India was like a sky-high tower of light
shedding its lustre on the surrounding countries, even on those at
the far ends of the earth, illumining the mind of man, exalting
his heart, ennobling his life and, above all, beckoning him on to
the realisation of his highest spiritual destiny. The story is indeed a romantic one of how India gave expression to this impulse of her soul and built up her cultural empire in the mind
and heart of humanity.

India realised the essential oneness of the human race, and
whatever she achieved, especially in her spiritual pursuits, was
regarded by her as the common property of mankind. The spirit
of service was ingrained in her racial being. And to her there is
no greater service than what is rendered through the gift of
knowledge. It was this gift which India throughout her history
has generously made to all countries with whom she came in
contact, without expecting any return or even an acknowledgment. 'Like the gentle dew,' said Swami Vivekananda, 'that falls
unseen and unheard and yet brings into blossom the fairest
of roses, has been the contribution of India to the thought of the
world. Silent, unperceived yet omnipresent in its effect, it has
revolutionised the thought of the world.'

The high purpose that prompted this selfless bestowing of

her knowledge had its origin in her hidden intention to help mankind to the attainment of its divine goal. This inner motive as well as the effort might not have been always externally visible. But the Shakti of India has all the time been working to that secret end in her own inscrutable way. A greater India was to her a necessity for fulfilling her highest mission. The laying of a cultural foundation for it started when Indian ideas began to spread beyond her physical frontiers and influence the thought and culture of many great peoples of history, as if to prepare the ground for the message which India would deliver in the future for the liberation of the human race. That would indeed be her crowning gift to humanity.

The sources so far available are not enough for reconstructing a complete story of how in the past India built up her cultural empire through the diffusion of her ideas in countries far and near. Nevertheless, thanks to the more liberal among the Indologists, we are now able to form some idea of it, and we shall try here to tell it in the following lines. In the first section we shall trace briefly the different ways in which India influenced the early expressions of Western thought. In the second, we shall take up a rapid survey of Indian influences in the continent of Asia. In the third and last, we shall give a short account of the spread of Indian ideas in modern times.

I

The early history of India cannot be said to have been completely recovered from obscurity and viewed in its proper perspective. The myth that India lived in isolation has however been exploded and the fact established that from very early times she had communication with various parts of the world far and near, her stately ships moved on the high seas, her merchants and missionaries made long treks, hazarding the perils of land journeys in the continent with which she is geographically connected. Barriers there certainly were for India and other countries against meeting and developing between them any commerce, cultural or material, in those dim days of the past. Yet archaeology has brought to light sufficient evidence that India did have intercourse with Europe as early as the tenth century B.C. when ships regularly plied between the mouth of the Indus and the Persian Gulf, when the people of the west coast of India knew those of the Levant. It was not that these ships carried from India only her 'ivory, apes and peacocks for the decoration of the palaces and the Temple of King Solomon.' They used also to have on board her cultural ambassadors to the royal courts and seats of learning which flourished on the shores of the Mediterranean.

Four times in history, says Sri Aurobindo, the stream of Indian thought has poured out upon Europe. The first attempt was the filtering, among others, of Indian wisdom through the thought of the Greek philosophers from Pythagoras to Plato and the Neo-Platonists; the result was the brilliant intellectual civilisation of Greece and Rome which prepared the way for the second attempt when Buddhism and Vaishnavism filtered through the Semitic temperament and entered Europe in the form of Christianity. The third was through the Arabs after the rise of Islam; the result was the reawakening of the European mind in feudal and Catholic Europe. The fourth and last attempt was the quiet entry of Indian thought into Europe, first through the veil of German metaphysics which inspired most of the modern developments of European thought, and then openly through the dissemination of ideas of the various schools of Indian thought by exponents both Indian and European; the result is the growing tendency today in Europe and America to acknowledge the superiority of India's spiritual values.

Scholars have recently begun to accept the view that India is the original home of the Aryans, the latest theory being that the whole of the north-western India and Iran was called Aryana where four successive movements took place through which the Aryan genius expressed itself, first in the Bactrian culture, secondly in the Indus Valley, thirdly in the Vedic, and lastly in the Avestan. Radha Kumud Mookerji has shown how no other region than India could be the cradle of the Aryans, where they must have lived for a very long time before they evolved their civilisation. Kalidas Nag says: 'The Aryan trail definitely began from India.' There are, besides, other evidences which point to this conclusion. Sri Aurobindo says that the hymns of the Rig Veda composed in India circa 3000 B.C., belong to a later period of a long anterior stage which witnessed 'more luminous dawns of the supreme knowledge upon the forefathers of the race.' There is therefore no doubt that the Aryan culture had taken its birth in India and then spread to different parts of the world by the early missionaries of the race who in those dim days hazarded the perils of land and sea and went to countries far beyond the borders of their own, carrying with them the treasures of that culture and thought of which they were the proud inheritors.

Traces of Hindu culture have begun to be found in various parts of eastern Europe. Archaeologists are of opinion that Russia and Siberia have regions in them where excavations may yield evidences of Indian influence. It is believed that Aswamedha (the horse-sacrifice of ancient Hindu kings) was one of the royal ceremonies in some parts of northern Europe. Lithuania observes even to this day many Hindu rites and customs. The names of the Lithuanian rivers are undoubtedly Indian in their origin. Tapti is one such name which is the name of a river in the Punjab; some of the others are Nemuna (Indian, Yamuna), Srobati (Indian, Saraswati), Narbudey (Indian, Narmada). The tribal or clan names of the Lithuanians such as Kuru, Puru, Yadav, Sudav are distinctly Indian: so also are the names of their gods such as Indra, Varuna, Purakanya (Vedic Parjanya). These are facts, however startling they may look. And they are traced to influences that had gone from India. Patient investigations may throw further light on this relation between India and Lithuania in pre-historic times. The eminent Lithuanian archaeologist Pulk Tarasenka in his book *Priesistoirie Lietuva* has made revealing observations on the early history of the Lithuanian tribes.

Researches have unravelled fragments of the story of how Indian ideas travelled to Greece and the neighbouring countries through Persia, Asia Minor and Alexandria, and became an inspiring factor in the development of thought in those regions. Centuries before Christ these regions were widely known for their numerous, crowded, many-sided seats of learning which were visited by seekers of knowledge as also by wise teachers from various parts of the world, who used to participate in the philosophical discussions for which these seats were reputed. And there can be no doubt that in these discussions representative thinkers of each country made their contributions. Authorities agree that India figured most prominently in these centres of intellectual fellowship and that her ideas were most popular among their members. Eminent scholars like Max Muller, Garbe and Winternitz believe in the factual basis of the Greek and Persian traditions that Brahmins from India visited those countries in very early days. It is to them that is traced the origin of the Orphic cult, of its rites and practices, which are neither Greek nor Semitic. Orphists flourished in the seventh century B.C. during which the Ionian philosophers were influenced by Indian wisdom.

Garbe, regarded as the greatest authority on Sankhya philosophy in Europe, holds that Sankhya ideas have exerted great influences on the doctrines of Heraclitus, Empedocles, Anaxogoras, Democritus and Epicurus. Winternitz is convinced that Pythagoras was influenced by the Indian Sankhya, nor has he any doubt that the Gnostic and Neo-Platonist philosophers have been influenced by Indian philosophical ideas. It is again the opinion of Garbe that the theory of Thales (600 B.C.), the father of Greek philosophy, that everything springs from water, that of Anaximander, that the first principle is not water but infinite atmosphere, and that of his disciple Anaximenes, that it is air which is the source of phenomena, are derived from similar Vedic theories which their Greek exponents are said to have been helped to conceive while they were in Persia on a 'mission of pilgrimage for philosophical studies.' The view of Heraclitus (500 B.C.) that 'all bodies are transformations of fire, and that everything that exists is derived from it and strives to return to it' is only an echo of a similar idea in the Chhandogya Upanishad. Garbe compares this with the Sankhya theory of 'the innumerable annihilations and re-formations of the Universe.' Empedocles's (450 B.C.) theory of the eternity and indestructibility of matter is only a restatement of the Sankhya principle of *satkaryavada* or the beginningless and endless reality of all products. He also believed in the transmigration of the soul and posited the evolution of the material world out of primeval matter, which is acted upon by the three qualities—lightness, activity and heaviness—which are nothing but the three *gunas—sattva, rajas* and *tamas*—of the Sankhya system. To Zenophanes (575 B.C.) the father of the Eleatic School, God and the Universe are one, eternal and unchangeable. According to Hiszar, the ideas of the Eleatic School were profoundly influenced by the teachings of the Upanishads. Says Erdmann: 'The absorption of all separate existence in a single substance, as taught by the Eleatics, seems rather an echo of Indian pantheism than a principle of Hellenic spirit.'

The indebtedness of Pythagoras (550 B.C.) to India is almost a fact of history. There is an Indian tradition that Pythagoras was a Hindu of the Sanskrit name Prithviguru, meaning a world-teacher who went to Greece to preach Hindu philosophy. Evidence however is lacking in support of this view. But that he came into touch with Brahmins in Persia, if not in India, is admitted by Max Muller. Jones was the first to point out the striking similarities between the theories of Pythagoras and those of the Sankhya system. Pythagoras's emphasis on number, i.e., Sankhya, Jones says, indicates his Indian inspiration. Pythagoras learnt from India the forty-seventh theorem of the Euclidean geometry which is found in the *Shulva Sutras* of Baudhayana. And it is also from India that he received his idea of the science of music, the importance of numbers and the existence of a fifth element, all of which were unknown to Greece and Egypt in those days. The origin of the Pythagorean doctrine of reincarnation is traced to India, as also of the 'holy tetractyls,' the swearing symbols of the later Pythagoreans, whose meaning may be found in the formula of diagrams for Vedic sacrifices (also in the Katha Upanishad) to which again is traced the origin of the decimal system of notation. The Pythagoreans regarded spitting before fire as a grievous sin, and they abstained from beans, both of which are Vedic conventions. D. N. Tagore has shown that all these ideas of the Pythagorean School are undoubted borrowings from India. Colebrooke says that the doctrines of Pythagoras were rooted in India. He says: 'Adverting to what has come to us of the history of Pythagoras, I shall not hesitate to acknowledge an inclination to consider the Grecian to have been indebted to Indian instructors.' Schrader declares India to be the birthplace of Pythagorean ideas.

The mention by Plato and Aristotle of the name of Zoroaster, and the study by Hermippus of the books of the Persian teacher, are among the evidences that the Persians were in touch with Greece and that their literature had many students in that country. We know that the Achaemenian empire touched the

borders of India and Greece and that Persia was a centre of
contact between these two countries. Besides, the fact is there
that not only Persians but Indians also visited Greece. Max
Muller is one of those who believe that in the fifth century B.C.
there were in Greece Brahmins from India. Rawlinson has brought
to our notice a statement of Eusebius which runs as follows:
Aristoxenus the musician, a pupil of Aristotle, tells the following story about the Indians. One of these men met Socrates at
Athens, and asked him what was the scope of his philosophy.
'An enquiry into human phenomenon,' replied Socrates. At this
the Indian burst out laughing. 'How can a man enquire into
human phenomena,' he exclaimed, 'when he is ignorant of divine
ones?' It is to this dialogue that some scholars trace the origin
of the mystical ideas that are found in the writings of Plato who
must have had them from his master. There is a view that Socrates
was more introspective in later-day thought, possibly due to the
influence he received from Indian sources.

    Plato (427-347 B.C.), the famous disciple of Socrates and
a great admirer of the Pythagorean School, is no less indebted
to India. It is said that Plato was out on a cultural tour in the
countries of Asia. He visited Persia and there is a view that he
was in India for some time. Hopkins says that Plato is full of
Sankhyan thought worked out by him but taken from Pythagoras. His ideas of the bondage of soul to matter and its liberation therefrom, as also his doctrine of reincarnation are distinctly
Sankhyan. His use of the simile of the charioteer and the horses
reminds us of the comparison in the Katha Upanishad 'of the
body with a car, the soul with the charioteer, the senses with
the horses, and the mind with the reins.' Urwick is one of those
scholars who are convinced that India is the birthplace of many
of the ideas which Plato set forth in his *Republic*. Plato's division of the ideal polity into Guardians, Auxiliaries and Craftsmen is nothing but the Hindu caste system in another garb. The
simile of the Cave with which the seventh book of the *Republic*
opens, reminds us of the Vedantic doctrine of Maya or illusion.
The Orphic legend that the Universe was formed in the body
of Zeus, after he had swallowed Phanes, the offspring of the
great 'World Egg,' resembles almost exactly the story in the tenth
book of the Code of Manu of how the Supreme Soul produced
by a thought a Golden Egg (Brahmanda) from which he was

born as Brahma. These similarities, says Rawlinson, are too close to be accidental. Max Muller says that the similarity between Plato's language and that of the Upanishads is sometimes startling. From the foregoing outlines we may conclude with Garbe that the historical possibility of the Grecian world of thought being influenced by India through the medium of Persia must unquestionably be granted, and with it the possibility of the above-mentioned ideas (of the Sankhya and Vedanta philosophy) being transferred from India to Greece. Declaring India as 'a parent civilisation' the great French thinker Voltaire said: 'Everything came to us from the banks of the Ganges where the first Greeks travelled for nothing but knowledge.'

The writings of Pliny, Strabo, Ptolemy and the anonymous pamphlet *Periplus Maris Erythraci,* published at Alexandria in the first century A.D., show that for centuries there was regular intercourse, both cultural and commercial, between India and Alexandria. Pliny says that there were a number of Buddhists in Syria, Palestine and Egypt and that the Gnostic School of Thought of Alexandria was directly under their influence. Its concept of man and Nature was distinctly Buddhistic. Towards the close of the third century B.C. Alexandria under the Ptolemies who were great patrons of learning, acquired considerable importance as a far-famed centre of culture. It attracted scholars from various parts of the world. Among the Buddhists here there must have been some who were missionaries sent by Ashoka, and there were Brahmins too, who carried with them the ancient lore of the Hindus. Evidence shows that these exponents of Indian thought wielded immense influence upon the scholars from different countries who assembled there, it is said, for the purpose of imbibing Indian wisdom. Through these great sons of hers, India made her distinctive contribution in the development of Gnostic and Neo-Platonist ideas as well as early Christian thought. It is admitted that Gnosticism grew out of a synthesis of Christian and Indian ideas. The Gnostic idea of the plurality of heavens and spiritual worlds echoes similar Upanishadic ideas, particularly the Mahayana doctrine of innumerable gods or Bodhisattvas. Mahayana Buddhism and Sankhya philosophy 'undoubtedly exerted considerable influence upon the intellectual life of Alexandria.' Fred. Chr. Baur says that the classification of men into three classes, according to a section of Gnostics, must have been derived from the Sankhya idea of the three *gunas*.

In the words of A. A. Macdonell: 'According to Greek tradition, Thales, Empedocles, Anaxagoras, Democritus and others undertook journeys to Oriental countries in order to study philosophy. The influence of Indian philosophy on Christian Gnosticism in the second and third centuries seems at any rate undoubted. The Gnostic doctrine of the opposition between soul and matter, of the personal existence of intellect, will and so forth, the identification of soul and light are derived from the Sankhya system. The division peculiar to several Gnostics of man into three classes, premnatikoi, psychikoi and hylikoi, is also based on the Sankhya doctrine of the three *gunas*. Again, Bardesanes, a Gnostic of the Syrian school who obtained information about India from Indian philosophers, assumed the existence of a subtle ethereal body which is identified with the *linga sarira* of the Sankhya system. Finally, the many heavens of the Gnostics are evidently derived from the fantastic cosmogony of the later Buddhism.'

A notable figure in the history of Alexandrian philosophy was Philo who lived in the first century B.C. Philo had contact with Indian Gymnosophists. He knew also the Buddhist communities called the Therapeutaes and the Essenes of Palestine. There is a view that Philo was himself a lay follower of the Buddhist faith. He propounded the doctrine of Logos which passed into Christianity (in the Gospel of St. John) and whose origin is traced to the Indian idea of *Vak* (Word) which is personified in the Rig Veda as a divine power. Ammonius Saccas (A.D. 200) was another Alexandrian philosopher whose thought reflects Indian inspiration. He is said to have had direct intercourse with travellers from various countries including India. It is however from the Indians he met that he had his initiation in Yoga of which he became a master. It may be noted that the disciplines he practised were unknown in Alexandria at that time. Mead says that Ammonius made such an impression in his time by his wisdom and knowledge that he was known as the 'God taught,' believed to be an appellation for a Yogi in Alexandria.

Ammonius was the teacher of Plotinus, the founder of the Neo-Platonist School whose influence on European thought is well known. That this School had much in its ideas which was derived from India was due to Plotinus being imbued with the truths of the Yoga and the Vedanta philosophy of the Hindus. Erdmann says that Plotinus had a desire to visit India, but no mention is found in the fragmentary account of his life whether he was able to fulfil it or not. But, thinks the same authority, there can be no doubt that he had deep knowledge of Indian mystical thought, particularly of the Vedanta School, which he might have received from his master whom he followed in his spiritual life. Like his master he led an ascetic life and practised Yogic disciplines. He used to remain most of his time in meditation and would often rise into those states of trance and ecstasy which are likened to states of Samadhi mentioned in the Yoga philosophy. The Good, the One Reality, of his system is the same as Brahman or Parmatman, the Supreme Self of the Upanishads. He declared with the Upanishads that the Absolute is inexpressible. His Universal Mind and World-Soul are respectively the Ishwara and the Hiranyagarbha of the Vedanta. What he called Nature is the Prakriti of the Sankhya. He believed in Karma and reincarnation. At the time of his death he said like a Hindu Yogi: 'Now I seek to lead back the self within me to the All-Self.' Plotinus looks upon the world as 'an outflow, a diffusion of the Divine,' echoing thereby the Vedic view of the desire of the One to be Many expressed through the divine utterance *'ekoham bahu syam.'* His idea of God as the One, the good, the pure thought, the pure actuality,' corresponds with the Sachchidananda connotation of Brahman in the Upanishads. The words of Plotinus that 'we say what He is not, we cannot say what He is' seem to be a mere repetition of the famous expression of the Upanishad, *neti, neti* (He is not this, not this). Plotinus declares that all worldly things are void of value, and that man's chief duty lies in freeing himself from the snare of illusion under which he sees reality in a world of phenomenon, and this he can do only by deep meditation, which will lead him to 'an ecstatic perception of God.' This is nothing but a restatement of the doctrine of Maya and the Yoga philosophy of the Vedanta. The influence of the Sankhya thought upon Plotinus is traced by Garbe in the explanation Plotinus gave of how the world happens to be in the bondage of matter and so of sorrow and suffering, and of how it could be redeemed and brought to 'a state of absolute cessation of pain.' This is only an echo of the Buddhistic view of Nirvana. It is not possible, says Garbe, to question Indian influence in the thought of Plotinus. And it is needless to repeat what an enormous debt Western thought owes to Neo-Platonism, first propounded by Plotinus.

Porphyry (A.D. 232-304), the celebrated disciple of Plotinus, followed Indian ideals more closely than his master. He was fortunate in having a personal acquaintance with the ideas of Indian philosophy through an access he got to an important treatise on India by Bardesanes, the noted Babylonian Gnostic teacher of the early third century A.D., 'who acquired authentic information about India from the Indian ambassadors who were sent to the court of Emperor Antoninus Pius.' An important passage from his work, copied by Porphyry and still preserved, reveals a very intimate knowledge of the Brahmins and the Buddhists, their discipline and their mode of life. He describes, in accurate detail, the life in a Buddhist monastery, and a visit to a cave temple in western India, containing an androgynous image of the god Shiva. Porphyry developed on some scientific lines the Sankhya doctrine of the contrast between the spiritual and the material world. But his strong insistence on abstention from animal slaughter and his denunciation of sacrifice for religious merit indicate the Buddhistic bias of his mental make-up.

Buddhism was a great force in the expansion of Indian culture. The name of the Buddha 'reached Bactria during the first century after his passing away'; and the presence of Buddhists in Bactria in the first century B.C., says Max Muller, is attested by several authorities: Mackenzie has shown in his book *Buddhism in Pre-Christian Britain* that Buddhism was prevalent in Britain in pre-Christian times. The ideal of *maitri,* universal brotherhood, inculcated in Buddhism, inspired Ashoka, 'the first internationalist of history,' to send out goodwill missions to Syria, Egypt, Cyrene, Macedonia and Epirus embracing the three continents Asia, Africa and Europe, besides Ceylon and other parts of Insulindia and Indonesia. Many of these missionaries settled in those countries and formed large and influential Buddhist communities.

Ashoka's is indeed a unique figure in history. There has never been a monarch who loved not only his own subjects but also the whole of mankind so sincerely as this Maurya emperor of India. His unexampled concern for the spiritual welfare of humanity marks him out as one of the greatest benefactors of the human race, the earliest and most notable builder of the cultural empire of India. Ashoka proclaimed the Indian ideal of world-peace and world-fellowship when he said that all men were his children and that the true conquest lay not in the way of the sword but in the conquest of men's hearts by the law of the Dharma.

Buddhism was well known to Clement of Alexandria in the second and third centuries A.D. He repeatedly refers to the presence of the Buddhists in Alexandria, and declares that 'the Greeks stole their philosophy from the barbarians.' He is the first Greek to mention the Buddha by name. The Therapeutaes of Alexandria and the Essenes of Palestine, who were so well known to the Greek world, were in fact communities of Buddhist Bhikkus (monks), practising Buddhist rites, preaching Buddhist doctrines and spreading the teachings of Gautama Buddha in the West. The word Therapeutae is only a Greek variation of the Pali word *Theraputta,* meaning son of the Buddha. *Thera* is the Pali form of the Sanskrit word *sthira* meaning 'settled in peace'; and *putta* is the Pali form of the Sanskrit word *putra* meaning 'son'. The Christian historian Mahaffy says: 'These Buddhist missionaries were the forerunners of the Christ.' Philosophers like Schelling and Schopenhauer, and Christian thinkers like Dean Mansel and D. Millman admit that the Essenes and the Therapeutaes arose through the influence of Buddhist missionaries who had come from India particularly during the reign of Ashoka.

There is plenty of evidence to show the influence of Buddhism on the development of the Christian faith. The parable style of the Bible is held to be an echo of the story-telling method of the Buddhist Jatakas, and that, says Vincent Smith, 'some orthodox forms of Christian teaching owe some debt to the lessons of Gautama.' Winternitz believes that 'in the combination of the Jewish and the Greek ideas on which the teachings of the Christian Gospels are based, there was also a small admixture of Buddhist thoughts and legends. Some undoubted borrowings from the Buddhist religious literature are also found in the Apocryphal Gospels.' The strong insistence of the orthodox form of Christianity on the observance of rituals, penance, celibacy and other rigid austerities is said to have been imbibed from Buddhism. The Gospel story of the Bible bears striking resemblance to the account of the Buddha's life given in such Buddhist works as the *Lalita Vistara,* which describe the Buddha's miraculous conception and birth, the star over his birthplace, the prophecy of the aged Asita, the temptation by Mara and the twelve disciples. But points of similarity between the Buddhist and the Christian parables are even more startling. Discussing the coincidence of the Jataka story of the pious disciple walking on the water with the similar story in the Gospels, Max Muller remarks that it can only be accounted for by some historical contact and transference, and the Jatakas are centuries older than the Gospels. The story of the Prodigal Son is found almost in the same form in the Buddhist work, the *Saddhamma Pundarika.* Another fact which confirms the possibility of Indian influence on Christianity was revealed years ago in a book called *The Unknown Life of Jesus Christ,* translated from a manuscript discovered in a monastery of Tibet by the Russian explorer, Lutovitch. The book fills up the gap of the Christ's absence from Jerusalem for twelve years by describing his itinerary in northern India during that period when he visited India's well-known cities and centres of learning and her great saints and scholars.

Indian knowledge was familiar to the Eastern churches of the Levant. A notable instance is furnished by the presence of Indian ideas in the writings of Origen (third century A.D.), who was one of the greatest of the Greek Fathers of the Eastern church and a writer of many authoritative books on Christian theology. Origen believed in reincarnation and showed extreme eagerness to imbibe Indian wisdom, 'those insights and illuminations from "the Christians that were before Christ." ' He was thrice persecuted, the last time to death, for holding 'un-Christian' views, one of which must have been on reincarnation. An eminent Christian thinker says that had not in the fourth century the Council of Chalcedon condemned reincarnation, then believed in by many Christian Fathers, the 'religion of love' would have been saved the disgrace of the cruel finality of everlasting punishment for the mistakes of this one life.

Many authorities have felt that India is the sourceland of the Water of Life, rich and constant enough in its yield to have fed all mankind's ecclesiastical channels. They think that

India influenced, directly or indirectly, that stream of lofty idealism and devotion which arose in the Rhineland in the spring of the Middle Ages. Indian ideas were transmitted through a succession of teachers and disciples like the Arabian monk Bar Sudali, also known as Dionysius the Areopagite, whose doctrines were more Vedantic than 'Synoptic.' Erigena and Eckhart were his spiritual sons. This was, as it were, a transplantation of Indian wisdom from the banks of the Ganga to those of the Rhine. In his book the *Flowering of Mysticism*, Rufus Jones has traced this movement of Indian ideas through Persia, Alexandria, Cordova, Padua and thence by Paris on to the Rhine, 'influencing and forming the thought and practice of the first great schools of Western mysticism.' Scholarship, says Gerald Heard, has now proved as fact of literature that the specific concepts which gave to Western religion its deepest insights and its most effective techniques were all imported from Indian areas.

There is positive evidence that Indian faiths and philosophies flourished in Asia Minor in pre-Christian times. Zenob, an early fourth-century classical writer of Christian Armenia, relates the episode of two Indian chiefs who as a result of their discomfiture in an insurrection against their king, left their country with their followers and settled in Taron in the upper Euphrates, west of Lake Van. There they built a town and erected temples for the worship of a deity called Giasne—a corruption of the name Krishna. This was about the middle of the second century B.C. They flourished in that region for more than four hundred years when about the year A.D. 304 St. Gregory appeared there in his temple-breaking campaigns and after overcoming stiff resistance razed the temples to the ground. There were at that time more than 5000 followers of the Krishna cult or Vaishnavism as we may call it. But, obviously enough, all of them could not be Indians.

The true fact is that the Syrian countries which formed part, first of the Persian and later of the Graeco-Roman world for nearly five centuries before the Christian era, were long exposed to Indian influence. They had intimate contact particularly with the Bhagavata (the worship of the Hindu Godhead Vishnu of whom Krishna represents an aspect) religion and Buddhism. There is a view that this impact of India upon Israel had much to do with the rise and growth of Christianity and that it was one of the reasons why Judaism became hostile, and remained so ever afterwards, to the new faith as something outlandish.

It is said that fables had their origin in the East. And India had always a rich stock of them, which spread to distant lands through sailors and merchants, round camp-fires on long caravan journeys. Like her thought, her fables too have influenced those of Europe. The *Panchatantra* and the *Hitopadesha* are among the oldest folk stories, which are woven into the fabric of European literature, the former having been translated into all the principal languages of the world, ancient and modern, including Chinese, Japanese, Arabic, Persian, Greek, Latin, French, German, Italian, Russian, English, Spanish, Swedish, Dutch and even Icelandic. With the exception of the Bible, there is probably no work which has been translated into so many languages as the *Panchatantra*. Arthur Ryder claimed that this work contains the most widely known stories in the world. 'If it were further declared that the *Panchatantra* is the best collection of stories in the world, the assertion could hardly be disproved.' These stories reached Asia Minor as far back as the sixth century B.C., and were translated into Greek by Aesop who lived in the court of Croesus of Lydia. Some of them appear in Herodotus. A Latin version of them is ascribed to Phaedrus in the time of Tiberius and another Greek version to Babrius of Alexandria about A.D. 200. The famous Indian story *Shuka Saptati* reached Europe in Persian form in the tenth century, as also the *Arabian Nights* which contains many Indian references, and the story of Sindbad the Sailor which is of Hindu origin. La Fontaine made use of the fables of the 'Indian Sage Pilpay' which name is believed to be a corruption of Vidyapat or Vidyapati.

That these stories of India form a substantial element in those of Europe is obvious. A few examples are given below. The animals and birds such as the lion, the jackal, the elephant and the peacock, which figure prominently in them, are mostly Indian ones. In the European versions the jackal becomes the fox. The well-known Welsh story of Llewellyn and Gelert is a direct adaptation from the *Panchatantra* story of the Mongoose and the Cobra with this variation that the dog and the wolf in the former become mongoose and cobra in the latter. Many

Indian fables are found in La Fontaine's famous work in French. Sir Thomas North adopted them in English and they are utilised by Shakespeare in a modified form in his plays. La Fontaine's fable of the milk-girl building 'castles in the air' echoes the Indian story of the Brahmin Beggar. India is held to be the source of numerous fairy tales in Grimm or Hans Anderson, including the Magic Mirror, the Seven-leagued Boots, Jack and the Beanstalk, and the Purse of Fortunatus, many of which are found in the *Gesta Romanorum*, the *Decameron*, and Chaucer's *Canterbury Tales*. The origin of the Pardoner's Tale is traced to the *Vedabbha Jataka*. A most striking example of the migration of a tale is furnished by the famous history of Barlaam and Josaphat, in which the Christian prince Josaphat, deeply moved by certain distressing conditions of life, renounces the world and becomes an ascetic. It was written in Greek by John of Damascus in the eighth century A.D. and was translated into Arabic during the time of Caliph Al-Mansur, and later, from Arabic into European languages. It has now been shown that Josaphat is no other than Bodhisat or Bodhisattva, and the story is that of Gautama Buddha's Great Renunciation, as told in the *Lalita Vistara*. Thus the Buddha is worshipped today in a garbled form in a church in Sicily dedicated to St. Barlaam. The Buddhist Jataka story of the 'Three Caskets' is also woven into the story of Josaphat, which was borrowed by Shakespeare for use in his *Merchant of Venice*.

Not only in the realms of thought and literature, but also in those of the exact sciences, India's influence on the West in early days was no less remarkable. The so-called 'Arabic' numerals and the decimal system were first developed in India and were transmitted to Europe through the Arabs. 'India hit on the brilliant ideas of a place-value system for numerals in contrast to the clumsy Greek and Roman methods of counting—inventions eagerly taken over by the Arabs and later passed along to Europe.' 'Zero, the most modest and the most valuable of all numerals, is one of the subtle gifts of India to mankind.' Algebra had its origin in India and came to Western Europe through the Arabs. Geometry was developed in India as early as in the Vedic age when the construction of sacrificial altars required its psychological application. Anatomy, Physiology and other branches of medical science were also highly developed by the ancient Hindus. Dr. Royle has shown that Hippocrates, the father of Western medicine, borrowed his *Materia Medica* from India. 'We find from the works of Charak and Susruta,' says the same authority, 'that the Hindus used minerals in medicine for the first time.' In the time of Alexander, says Garrison, Hindu physicians and surgeons enjoyed a well-deserved reputation for superior knowledge and skill, and Aristotle is believed to have been indebted to them. Julian Huxley says that the Hindus were acquainted with the science of evolution before Paul of Tarsus. Sir Monier Williams avers that the laws of evolution were known to the Hindus at least a thousand years before Darwin. Mention is made in the Jewish Encyclopaedia that the theory of Copernicus that the earth is round and revolves on its axis was known to the Hindus long before Copernicus. It is well known that more than seven hundred years before Newton Bhaskaracharya developed the theory of gravitation. There is plenty of evidence to show that the sciences of Astronomy, Physics, Chemistry, Botany, Zoology and Metallurgy were widely cultivated in ancient India. *Sukraniti-sara* and *Brihatsamhita* are among the works in which we find a systematic treatment of these sciences. In 1952 Jagadguru Shankaracharya of Jyotir-pith demonstrated before the staff and students of the Banaras Hindu University the application of the sixteen basic principles of the Vedic mathematics known to the modern world. He covered such a wide field as the first four principles, recurring decimals, quadratic equations and calculus. He asserted that the various 'Sutras' of the Atharva Veda, if deciphered correctly, could any day solve the problems that mathematicians have struggled and failed to. He claimed that Vedic mathematics could yield the result of pie upto one thousand decimal places, whereas it is upto only seven hundred that the value of pie has been acheived.

The science of music was systematised in India many centuries before it could be called a science in other countries. Wagner is said to have got familiar with Hindu music through Latin translations and is indebted to it for his principal idea or 'leading motive.' Beethoven was not untouched by India.

It is not possible within the brief scope of a short chapter to give further details of the story of the diffusion of Indian ideas in the Western world in early times. What however we have so far been able with the help of authorities to say about the main movements and personalities in it, suffice to show that India left the indelible stamp of her individuality upon the culture of those regions in the West with which she came into contact.

Time was when India not only achieved great things, perhaps the greatest, both in the inner and outer fields of her activity, but the exalting sublimities of her culture and thought have been for ages the perennial source of inspiration to many a people for all their strivings after a high degree of refined existence. We may sum up this unique phenomenon of cultural influence in the reverend words of Will Durant, the eminent American thinker and historian: 'India was the motherland of our race, and Sanskrit the mother of Europe's languages; she was the mother of our philosophy; mother, through the Arabs, of much of our mathematics; mother, through the Buddha, of the ideals embodied in Christianity; mother, through the village community, of self-government and democracy. Mother India is in many ways the mother of us all.'

II

Coming nearer home we find that almost the whole of the mental soil of Asia was watered and fertilised by the streams of religious and cultural ideas that flowed from India for an unbroken period of nearly two thousand years. Says Aurel Stein: 'The vast extent of Indian culural influences, from Central Asia in the north to tropical Indonesia in the south, and from the borderland of Persia to China and Japan, has shown that ancient India was the radiating centre of a civilisation which by its religious thought, its art and literature was destined to leave its deep mark on the races wholly diverse and scattered over the greater part of Asia.' Alfred C. Lyall in his paper on *Natural Religion in India* says: 'As from some high ridge or plateau the rivers rise and run down into distant lands, so from India there has been a large outflow of religious ideas over Asia. It has, of course, been the fountainhead of Buddhism, which has flooded, as I have said, all eastern Asia; while I believe that the influence of Indian theosophy spread at the beginning of the Christian era as far as Alexandria and Antioch. I am told that it profoundly affected the ancient religion of Persia; and it may be traceable later in the mysticism of the

Persian Sufis. The religious thought of India has thus radiated out east and west across the Asiatic Continent.' Sylvain Levi, the eminent French Indologist, stresses India's influence over 'one-fourth of the human race.' 'From Persia to the Chinese Sea, from the icy regions of Siberia to the islands of Java and Borneo, from Oceania to Socotra, India has propagated her beliefs, her tales, and her civilisation. She has left indelible imprints on one-fourth of the human race in the course of a long succession of centuries. She has the right to reclaim in universal history the rank that ignorance has refused her for a long time, to hold her place among the nations, summarizing the spirit of Humanity.'

Before we begin our survey of India's cultural empire in her mother continent, we may digress for a moment to trace briefly the spread of Indian ideas in pre-historic times. The extensive maritime activities of India in the ancient world brought her into contact with many countries, such as Egypt, Babylon, Assyria, Judea and prehistoric America. Evidences are not rare which show that India had cultural intercourse with almost all of these countries. Inspiration from India is traced in the Egyptians' apotheosis of the forces behind natural phenomena, particularly of the solar deities of whom Horus is said to be a variation of Surya, the Sanskrit word for the sun. Their god Osiris and his consort Isis are believed to be adapted from the Vedic gods Ishvara and Ishi. The ancient Egyptians had a caste system 'similar to that of India.' In the Puranas of the Hindus Egypt is mentioned as *Mishra-desha* (a country of mixed people, so called because people from different countries used in those days to gather there for cultural and commercial purposes), from which is derived its present Indian name *Mishar*. Herodotus wrote that some of the customs of the Egyptians were essentially Aryan. The discovery by Sir Flinders Petrie of statues and other Indian relics at Memphis, the ancient capital of Egypt, led that famous British Egyptologist to believe in the existence of an Indian colony in ancient Egypt about 500 B.C. Madame Blavatsky in her book *The Secret Doctrine* says: 'If Egypt furnished Greece with her civilisation and the latter bequeathed hers to Rome, Egypt herself in earlier antiquity received her laws, her social institutions, her arts and her sciences, from India. Similarly the Babylonian civilisation was neither born nor developed in that country. It was imported from India and the importers were Brahminical Hindus.'

It was the Babylonians who gave the name *Sindhu* to the *Muslin* because of its being manufactured by the Aryans of Sapta-Sindhu at 'an amazingly early period.' The story of Manu's flood, and other legends and religious traditions of India were current in ancient Babylon and Assyria. The Vedic influence is traced in the Babylonian theory of creation. The science of Astronomy in which the Babylonians excelled was a gift from the Aryanised Dravidians of India. The figure of Anu, the highest god of the Assyrians, is said to be a symbol of Brahman of the Vedanta. The term *Asura,* deciphered in some Assyrian inscriptions, is believed by some scholars to be the Asura of the Vedas. There is also a view that the Assyrians migrated from India. Sayace and Haddock trace the origin of Sumerian culture to the culture of the Indus Valley in India. The old Testament refers to a people 'who journeyed from the East and came into the plain of Shinar (lower Mesopotamia).' Hall says: 'The Sumerians were decidedly Indian in type. They bear most resemblance to the Dravidian ethnic type, so far as we can judge from their monuments. They were very much like the South Indian Hindus of the Dekkan. And it is by no means improbable that the Sumerians were an Indian race.' Dr. A. L. Waddel in his book *Indo-Sumerian Seals Deciphered* maintains that the Sumerians were Aryans and that their names can be identified in the Vedas and the Puranas. Antiquities and monuments unearthed in Sumeria are believed by him to be associated with Vedic kings and priests. There are also other scholars who support the view that the Sumerians derived their culture from India. It is interesting to know that the word 'Sumeria' is derived from the Sanskrit word 'Sumeru' meaning good mountain. V. G. Childe holds that the characteristics of the proto-Sumerian civilisation as revealed by its relics and antiquities are not so much native developments on Babylonian soil as results of Indian inspiration. It is most likely that the Sumerians came from the Indus, or at least from regions in its immediate sphere of influence. The striking similarity between the central story of the Yahvist sections of the Pentateuch, Joshua and Samuel, and the Kurukshetra War of the *Mahabharata* has led some scholars to opine that the Semites of Judea were influenced by the Aryans of India.

About 1800 B.C., the Kassites, a branch of the Indo-Aryans, were in possession of Babylonia. They worshipped Indra-Bhaga and the sun-god Surya. Similarly, the Mittannians ruled over the

northern part of Mesopotamia in the fifteenth century B.C. Contemporary with the above two, were the Hittites who ruled over
a greater part of Asia Minor, Syria and Palestine between the
years 2000 B.C. and 1200 B.C. The real name of the Hittites,
as revealed by their inscriptions, was Khatti—a corruption of
Kshatri or Kshatriya.

It is noteworthy that the land of Syria which was ruled
over by the Hittites, continued to be called Khatti from the
second millennium B.C. to the time of the Assyrian king Nebu-
chadnezzer (sixth century B.C.). Long after the Hittites were wip-
ed out of that land, Boghaz-Keui, the capital of the Hittites, was
called Khattishash, meaning that it was founded by the Khattis.
Excavations there have brought to light inscribed tablets recording a treaty concluded in the fourteenth century B.C. between
two belligerent tribes, the Hittites and the Mitannians, in terms
of their respective customs which included, as the inscriptions say,
the invocation of the Vedic gods Mitra, Varuna, Indra and the
Nasatyas (the twin Aswins) for their blessings so that the tribes
might grow in their friendly relations. Inscriptions on other tablets excavated in the same region by the German archaeologist
Winckler, describe a treatise on the management of horses and
chariot-races, in which occur such pure Sanskrit terms as *aika-
vartana* (in one turning), the *trivartana* (in three turnings).
Besides, these inscriptions mention a class of military nobility,
the so-called 'mariannu' who played an important role in Syria
and Mitanni and whose name is derived from the old Indian
'marya' meaning a youngman, a hero. The name of a certain
Palestinian king was Subandhu, a Sanskrit name.

From Tel-el-Amarna letters we know that between the years
1470 and 1400 B.C. there reigned in Mitanni four kings whose
names were Artatana, Artasuma, Sutarna and Dasharatta, all of
which are derived from Sanskrit. These and similar other inscriptions show that Indian ideas penetrated the upper valley of the
Euphrates in those early days.

Before the rise of Islam, there lived in Arabia many Hindus,
mostly Brahmins, who settled there observing Hindu religious
customs including the worship of Shiva as Makkesha from which
the name of Mecca is said to have been derived. The famous
astronomer Yavanacharya was born of one such Brahmin family.
It was from these Brahmins that the Arabs learnt much of the

science of Mathematics, Astronomy, Algebra and Decimal notation, which, as already seen, were first developed in India.

Traces of Indian culture in pre-historic America lend support to the view that the word *patala* (antipodes) in the Hindu
Puranas signifies America. Humboldt says that Hindu customs
and manners were prevalent in America when the Europeans
first founded colonies there. An icon discovered in Mexico shows
that the Hindu god Ganesha was worshipped there. The art
of Maya civilisation resembles in many respects some South
Indian carvings. Temples in Mexico are modelled on those of
South India. There is a striking similarity between the life led
by the people in Mexico and that led by the people in India.
The legend is still current in Mexico that the Mahabharata hero
Arjuna, in the course of his *digvijaya* (world-conquest), came to
Mexico and broke his vow of celebacy by marrying a local princess. The people of India had the cipher long before the Maya
people whose extreme emphasis on the Zero, says Elliot Smith,
'acquires a special significance as further corroboration of
America's debt to India.' A sculptured representation of a typical
elephant at Copan in Central America is held to be a representation of the Indian elephant with Indian embellishments and addi-
tions of a symbolic import. Sir William Jones says the ancient
Peruvians of South America claimed descent from a solar generation and were worshippers of the Sun-god. The ancestors of
the Peruvians, says Prococke, were connected with the Indians.
No wonder that the story of the *Ramayana* should be current
among the Peruvians, whose greatest festival is called *Rama-Sitoa*
which is even now observed in Peru very much in the same
fashion as Ramalila is observed in North India. The poetry of
Peru bears the imprint of the *Ramayana* and the *Mahabharata*
on each page. Ambassador Miles Pointdexter of the United States
who spent several years in Peru and made personal investigations from the descendants of the Inca rulers says that the founders of the Inca dynasty of South America were four 'Ayar'
(having phonological connection with Arya) Brahmins. The Incas
observed the caste-system and performed the sacred thread rite
more or less exactly as it is performed by the Brahmins of India.
The language of Peru has more than a thousand Sanskrit roots.
Peruvian music is based on Hindu music. Chamanlal in his book
Hindu America says: 'The belief of these Americans in the four

Hindu Yugas (epochs), their *Gurukula* scheme of education, *Panchayat* system, worship of Indra, Ganesha and other Hindu gods, practices of Hindu religious dances, and childbirth, mar riage and death ceremonials including *Sati,* prove beyond doubt that the Hindus were the first to discover America.'

Artistic treasures and manuscript materials that have yielded to the spade of the archaeologist in various parts of Central Asia, at Bamiyan, Bactria, Khotan, Miran, Kucher, Turfan and Tun-huang, reveal the vastness of Indian influence in those regions. The manuscript remains of Turkestan have brought to light a formidable mass of Buddhist literature. It is now a fact of history that a large number of Indians migrated from the Punjab and Kashmir and settled in the basin of the Tarim and built up a series of cities, studying and interpreting Buddhist culture for several centuries from about the second century of the present era. Relics of numerous *stupas,* monasteries and *viharas* have been found in Khotan and its surrounding regions. It is said that Khotan derived its name from the Sanskrit word *Go-dana* meaning gift of cows, which seems to suggest its connection with Brahminical culture. A saint of Kashmir named Virochana introduced Buddhism in Khotan which grew into an important centre of learning. Gotami-Vihara, the famous University of Mahayana studies, attracted scholars from different parts of Asia. Buddha-Sena, its Chancellor, came from India. Sanskrit and Pra-krit which was then the current language of North-West India, were in use in those distant outposts of Indian culture. The Gupta and the Kharosthi were generally the prevalent scripts in most of those regions. The influence of Ajanta is traced in the frescoes of the grottos there, but the sculpture and architecture, though derived from original Indian sources, are expressed in local media. Some of the frescoes describe Jataka stories, and a number of palm-leaf manuscripts give the dramas of Ashva-ghosha in the script of the Kushana period of Indian history. Another manuscript gives the whole of the Dhammapada in Pra-krit. Central Asia was verily a stronghold of Indian culture, and therefore an important part of India's cultural empire.

India's cultural intercourse with China is an event of out-standing importance in the history of Asian culture, as also in that of the expansion of Indian ideas in the East. The *Manu Samhita* mentions the Chinese as mixed Kshatriyas, and the *Maha-*

bharata calls them allies of king Bhagadatta of Assam who fought against the Pandavas in the Kurukshetra War. The *Shakti-mangala Tantra* refers to Maha-China as belonging to *Ratha-Kranta,* one of the divisions of greater India. There is a view that China was a centre of Tantrik culture and that the idea of the Universal Mother in Taoism is an echo of it. But recorded history assigns the commencement of India's contact with China to the year A.D. 60 in which the Chinese Emperor Ming-ti saw a vision of the Buddha and sent a delegation to India to collect information about Buddhism. Since then China began to be visited by scholars and missionaries from India, and India, by devout pilgrims and religious seekers from China, with the result that these two oldest peoples of history became united by a deep bond of cultural friendship.

It is interesting that the earliest missionaries of Indian culture to China were, many of them, monks of mixed race-origin, having connections with the nomad tribes of Central Asia, particularly the Scythians and the Yuechi. Indian culture had already struck deep roots among these tribes even before it reached China in the historical period. The first Indian scholars to arrive in China were Kasyapa Matanga and Dharmaraksha of Scytho-Indian parentage. And the first Buddhist monastery in China was the one built in their honour. It became the most important centre of Sino-Indian cultural collaboration for more than three centuries. With the spread of Buddhism in China other centres were soon established in different parts of the country, in all of which the main work done was the study of Indian texts and their translation into Chinese.

Kashmir, then a renowed seat of Sanskrit learning and Buddhist studies, supplied the bulk of Indian scholars who in the earlier period took a leading part in the dissemination of Indian culture in China. Madhyadesha and Gandhara were not without their share in this noble mission. The four centuries of T'ang reign in China was the most glorious period of Sino-Indian cultural fellowship, during which Buddhism was in a most flourishing condition in China. There were thousands of Indian merchants, monks and scholars in the metropolitan cities of China. Many eminent scholars of the Nalanda University were working in China during this period, and the results of their work is found in the Chinese Buddhist Canon which contains thousands of volumes of translations of Indian texts whose originals were lost in India owing to the depredations of Muhammedan iconoclasts who destroyed hundreds of Buddhist seats of learning in northern India, including the world-famous Nalanda University. India now looks to China for a recovery of those vast literary treasures of her past. In fact, the work has been already started in Visva-Bharati—the celebrated institution embodying Tagore's vision of cultural fellowship—under the direction of the eminent Chinese savant Tan Yun-Shan.

Indian influence in China is not confined to the sphere of religion alone. It is evident also in her arts and crafts, in her music and sciences. Inspiration from India is obvious in the stone sculptures and bas-reliefs of the Han period before which the art of China was generally in bronze, wood and jade. The Tun-huang and Yun-kang grottos contain superb relics of Buddhist sculptures, which reflect direct influence from India. The pagoda type of temples, so much in vogue in China, is regarded by some scholars as of Indian origin. One type of such storied structures was in fact known in China as well as in Japan as 'Indian style of architecture.' The old paintings in the caves called Tzu-hsia Tung near Nanking and in the famous Pagoda in Kai-fong depict figures looking like and dressed exactly as Bengali Brahmins. The paintings in them of religious musical gatherings resemble in every way the figures of the Sankirtan singers of Bengal. The eminent artist, Nandalal Bose, who visited these temples, is of opinion that these pictures are without doubt those of Bengalis. Inscriptions, including those of Tantrik *mantras* in Bengali letters in a temple in Peking called Wu Ta-ssu (that is, roofed by a group of five spires), which is built in the famous Pancharatna (five jewels, i.e., five spires) style of Bengal, show the influence of Bengal in China. The nobles of ancient China were great patrons of Indian music, and especially of the stringed instruments and certain modes of dancing, which had been adopted by the Chinese. The study of Indian astronomy and mathematics was encouraged in China. A T'ang emperor appointed several Indian astronomers to work in the Imperial Astronomical Bureau and help in the preparation of new official calendars. Indian arithmetical rules were translated into Chinese, as also books on Indian medicine. Many Indian drugs found place in the Chinese pharmacopoeia. The Chinese speak of children's dolls, and sometimes the children themselves, as little *bodhi-sattvas* (hsia p'usa), the previous incarnations of the Buddha. An Empress Dowager of China was addressed as 'Old Buddha.' The Buddhist Goddess of Mercy and the smiling Buddha are household words in China. Dr. Tan says that in the culture of China a deep permeation of Indian ideas is unmistakable.

From China Korea received her initiation in Buddhism about the middle of the fourth century. In Silla, an ancient city of Korea, decorations in purely Indian style can be seen today on a temple, eracted by a king to commemorate an Indian priest who lived there and was described as black—probably a Dravidian Indian. Gradually Buddhist culture deepened in the soil and became in course of time the national culture of Korea.

Japan was blessed with the light of Buddhism, but not by India direct. In A.D. 538 Korea made the first official presentation of a gilt statue of the Buddha and some beautiful banners and sacred texts to the Japanese Court as a token of her homage and friendship. The message that accompanied the gift runs as follows: 'Buddha Dharma, the most excellent of all laws, which brings immeasurable benefit to all its believers, has been accepted in all lands lying between India and Korea.' With the introduction of Buddhism, Japan felt the impulse of a new life, of which a distinct reorientation of her arts and letters was the immediate outcome. So deep was the influence of this new cult on Japan that the Emperor Shomu of the eighth century took pride in calling himself 'the slave of the Buddhist Trinity' and erected a colossal figure of the Buddha at Nara, the largest cast bronze statue in the world. The fresco paintings of the same period on the walls of a temple at Horiyuzi followed almost faithfully the technique and convention of Ajanta. The ancient 'Bugaku' or dance-music of Japan has been characterised as a combination of Chinese and Indian styles. The most favourite Japanese musical instrument called 'Biwa' is said to have been derived from the Indian Veena. Traces of the influence in Japan of Hindu religion could be found in the artistic figurations of Hindu gods and goddesses as Maheshwara, Kali and Saraswati which were brought to that country by the Brahmins who were invited by Japan when later she had direct intercourse with India.

About the middle of the fifth century, the marriage of a

Tibetan king with a Nepalese princess who brought her Hindu gods and sometime later, with a daughter of the T'ang emperor who brought her Buddhist deities, heralded the dawn of Indian influence in Tibet, where with the progress of religion there was a marked rise of art in paintings and bronzes which kept to the traditions of Indian art. History records in glowing terms how regardless of his poor health Shrijnan Dipankar, the eminent Buddhist savant and saint of Bengal and Chancellor of the University of Vikramashila, undertook the perilous journey to Tibet at the request of its king and founded there a School of Tantrik Buddhism. In many monasteries of Tibet, Dipankar is worshipped as next to the Buddha. But Dipankar had been preceded by other Indian scholars among whom may be mentioned Shantarakshita and Padmasambhava, who together visited Tibet in the eigth century and helped in spreading the doctrines of Buddhism there.

Tradition has it that in the fourth century B.C. Vijayasingha, an enterprising prince of Bengal, sailed over the rough waters of the bay and built up a colony in Ceylon whose old name Singhal is derived from his name. Linguistic and other cultural affinities that still exist between the present Bengalees and the Sinhalese point to this ancient bond. India's political and cultural relations with Ceylon are attested by the Pali chronicles of Ceylon to whom the world is indebted for much of the literature on Hinayana Buddhism. Even to this day Ceylon continues to be a seat of Buddhist learning. In the third century B.C. Buddhism was carried to Ceylon by Mahendra, a younger brother of Ashoka. The famous Buddhist apostle Buddhaghosha, called the Shankaracharya of Buddhism, went to Ceylon about the middle of the fifth century and there edited some very important Buddhist texts of the Hinayana School, and prepared learned commentaries on them which are held as authoritative interpretations of the Buddhist faith. Indian influence on the art of Ceylon is clearly discernible in the statues of the Buddha in such old centres of culture as Sigiriya, Anuradhapura, and Polonnaruwa; the last named has also a series of Hindu temples built in the Chola style at the time of the Chola occupation in the early part of the eleventh century. The frescoes of Sigiriya, executed during the reign of Kasyapa I towards the close of the fifth century, bear striking resemblance to those of Ajanta and Bagh.

It is now generally accepted that there were Hindu settlements in Burma in the first century A.D., though legendary accounts go back to a much earlier period when emigration from India to Burma had first taken place. Literary and archaeological evidences prove beyond doubt that the entire culture and civilisation of Burma was of Indian origin. According to the Ceylonese Buddhist tradition, Ashoka's missionaries visited Suvarnabhumi, lower Burma. In the third century A.D. central Burma had a Buddhist population of 100,000 families including several thousand monks. The Hindu colonisation however had begun much earlier. Written records explored in Prome, Pegu, Thaton and Pagan covering a period from the third to the tenth century A.D. show that the languages and literatures of Sanskrit and Pali and the various cults, both Brahminical and Buddhistic, were most popular in those regions during that period. There were many sects belonging to Shaivism and Vaishnavism, as well as to the Hinayana and Mahayana Schools of Buddhism. Prome was then known by its Hindu name Shrikshetra. The colonists who settled in the deltaic regions of Burma had most of them gone from Kalinga or Andhra. A prince of Varanasi founded his kingdom in Arakan whose ancient Indian name was Vaishali. Many kings of Burma re-christened their dominions after the names of famous Indian cities.

A vast Pali literature on different aspects of Buddhism, its doctrines, monastic discipline and philosophical speculations has been found in Burma. A long list of Sanskrit works shows that knowledge of that language was cultivated in Burma as far back as the early centuries of the present era. The influence of Sanskrit is perceptible in the Budhist Dhammasathas (Law) which were based on Sanskrit originals, the Dharmashastras of Manu, Narada and Yajnavalkya. The art of Burma, as expressed in her architecture, sculpture and painting, is mostly Indian in spirit and workmanship. The Ananda temple in Pegu—that finest piece of sacred architecture—was, according to Duroiselle, planned and built by Indians. Everything in it, from Shikhara to basement, as well as the numerous stone sculptures found in the corridors and terracotta plaques adorning its basement and terraces, bears the indubitable stamp of Indian genius and craftsmanship.

Cambodia, the ancient Kambuja, was one of the earliest to receive the culture of India. The name of its river Mekong is derived from Ma-Ganga, *Ma* meaning mother, an appellation of the river Ganga of India. In the first century A.D. a Brahmin called Kaundinya came to Kambuja from the Pallava capital of Kanchi in South India, married a princess there and was elected king of the country by its people. But the organised Indianisation of Kambuja is attributed to Shrutavarman who ruled there in the fifth century. Bilingual inscriptions in South Indian (Pallava) script reveal a knowledge of the Vedas, the Puranas and the epics. Kambuja rulers followed Kautilya's *Arthashastra*—Hindu Polity —in administering the country. Pauranik Hinduism was the popular religion of the people. Shaivism had however more adherents than Vaishnavism or Buddhism. The worship of Shiva-Vishnu was a peculiar feature of the religious practices prevalent in Kambuja. A general form of the Hindu caste system was the basis of its social structure. Sanskrit language and literature were widely cultivated, and mention is made in the inscriptions of the Dharma-shastras as also of treatises on Hindu science and medicine.

A careful study of the inscriptions of Cambodia brings out the fact that the people were generally of a religious turn of mind and that in many of them there was an earnest endeavour to attain the spiritual end of life. The intimate association between the secular and spiritual heads is an interesting characteristic of Kambuja court-life, reminding one, as it does, of a similar practice in ancient India. In their early life the kings of Kambuja, like those of India, had to receive their training under eminent religious *acharyas*. Kambuja had many *ashramas,* centres of learning, which were richly endowed by kings and presided over by Brahmin sages.

The early temples of Kambuja resemble the Gupta temples of India, though their sculpture is more Gupta in style than their architecture. Groslier is of opinion that the images and temples of the later period are the work of the artists and craftsmen brought by the Indian colonists. The divine expression, especially the smile, of the figures suggesting inward illumination or peace of the supreme Buddhist beatitude is a remarkable feature of Kambuja sculpture. The Brahminical images too are marked by the same quality. And do not these images both Buddhistic and Brahminical reflect the heavenly glow of their Indian prototypes? The scenes in the bas-reliefs which adorn the temples are almost all of them drawn from Indian epics. The most famous of the monuments of Kambuja is the Angkor Vat—that wonderful epic in stone—which was built in the twelfth century by king Surya-varman II. It is a marvellous combination of the styles of India's temple architecture prevailing in the north and the south.

It was in the first century of the present era that Indian ideas began to flow out to Siam and permeate her mental soil. Much interest attaches to the fact that the predominant influence which the culture of India exercised all over the country exists even to this day. Temples and sculptures, both Brahminical and Buddh-istic, all built in the Gupta style, have been found all over the country. A Sanskrit inscription of the fourth century along with Shaiva and Vaishnavite sculptures are among the finds in Mung Si Tep, near Pechabun. Sculptures in bronze have also been unearthed in many places. The bronze Buddha image found in Pong Tuk belongs to the Amaravati school of art of the second century A.D. The sculpture of the Dwaravati period (seventh century) is derived from the Gupta art of the Sarnath school. The temple architecture of Siam (Thailand) is a blend of the Shikhara styles of the North and South India. The two Yunan bells of the eleventh century with inscriptions in Chinese and Sanskrit are clear evidences of the influence of Buddhism. The king of Nan-Chao had the title Maharaja and also another Hindu title which means the king of the east. The Hindu idea of Mount Meru as the centre of the universe is even now a common theme of Siamese religious books and paintings. The *Ramayana* episodes are illustrated on the walls of the Royal temples at Bangkok. The Swing festival of the Hindus in the spring season is still extant in Siam with slight local variations.

Champa, the present province of Annam, figures prominently in the story of India's cultural expansion. It was about the second century A.D. that Indian ideas began to enter this region. The dynastic history of its kings is full of Hindu names who ruled over the land for centuries, but more remarkable is the way in which they helped to extend the cultural empire of India in Champa. Literary and inscriptional evidences show that the Indian colonists in Champa tried to build up a society of the orthodox Hindu type. The Hindu caste system dividing the people into four principal castes was there in a slightly modified form. As in India, the Kshatriyas were sometimes given a superior position in society.

The ideals of marriage, the relation of husband and wife were distinctly Hindu. The *sati* system was also prevalent there. The various forms of dance and music in Champa were direct borrowings from India.

Sanskrit language and literature were highly cultivated in Champa and the language of the court was also Sanskrit. The Sanskrit inscriptions, more than one hundred, discovered there, show that books were not only imported from India but many new ones in Sanskrit were also written there. The kings like Bhadravarman, Indravarman and Indravarmadeva were versed in the Vedas and other branches of Sanskrit literature. The great epics of India, the Puranas and the texts of Mahayana Buddhism were familiar subjects of study in Champa.

Shaivism was among the most popular cults of Champa. In fact, Shiva as Bhadreshwara was regarded for centuries as a national god. Shakti, Mahadevi, had not an unimportant place in the religious life of Champa. There were worshippers of Vishnu too. Following the Hindu tradition, some of the kings proclaimed themselves as incarnations of Vishnu. Evidences of Buddhist influence in Champa are no less remarkable. And it would be enough if we mention one of them. A victorious Chinese general carried away as many as 1350 Buddhist works from Champa. The temples of the country evolved out of the South Indian style of the Mamallapuram Rathas and of the temples of Conjeevaram and Badami. In some of them can be traced the Shikhara style of North India.

The group of islands known as Malay Archipelago is another renowned outpost of Indian culture. The Indian immigrants there are still called Orang-Kling, a survival of the name Kalinga by which the people of Orissa were known. In the third century A.D. the Kalingas and the Andhras of Orissa and Vengi laid the foundations of Indian and Indianised states in these islands. Shrivijaya, modern Sumatra, was a well-known seat of Buddhist culture where as many as one thousand Bhikkus had settled and formed a community for the study and practice of Buddhism. The fame of this culture-centre attracted scholars from all parts of India and Asia. A most notable visitor to it was Shrijnan Dipankar, Chancellor of the University of Vikramashila in Bengal. Dipankar met there Acharya Chandrakirti, the eminent Buddhist scholar. He declared Shrivijaya to be the headquarters of Buddhism in the East. Dharmapala of the University of Nalanda is said to have passed his last days in Sumatra.

The expansive movement of Indian culture witnessed its heyday in Java, the Hindu basis of whose culture is a marvel of India's cultural colonisation. It was a prince of Kalinga who inaugurated this movement by founding a Hindu state in Java in the first century of the present era. Later, there came into existence another Hindu kingdom in central Java, which was called Ho-ling or Kalinga, after the name of the original homeland of the colonists. In the fourth century when Fa-hien visited Java, he found Brahminism flourishing there. It was Gunavarman, a prince of Kashmir, who introduced Buddhism into Java by first converting the queen-mother to Buddhism. The art, language, literature, political and social institutions of Java bear an unmistakable impress of Indian ideas even to this day. The spirit of Javanese poetry, drama, music, and dancing is directly Indian, the *Ramayana* and the *Mahabharata* having played a most prominent part in the development of these forms of fine art in Java. The epics of the Hindus as well as many of their Puranas are still available in Java in Javanese versions. Some of the scientific and medical texts of India are among the literary remains of ancient Java.

Shiva was a popular deity of the ancient Javanese; so also was Shakti or Devi. The images of Ganesha and Kartikeya, the war-god, have been found in Java. Vishnu with his carrier Garuda, as also his ten incarnations are represented in the sculptures found there. Later, Mahayana Buddhism dominated the religious life of Java. The Shailendra kings of Java were in close touch with the political powers of India. Under their patronage a large number of Buddhist preachers hailing from Bengal, exercised an enormous influence on Javanese Buddhism.

The art of Java is a most glorious creation of Indo-Javanese collaboration. Indian influence on it is as distinct as it is powerful. It excelled in sculpture and architecture and evolved forms that are a marvel of the artistic expression of the culture from which it derived its theme and inspiration. The temples of Dieng plateau, called after the heroes and heroines of the *Mahabharata,* look like direct adaptations from Indian temples of the Gupta period. The Brahminical images in them are more Indian than Javanese. The famous Barabudur is a veritable

masterpiece of temple architecture and the greatest monument of
Indo-Javanese art. Fergusson holds that the builders of the
temples of Java including Barabudur came from eastern India.
The sculptures in Barabudur describe the life and deeds of the
Buddha, Jataka stories, etc. Its images of the Buddha are among
the finest examples of Indo-Javanese sculpture bearing the classical
excellence of the similar figuration evolved in India.

Indian influence in Borneo is attested by several Sanskrit
inscriptions of the fifth century A.D. acknowledging gifts of gold
and cows to Brahmins. It is said that Brahmins formed an
important element of the population there and Brahminical rites
and ceremonies found great favour at the Court. Sandstone
images unearthed in Borneo, include those of the Hindu gods as
Shiva, Ganesha, Nandi, Agastya, Brahma and Mahakala. A few
among them are Buddhistic. Mention may be made of the seven
gold figures of the Buddha and several of Bodhisattvas recently
discovered in West Borneo. The exquisite style and fine workmanship of these images are characteristically Indian.

The island of Bali stands unique in the history of India's
cultural empire, since it is the only colony which is still Hindu in
its culture and civilisation, a fact which is enough to show how
deeply Indian ideas have shaped the life and thought of the
people of this island. The evening gatherings of men and women
to hear readings from the *Ramayana* and the *Mahabharata*
recall similar scenes in India. Bali had her Hindu initiation direct
from India. Her subsequent conquest by Java has helped to
deepen this influence.

Researches into the cultural and racial origins of the
Philippines are more and more lending support to the view that
the country was once colonised by the people from South India.
That the former had some relation with the latter is evident from
the fact that the scripts of the Filipino have striking similarities
with those of South India. Justice Romualdez, a distinguished
Filipino, says: 'Our dialects belong to the Dravidian family.' The
names of some of the places on the shores of Manila Bay and
the coast of Luzon show their Sanskrit origin. Saleeby says: 'The
head-gods of the Indian triad and the earliest Vedic gods hold
the foremost place in the minds and devotions of the hill-tribes
of Luzon and Mindanao.' The statue of a Hindu god, preserved

at the Ateneo de Manila, is held by a Dutch archaeologist to be that of Ganesha. According to Kroeber, most of the folklore of the Philippines is of Hindu origin. Indian influence is most obvious in the handicrafts and in the old names of the coins used there. Many of the social and religious customs at present current in the Philippines bear close resemblance to those of India. Beyer says: 'India has most profoundly affected the Philippine civilisation.'

Indian influence in Polynesia, a group of islands in Oceania, was unknown to Indian scholars till a few years ago when the late P. Mitra of the Calcutta University took up the subject and in collaboration with some Polynesian scholars unravelled the story of the spread of Indian ideas to those distant islands. It is difficult to say exactly when this intercourse began. The islands were reached by man sometime during the early centuries of the present era. The physical appearance of the Polynesians is more like that of the Indo-Aryans than that of the peoples of the neighbouring islands. And their language has closer affinity to the language of the tribes like the Mundas and the Santhals of India. Many of the religious beliefs and social customs of the Polynesians are held to have been derived from India through Indonesia. Their use of the conch-shell and the nose-flute is most liktly to have come from India. The Hula dance of Hawaii and the Shiva dance of Samoa are very similar to some of the folk-dances of Bengal. Skinner says that many decorative designs of the Polynesians are traceable to India and Cambodia. Some of the staple foodsuffs and domestic animals of Polynesia are, according to specialists on the subject, indigenous to India from where they were carried to Polynesia. In the mythology of the Polynesians are found the idea of Brahmanda or Cosmic Egg of the Hindu Puranas and the Gita's conception of the world as the branches of a tree of which the roots are in the Brahmanda. Craighill Handy says: 'As examples of old Polynesian culture-traits derived from the Brahminical civilisation, I may mention the craft traditions, rites for the first-born, the ancestral cult with its use of genealogies and images, phallic symbolism and representative art, ritualistic conventions, priestly traditions and orders, *mana* and *Tapu,* walled temple with tower-like shrines....and finally the remarkable dualistic evolutionary cosmogony.'

III

The story of India's cultural empire does not end with the dawn of the modern age or with the political changes that then took place in the countries of Asia and other parts of the world. It is true that the impact of European culture tended to create a new outlook in many of them, but the fact cannot be doubted that the contribution of India to the culture and civilisation of mankind has come to stay as a perennial source of inspiration. Though centuries of Muslim rule in India gave a set-back to the movement of her cultural expansion, yet the work done by the forebears of the race was enough to lay the cultural foundation for the larger empire of the Spirit which India was to build up in the future. There can indeed be no better acknowledgment of this debt to India by the countries of the world today than the ready response they are making to her call upon them to rise into greater endeavours, to wake up to the truths of a higher life. In the recent Inter-Asian Conferences in Delhi, the representatives of almost all the countries of Asia expressed in one voice and in the language of their heart their 'unbounded gratefulness' to India, 'the Mother of our culture and civilisation.' The seeing minds of Europe and America have already begun to appreciate the unique greatness of India in the world of the Spirit. Her stupendous cultural achievements in the past have found their votaries in these continents.

The year 1671 is a landmark from which to date the beginning of a new phase in the movement of India's cultural expansion in modern times. It was in this year that the French traveller Bernier carried to France a manuscript translation of the Upanishads in Persian by the Mughal Prince Dara Shikoh. He was followed by several French missionaries and German Jesuits who published translations of Vedic and other Sanskrit texts, one of the latter having written a book on Sanskrit grammar too. Voltaire's love of India and her wisdom, and later Amiel's insistence on the need of 'Brahmanising souls' for the spiritual uplift of humanity are doubtless due to the contact with Indian thought they had through the above and other sources which began to multiply with the growth of Europe's interest in India, commercial at the beginning, then proselytising, afterwards cultural, when the superiority of Indian thought became more and more evident to the scholars of Europe.

In the eighteenth and nineteenth centuries the most outstanding figures who brought to light the wide range of Sanskrit literature and organised its systematic study and dissemination were the three Englishmen Sir Charles Wilkins, Sir William Jones and Colebrooke, all of whom 'aimed at a union of Hindu and European learning' and did much to introduce the ancient Sanskrit classics to the Western world. Wilkins' earliest work was a translation of the Gita. Jones, who founded the Asiatic Society of Bengal in 1784, edited, among other works, Manu, *Shakuntala* and several other Sanskrit plays. Colebrooke, the founder of Indian philology and archaeology, wrote extensively on various aspects of Indology and edited several Sanskrit texts, such as the grammar of Panini and the *Hitopadesha.*

In the latter part of the eighteenth century Sir William Jones startled the world of scholarship by declaring that Sanskrit was cousin to all the languages of Europe, and an indication of Europe's racial kinship with the Vedic Hindus. These announcements almost created modern philology and enthnology. Sir William Jones' translation of *Shakuntala* in 1789, re-rendered into German in 1791, profoundly affected Herder and Goethe and— through the Schlegels—the entire Romantic movement of the West. It may be noted that all these happened during the early days of the East India Company when it was engaged in political and economic conquest of India.

France however was among the earliest centres of Sanskrit studies in modern Europe. Most of the early German Indologists learnt Sanskrit in Paris. The first collection of Indian manuscripts was that of the Bibliothèque Royale de Paris (now the Bibliothèque Nationale) which included manuscripts of Vedic literature. The Asiatic Society of Paris was first instituted long before that of London and Berlin. It was the College de France where teaching of Sanskrit was inaugurated first in Europe. By a Royal decree in 1816 a Chair of Sanskrit Professorship was created. Louis de Chezy was its first incumbent. He was followed by Eugene Burnouff who put Sanskrit studies on a permanent footing in Europe. The great philologist Rudolp, and the eminent Max Muller, were his illustrious students. Langlois who translated the Rig Veda was also his student.

Germany also was one of the pioneers of Indian studies in Europe. Early in the nineteenth century her scholars discovered the treasures of Sanskrit literature the study of which influenced the German thinkers in so many ways. It was Germany which was the first in Europe to discover the hidden treasures of Sanskrit literature early in the nineteenth century and give a fresh impetus to its study, a result of which was the influence it exerted on the German thinkers. To Schopenhauer the Upanishads came as a new Gnosis, as a revelation. He said: 'In the whole world there is no study so beneficial and so elevating as that of the Upanishads. It has been the solace of my life, it will be the solace of my death.' Kant's central doctrine that things of experience are only the phenomena of the thing-in-itself has been acknowledged as essentially a doctrine of the Upanishads. The influence of Kalidasa's *Meghaduta,* 'The Cloud Messenger,' on Schiller's *Maria Stuart* is most obvious. Goethe modelled his Prologue to *Faust* on the prologue to Kalidasa's Sanskrit *Shakuntala,* for which the German poet's rapturous praise is too well-known to require mention. Says Max Muller: 'Of all systems of Philosophy in the world, Vedanta is unrivalled. There is no philosophy which has not been influenced, directly or indirectly, by it.'

'Russia is more oriental than China' were the words of Maxim Gorki. And those of Dostoievski were: 'It would be useful for Russia to forget Petersburg for some time and to turn her soul towards the East.' A typical example of this tendency was H. S. Lebedev, a Russian musician, who lived in Calcutta in 1795, and built a playhouse called 'The Bengali Theatre.' He recruited and trained Bengali actors and actresses, prepared the Bengali version of the English comedy *The Disguise,* and staged it. He was not merely a musician and producer. He was an Indologist and a pioneer of Oriental learning in Russia. He translated several Indian classics into Russian, wrote a Bengali grammar, compiled a Bengali dictionary and published several papers on Hindu philosophy. In 1802 he published in London his English work *A Grammar of the Pure and Mixed East Indian Dialects.* He knew Sanskrit and Bengali and was a keen student of the language and literature of Bengal. He translated a Russian play of his own into Bengali, and set to music verses of the famous Bengali poet Bharatchandra Roy. He used four lines from

Bharatchandra's *Vidyasundar* as the motto of the title page of his grammar.

About the period of Lebedev were published Russian translations of the Gita and *Shakuntala*. Early in the nineteenth century Count S. S. Uvarov and several other Russian admirers of India founded the Asiatic Academy at St. Petersburg, and a Chair for Sanskrit in it. Russian translations of Sanskrit plays and some works of Kalidasa were the result of this endeavour. Between 1855 and 1875 was published the monumental St. Petersburg Sanskrit dictionary in seven volumes. During the same period rose Prof. I. P. Minayev, the greatest Russian Indologist of his time, who knew Sanskrit, Pali, Prakrit and more than one modern Indian languages. He visited India twice and wrote a number of books on Indian languages and religions including Buddhism. Minayev was followed by his brilliant pupils Kudryavsky, Oldenburg and Stcherbatsky, all of whom are internationally famous for their remarkable contributions to the growth of Russia's interest in Indian culture.

Another notable event in the expansion of Indian culture in the nineteenth century is the American Transcendentalist Movement. In Concord, Massachusetts, there used to gather together in the 1840's famous poets, authors and thinkers of America, to whom Emerson would read and re-read the Gita and the Upanishads. After reading Manu, Thoreau, the famous author of *Walden* and a member of Concord, wrote: 'I cannot read a sentence in the book of the Hindus without being elevated.' He recognised the Sankhya system as the only possible one for the masses. The following words of Thoreau show how deeply moved was he in his soul by the mystic lore of the Vedas of India: 'Whenever I have read any part of the Vedas, I have felt that some unearthly and unknown light illuminates me. In the great teaching of the Vedas, there is no touch of sectarianism. It is of all ages, climes and nationality and is the royal road for the attainment of the Great Knowledge. When I am at it, I feel that I am under the spangled heavens of a summer night. Slowly the full moon appears with its soothing beams and innundates me with an indefinable sublimity of celestial origin.' Walt Whitman, the poet, came into intimate contact with Emerson and had from him his initiation in Indian thought. His poem *Passage to India* is a plan for uniting the intellectual life of the West with the spiritual life of the East.

Edward Carpenter indicated parallels between Whitman's *Leaves of Grass* and the Upanishads of India. Emerson's humorous remark that *Leaves of Grass* was a mixture of the Bhagavat Gita of the Hindus and the *New York Herald,* is no less significant. And whatever Emerson himself has written is mostly Vedanta. His essays like *The Over-Soul* and *Circles* and poems like *Brahma* are nothing but Upanishadic thought. He once wrote: 'Nature makes a Brahmin of me presently.' And on another occasion the Sage of Concord said: 'In the great books of India an empire spoke to us, nothing small or unworthy, but large, serene, consistent, the voice of an old intelligence which in another age and another climate had pondered and thus disposed of the same questions that exercise us.' The Transcendental Movement of which Emerson was leader, and Thoreau and Alcott staunch supporters, was in a sense the forerunner of the Vedanta movement of Swami Vivekananda.

The Vedantic note in Carlyle's writings is too well known to require mention. And the Gita was the only book he chose to present to Emerson when the latter met him for the first time. There is a leaven of Vedantic thought in the poetry of Robert Browning: some of his lines read like paraphrases of Upanishadic verses.

Indian culture began to enter the mind of Europe and other countries more widely and deeply when in modern times distance was annihilated by quicker and easier means of communication. Indeed, the subjective tendency of the present age is to a great extent the result of the infiltration of Indian thought into the mind of humanity. An inner seeking is evident everywhere, an urge to know the deeper meaning of things. Receptive America has been able soon enough to accept and understand the light from India. In Europe the critical study and exposition of the various aspects of ancient Indian culture has taken shape in the subject of Indology. A galaxy of scholars have by their researches made invaluable contributions to the reconstruction of India's past. There have been attempts too on the part of India to interpret her culture and thought to the world, to reveal to it the truth that shines undimmed in the adytum of her soul. Among the inspired sons who voiced the message of Mother India, Swami Vivekananda stands out as a stately tower of light. His prophetic words were: 'Once more the world must be conquered by India: this is the dream of my life.... We must go out, we must

conquer the world through our spirituality and philosophy. There is no alternative. We must do or die.'

This mighty son of India, made all the more mighty by his Master's grace and power, thundered out to the world the central message of the Vedanta: 'Thou art That.' Never before was there one who had spoken of the divinity of man with such an electrifying intensity of conviction as that soldier of the Light, that indomitable exponent of India's spirituality. His luminous interpretation of the Vedantic thought and its application to the practical life of man attracted seekers from almost every part of the world, who formed the first nucleus of a universal fellowship based on the intrinsic unity of man in the world of the Spirit. Whether it was America or England or the Continent, wherever he went, people of all classes flocked to him only to be illumined in their soul by a new light. Spiritual India, reawakened after a long sleep, found in him an inspired champion of the divine heritage of man; and the materialistic West bowed its head before the majesty and sublimity of his message. The Math and the Mission, started by the Swami with the express object of giving form to the ideal he stood for, have since grown and expanded into a network of organisations of social and spiritual service spread all over the world, America having the largest number of them. An American writer[2] characterises this movement as an invasion of the New World by Indian thought. Says another American, Mrs. Annie Smith, a friend of Swami Vivekananda: 'I found the spiritual seed of the Swami's planting springing up all over the Pacific coast; for he vitalised American religious sects as well as Hinduism.' Indeed the future of America is big with great possibilities. The call of the Spirit came to her first in modern times; and her response to it was the first stirring in the heart of humanity which has since then been growing so that there can come about a mighty resurgence of the world's soul, an utter awakening to the truth and light of a divine perfection man is destined to attain as the end and summit of his spiritual evolution. And America will be called upon to play her part also in that glorious future of mankind.

But Vivekananda's influence has always been much deeper and wider than we generally feel and know. He has been a force,

---

2. Wendell Thomas in his book *Hinduism Invades America.*

a great dynamic force, from whom millions derive inspiration and the exalting strength of the divine light which he embodied. This is how he has helped mankind to grow in readiness for the greater future that is to come to it as the end and consummation of its strivings through the ages. Thus by Vivekananda was given a new tempo to the work of India towards the building up of her spiritual empire in modern times.

Annie Besant dedicated almost the whole of her life to the cause of India's social, cultural and spiritual uplift. Her interpretation of Indian thought ranks her among those who have raised India in the estimation of the world. The work of the Theosophical Society in disseminating the truths of Indian culture through its centres and exponents all over the world must be recognised, as also that of the Arya Samaj which emphasised the Vedic basis of Indian life and thought. Swami Rama Tirtha, who voiced Vedantic ideas in accents of fire is still adored in Japan and America as an inspired messenger of India. Baba Premananda Bharati's Shri Krishna Home in America attracts hundreds of devotees from various parts of that country. Yogada is another centre of spiritual culture there. The India Society and the International School of Vedic and Allied Research, organised by the Indians in America are furthering the cause of Indian culture to which great service was rendered by that famous Irish poet and critic, James H. Cousins, who in his lecture tours undertaken on several occasions unravelled to big American audiences the depth and profundity of India's aesthetic expressions, their psychology and motivation. The masterly and revealing exposition of Indian art and culture by Ananda Coomaraswamy has opened America and the world to the intrinsic significance of India's creative genius, of its achievements through the ages, whose subjective and objective history he has for the first time presented from the standpoint of their integrality. Coomaraswamy was verily an institution by himself, a dynamic centre of Indian values, whose influence was as wide as it was illuminating. Indeed his stay in America for nearly thirty years as the Curator of the Indian Section of the Boston Museum of Fine Arts proved to be a most fruitful factor in the expansive movement of Indian culture in that country.

Circulo Esoterico da Communhao do Pensamanto in Sao Paulo, Brazil, is an institution whose professed aim is 'to com-

prehend the spiritual wisdom of the world and particularly that of India.' Lately it has organised researches into Vaishnavic thought. One of the many members of this Society who are devoted followers of Shri Chaitanya of Bengal, has started an inner circle called 'Tattva Shri Chaitanya.' Vicente Avelino who was the Consul-General for Brazil in India in 1930 belonged to this circle. He was a devout Vaishnava and an ardent admirer of Shri Ramakrishna. In an address at Panihati, near Calcutta, on the occasion of a religious festival organised by the Shri Gauranga Grantha Mandir to commemorate Shri Chaitanya's visit to that place, he said: 'India is the only country which has known God and if any one wants to know God he must know India.' Latin American countries are becoming more and more interested in India. For more than three decades there has been existing in Santiago an organisation called Suddha Dharma Mandal (a Sanskrit name meaning an institute of pure religion) where the Gita is being regularly studied. Sanskrit has already acquired a popular position with the scholars of various parts in South America. The State University of Santiago has a Chair in Sanskrit.

Nor does the Jewish world remain untouched by India and her thought. The Hebrew Encyclopaedia is so far the only work of its kind which carries a detailed account of Sri Aurobindo's life and work. In the course of a letter to the journal *India and Israel*, Dr. Hugo Bergmann, Professor of Philosophy at the Hebrew University, Jerusalem, wrote: 'Sri Aurobindo's message about the arising of a new humanity touches the heart of Jewry.... He has revived the Messianic ideas and hope in their full cosmic meaning and implications.... This great spiritual leader of mankind gives his message not only to Free India but also to Free Israel.' In his greetings to the 1950 Silver Jubilee Session of the Indian Philosophical Congress, Dr. Leon Roth of the Hebrew University said: 'India has always implied for the world at large the inward light of the spirit; and this light is the more needed today because of the dark mists of scientific barbarism, which seems to be closing in upon the world from all sides.'

Indian spirituality has of late been attracting an increasing number of American adherents through the International Society for Krishna Consciousness which has its headquarters in New York. The Vaishnavic centres in America and England are spreading the Holy Name of Shri Krishna among very many seekers of those countries who 'feel spiritually exalted by the utterance of that name.'

Ireland's interest in India deserves mention. It is said that the inborn spiritual inclination of this Celtic people is Aryan in origin and inspiration. The eminent Jurist Maine has shown that the old Brehon laws of Ireland are derived from the Vedic laws of India. The infusion of Indian ideas into the mind of modern Ireland, which began towards the end of the last century, roused her sense of cultural kinship with India. This new illumination is acknowledged as one of those factors that heralded the great Irish literary and dramatic revival, which proved a powerful incentive to the political resurgence of Ireland. George Russel (A.E.) and Yeats, both poets of world-wide fame, were the two chief inaugurators of this movement. They showed a strong predilection for the spiritual thought and life of India and the poetry of A.E. at its best is literally soaked in Indian mysticism and rises to heights unattained up to now by any other Western poet. In an appreciative article on Sri Aurobindo's philosophy, called *Divine Becoming,*[3] Morwenna Donnelly, a noted Irish writer, says: 'Since he is poet as well as a mystic, Sri Aurobindo's vision is both creative and prophetic. I believe there is no greater mystical thinker in the world today.'

Sir John Woodroff's achievement in the exposition of Tantrik thought cannot be over-estimated. Himself a follower of the Tantrik cult, this great Englishman edited in a masterly way a number of Tantrik texts and most of his views on them are regarded as authoritative. It is mainly through his writings—a rare combination of insight and scholarship—that the ideas of the Tantras began to enter the mind of the West in modern times. Influence of Indian thought is most obvious in the philosophical writings of well-known English thinkers like Gerald Heard and Aldous Huxley. Distinctly Indian is their idea of a new community of neo-Brahmins, which, according to them, is to emerge in the future as the next higher stage in the evolutionary ascent of man. In the thought of Gerald Heard is a clear note of Sri Aurobindo's teachings. In the Yoga School, started by these two English thinkers, many Europeans are having training in Indian methods of self-discipline. Mention

---

3. See the London Quarterly *The Wind and the Rain,* Vol. V, No. I.

may also be made here of the 'California Group' which they have formed in America along with Christopher Isherwood and which follows the esoteric teachings of the Vedanta. The greatest English novelist, Somerset Maugham, advises prospective writers to come to India for knowledge of the higher values of life. The largest Yoga colony in London is Hari Prosad Sastri's Shanti Sadan, the centre of Indian Adhyatma Yoga in the West—a two hundred strong colony of European disciples, some of whom have been meeting there for the last fifteen years. Dr. Kenneth Walker, the eminent English thinker, presiding over the Shri Ramakrishna birthday anniversary meeting in London in March 1949 said: 'If the two great nations, India and England, cannot be united by political chords, the ties of spiritual and intellectual co-operation will certainly prove a stronger bond of union. India, the greatest spiritual force of the world, even maintains today those fountain sources of eternal life, which are the only hope of the spiritual resurrection of humanity.'

Many in the West have come to believe that perhaps India will ultimately offer a way out of the present morass. Certain it is that India will become ever more important in future decades and will play a larger role in world affairs. Prof. F. S. C. Northrop of Yale University in his book *The Meeting of East and West* writes of the coming together of cultures and of India's possibilities for leading mankind out of the dark night that surrounds it. From England comes a similar voice. Dean W. R. Inge sees a ray of hope in India. History, he says, shows that progress usually follows from the fusion of two cultures. History also shows that religions, and revivals of religions, are born in the East. After speaking about Russia, he says, 'Perhaps a more likely source of inspiration is India.'

The eminent French savant, Romain Rolland, is noted for his deep understanding of the intrinsic meaning of Indian culture. His works on Shri Ramakrishna and Swami Vivekananda show the reverence with which he studied them and his appreciation of these two mastermen of modern India is remarkable for its perspicacity. He called Sri Aurobindo 'the King of Thinkers' and saw in him 'the completest synthesis of the culture of the East and of the West, holding in his outstretched hands the bow of Creative Impulse, the promise of a greater Tomorrow.' Paul Richard, that renowned French mystic, in the course of a talk in Paris in 1927 said: 'Sri Aurobindo is verily Shiva[4] himself. There is none like him in the whole world.' Earlier in 1919 in a lecture in Tokyo, he uttered the following words on Sri Aurobindo: 'Now, the day is coming when after having been in the obscurity of his silence and retreat, the saviour of India, he will become in the full light of day the Guru of Asia, the Teacher of the world.' India must never forget the valuable work done by French scholars in the world of Indology. Sylvain Levy's is a cherished name in this connection. Institut de civilisation Indienne is a well-known institution in France which aims at promoting the study and understanding of Indian life and civilization in its various phases of development. While in India Louis Renou of the University of Paris, the well-known Indologist and Sanskrit scholar of France, in the course of a talk at Santiniketan in January 1949, said that the best writers and thinkers of France had been influenced by Indian thought and culture, and the intuitive sense of affinity between France and Indian culture had developed into devotion. In another talk Prof. Renou said: 'India has the good fortune of being the repository of the noblest spiritual tradition, the only one in the whole world which has been alive throughout the centuries. And Sanskrit has been the privileged instrument of this tradition.'

The famous German thinker, Count Hermann Keyserling declared that 'India has produced the profoundest metaphysics that we know of.' He spoke of 'the absolute superiority of India over the West in philosophy.' His School of Wisdom at Darmstadt was often attacked for the very reason that 'he was transplanting Indian recognitions into the West.' The Summer School for Spiritual Research in Ascona, Switzerland, has the religions of modern India as one of its special subjects of study. Swami Ananda Acharya's Ashram in Norway attracts a large number of men and women from different parts of Europe, to whom it gives not only training in India's yoga but also ideas about her culture. The Academy of Sciences of Russia and its Eastern Institute Section have for years been engaged in the study of Buddhism and other religions of India, the epics also being included in their subjects of research and translation. The Eastern Institute is taking keen interest in modern Indian languages, such as Hindi, Tamil and Bengali. Its scholars have already translated Tulsidasa's

---

4. Godhead of divine peace and benignity.

Hindi *Ramayana* and some Bengali works of Bankimchandra Chatterji and Rabindranath Tagore. The Kern Institute in Holland and the Oriental Institute in Italy are reputed centres of research where under the direction of eminent European scholars important original work is being done on Indian art, archaeology and literature.

Among the Indologists of Europe in the present century Sten Konow of Norway is noted for his researches on the evolution of the religious thought of India; Glassenhap of Germany, for his commentaries on many Sanskrit philosophical texts including one of Madhwacharya (his father, also an Indologist, wrote a beautiful poem on Shri Chaitanya); Winternitz of Czecho-Slovakia, for his monumental work on the history of Indian literature; Tucci of Italy for his studies in Vaishnavic thought. Stanislav F. Michalski, the great Sanskrit scholar of Poland, devoted his whole life to the study of Sanskrit and ancient Indian literature. He is the founder of the Oriental Section of Warsaw Scientific Society and was Professor of Sanskrit language and literature at the University of Warsaw. He has published books on the Gita, the Upanishads, the *Ramayana* and other Sanskrit classics. An Indian visitor, who met him in Poland, wrote about him: 'He knows more about our culture than we do ourselves.' When Prof Stasiask of the Crakow University visited Santiniketan in 1935, he surprised the writer by the fluency with which he spoke Sanskrit. Macdonell, Rapson and Smith are England's eminent historians of Indian culture and thought. The India Society and the Society for Cultural Fellowship with India show how England wishes to deepen her cultural relations with India. It is not that the interpretation of Indian thought by these and other scholars of Europe and America has always been authentic. In fact, the spiritual, therefore the real, intention in India's cultural development has often been missed by most of them. Yet by their pioneer work they have all of them helped to rouse the world's interest in India and strengthen the foundation of her cultural empire.

The revival in Germany after the Second World War of the India Institute of the Deutsche Akademie, started in 1928, points to a revival of Germany's interest in Indian culture, in which she had once no equal in the whole world of Indology. The Oriental Institute in Praha (Prague) has also started functioning by organising lectures on India and publishing books on India and

Indology. V. Lesny, the eminent Indologist and the author of a comprehensive study on Tagore edits a magazine called *Novy Orient* (New Orient) in which articles on India find regular place. The Praha University has Chairs of Indian languages including Sanskrit, Hindi and Bengali.

The rise of Rabindranath Tagore to world-wide fame is another cause of India's figuring more prominently in the intellectual horizon of humanity. Nature chose him as the one man in history to receive for his poetry the unstinted homage of the whole of mankind during his lifetime. The poet of India was acclaimed as the poet of the world—a fact which together with his Visva-Bharati embodying his vision of the cultural oneness of mankind, has certainly furthered the cause of India's cultural expansion in modern times. 'Visva-Bharati,' in the words of the Poet, 'represents India where she has her wealth of mind which is for all. Visva-Bharati acknowledges India's obligation to offer to others the hospitality of her best culture and India's right to accept from others their best. It is India's invitation to the world, her offer of sacrifice to the highest truth of man.' Eminent scholars and Indologists including many of those mentioned above responded to this call, came and stayed there in pursuit of their respective subjects of study, imbibing all the time the life of India and the spirit of her culture. A note of deep regard for India is perceptible in all their writings about her.

The works of Radhakrishnan and his lectures in Europe and America have enormously increased the interest of these continents in Indian thought. Indeed his brilliant exposition of the religious and cultural ideals of India has a stirring appeal for the mind of modern man. And has it not raised India in the estimation of the world? The election of Radhakrishnan as Chairman of the United Nations Educational, Scientific and Cultural Organisation, and the part India's representatives are playing today in the various assemblies and councils of the United Nations Organisation clearly indicate the importance India has acquired in matters of international interest.

The aesthetic eye of man has already opened to the splendour of ancient Indian art. Sister Nivedita and Havell are among those from outside who caught the true spirit of India's artistic expression and revealed it to humanity. A striking revival of this spirit in the works of many modern Indian artists has won for them fame and appreciation from various parts of the world. Abanindra-nath Tagore, the founder of the new School of Painting, and Nandalal Bose, his worthy disciple, are the great masters, the artist-exponents of modern India's aesthetic intuitions. In an exhibition of Abanindranath's paintings in Paris in 1914 distinguished French art-critics saw 'authentic evidence of modern Indian renaissance.' On seeing the famous painting 'The Buddha carrying the kid' by Nandalal, shown in an exhibition in Geneva, a Swiss critic remarked: 'I see behind this picture a great civilisation.' Indeed the mind of Europe has begun to open to the greatness and glory of the art-expressions of India. An exhibition of Indian art, held in London in 1948, evoked warm appreciations both from the press and the public of England. *The New Statesman and the Nation* characterised it as 'a splendid but compelling proof of India's artistic genius.'

Big gatherings in Europe and America burst into ecstasy as they witnessed the dance of Uday Shankar. Eminent art-critics of these continents showered on him rapturous praises not only for his mastery of the art but also for his marvellous blending of modern ideas with the traditions and techniques built up by his country for centuries. An American critic called his art 'rhythms that are wonderfully graceful, dynamically exalting.' Indian music has also its ardent admirers in the West. During the years immediately following the first World War, large audiences in France, Germany, Hungary, England and Scotland listened with rapt attention to the exposition and demonstration of Indian music by Dilip Kumar Roy, the celebrated poet and composer of India. On hearing him Romain Rolland[5] told Dilip Kumar that by his capacity for continuous improvisation, the executant in Indian music was always a creator, while in European music he was only an interpreter. Madame Fullop-Muller, the famous Hungarian opera-singer of Vienna, held similar views about the creative power of the Indian musician. 'Your music strikes a new chord in my heart,' said Georges Duhamel,[6] the eminent French author and critic, to Dilip Kumar, 'it is indeed a novel but delightful experience with me. The music of India is without doubt one of the greatest proofs of the superiority of her civilisation.' Leopold Stokowski, the famous conductor of the Philadelphia Orchestra,

5. Dilip Kumar Roy, *Among the Great.*
6. Dilip Kumar Roy, *Aedeshay-Odeshay* (Bengali).

wrote to Dilip Kumar speaking in glowing terms of the subtle intricacies of Indian rhythm from which, so he wrote, the West has much to learn. In more recent times almost the whole Western world acclaimed Ravi Shankar as 'a maestro of the first order' and this for his 'exquisite performance' on the Indian stringed instrument Sitar. By her 'wonderful' recital of South Indian Carnatic music M. N. Subbulakshmi won the hearts of very many American audiences.

India has contributed not inconsiderably to the advancement of modern science. An Indian name is now associated with Einstein's Theory of Relativity. There are some notable Indians among the luminaries in the worlds of physics and chemistry. For their outstanding contributions in physics, C. V. Raman was made a Nobel Laureate, and Meghnad Shah, a Fellow of the Royal Society of Great Britain. Einstein's epoch-making work on Mathematical Physics is now mentioned with that of S. N. Bose. P. C. Roy, J. C. Ghose and S. S. Bhatnagar are known all the world over for what they have done in the sphere of chemical sciences. Writing about J. C. Bose's discoveries on plant life, Collum in his book *Life's Unity and Rhythm* says: 'Bose is a landmark, a point from which to date the dawn of a new thought.' In the world of astronomy S. Chandrasekhar stands as a most notable figure. He was invited in 1949 to deliver the Russell Lecture, the highest honour that America can bestow on an astronomer. He is a Fellow of the Royal Society, and for his original work in Steller Dynamics, is today an international scientist. S. Ramanujan, by far the greatest mathematician that India has produced in recent times, was called by Julian Huxley the greatest mathematician of the century. The first Indian to be elected a Fellow of the Royal Society of England, Ramanujan did work of profound value and astonishing originality. His amazing insight into algebraical formulae transformation of infinite series made Prof. Hardy remark that he could be most certainly compared to only Euler or Jacobi, the two mathematical wizards of the past.

China's desire to renew her ancient bond of friendship with India finds expression in the writings and activities of her eminent scholars and thinkers, of whom may be mentioned the names of Tan Yun-Shan, Jen Foo Kan and Ngo-Chang Lim. The foundation of the Sino-Indian Cultural Society by Dr. Tan is the great beginning of a significant movement which bids fair to usher in a new era of cultural fellowship between these two oldest peoples of history. The growth and expansion of its activities will mean preparation for a greater work in the future, the work of building up a new, better and united world through the joint efforts of India and China. In all her social and political thinking China regarded the unity of mankind as the one aim worth striving for. Dr. Tan asserts his faith in that great ideal of his country and makes its attainment the ultimate goal of his Society. He appeals to India for help and co-operation in this noble endeavour, since he believes that India alone can give that spiritual strength without which the aim can never be realised. After he saw Sri Aurobindo in his Ashram at Pondicherry, Tan in a press interview said that as in the past China was spiritually conquered by a great Indian, so in the future would she be conquered by another great Indian, Sri Aurobindo, the Maha-Yogi of India, who, as he said, 'is the bringer of that Light which will chase away the darkness that envelopes the world today.'

Indeed the ideal Sri Aurobindo stands for is the only hope that mankind has before it at the present hour of its distress. A new Light comes to his vision, a Light that is descending on earth to remould man into a divine perfection. The gloom that thickens everywhere is the deepening darkness of the night before dawn. The chaos and conflicts are the travail on the earth before its birth into a higher consciousness. Sri Aurobindo calls upon man to wake up and be ready for this glorious Dawn, the consummation of his earthly existence. He works through the Mother helping seeking souls and preparing the inner life of humanity. And response has already started coming from different quarters of the globe.

On reading Sri Aurobindo's *magnum opus, The Life Divine,* the well-known English thinker Sir Francis Younghusband wrote: 'I really do quite genuinely consider it the greatest book which has been produced in my time.[7] The intuitive insight of an English mind is reflected in an appreciative review by Rev. E.F.F. Hill of some of Sri Aurobindo's works, published in the October (1949) issue of *World Review*. Hill writes: 'Aurobindo is the greatest contemporary philosopher and great in the company of the greatest mystics of all time.... The work of Aurobindo compels,

---

7. *The Times Literary Supplement.*

not comparison, but concordance with the Fourth Gospel. Here are two men, peers in their own right in the realm of highest knowledge, and peers in relation to each other. Separated by twenty centuries, drawing their sustenance from different cultures but their inspiration from one spiritual source, "ye shall know the Truth and the Truth shall make you free," is one common aspect of their message.... We are at a turning point in the spiritual history of man. Aurobindo is the embodiment of a revolution in human life which new knowledge, new powers, new capacities, are creating at this hour.... Because Aurobindo is in the world, the world is becoming able to express progressively Unity and Diversity instead of Division, Love instead of Hatred, Truth-Consciousness instead of Falsehood, Freedom instead of Tyranny, Immortality instead of Death; it is becoming progressively that which it is: a movement of the Spirit in itself.'

Another instance of England's interest in Sri Aurobindo is the publication in 1949 of a book on him by the Royal Society of England. Prof. G. H. Langley, the author who was formerly Vice-Chancellor of the Dacca University in Bengal, presents in it for the Western readers an introductory but illuminating exposition of Sri Aurobindo's thought and a fine study of his poetry. The author speaks of 'the reasonable depth of insight in his poetical utterances; and quoting the poem 'Rose of God,' characterises it 'as the most impressive and perfect expression of the poet's mystic experience of oneness with the Divine.' In a Foreword to the book the Marquess of Zetland, cites an extract from Sri Aurobindo's political writings, which, he says, contains the mainspring of Sri Aurobindo's revolutionary political activities, and in which also could be found a glimpse of the philosophy Sri Aurobindo was to formulate later. The extract is: 'It is India who must send forth from herself the future religion of the world, the Eternal Religion which is to harmonise all religions, sciences and philosophies and make mankind one soul.' Sir Eugen Millington-Drake, Vice-President of the Poetry Society of London, who toured India in 1949-50 addressing many Universities and Literary Societies on Poetry, particularly that of Indians, paid in almost all his lectures a glowing tribute to Sri Aurobindo as a poet. He read his poems before his audiences and often the one called 'Invitation' which, he said, 'is a matchless one, comparable to the great speech of Mr. Winston Churchill delivered during the

World War II when he called upon the British nation, at a critical hour, to cooperate with him in the uphill task of gaining victory.'

Chile's Nobel Laureate Gabriele Mistral says: 'While Tagore awakened the latent music in me, another Indian Sri Aurobindo, brought me to religion. He opened the way to my religious consecration. Indeed my debt to India is very great and is due in part to Tagore and in part to Sri Aurobindo.'[8]

In an article in the *Mother India* of Bombay in April 1950, Dr. Juan Marin, Chile's Charge d'Affairs in India, wrote: 'Sri Aurobindo's books have no equals in the European literature for their precious content of spiritual nourishment. The Seer of Pondicherry is a sublime "Adelantado" who travels and guides us toward worlds of which we have only a pale glimmer at present.'

That there is a growing interest in America in the teachings of Sri Aurobindo is becoming more and more evident. The Cornell University of New York has prescribed Sri Aurobindo's *The Life Divine* for the graduate seminar studies in Philosophy. E. A. Burtt, the Head of the Department of Philosophy of that University, who visited Sri Aurobindo's Ashram in Pondicherry, India, in 1947, and who is responsible for the introduction of the above-mentioned book in the University, himself conducted the seminar. P. A. Sorokin, Chairman of the Department of Sociology, Harvard University, took a keen interest in the philosophy and Yoga of Sri Aurobindo. In a message on Sri Aurobindo's birthday he wrote: 'From scientific and philosophical standpoint, the works of Sri Aurobindo are a sound antidote to the pseudoscientific psychology, psychiatry, and educational art of the West. Sri Aurobindo's *The Life Divine* and other Yoga treatises are among the most important works of our time in philosophy, ethics and humanities. Sri Aurobindo himself is one of the greatest living sages of our time; and a most eminent moral leader.' Raymond F. Piper of the Syracuse University says: 'The greatest gift of Sri Aurobindo to me as a philosopher is his magnificent perspective of existence.... His sustained song of the nature and divine potentialities of the human mind comes as a refreshing breeze over the fragmentary, superficial, earth-bound glimpses of the self in West-

---

8. *The Aryan Path*, February, 1947.

ern psychology and epistemology. He helps me to discover what
I am, and what I really and deeply want of existence. His new
thoughts change in my mind into clear recognitions of truths about
myself which I wonder I had not found before. His writings have
extraordinary power to awaken the mind to philosophic insight.
The Life Divine is in large part a declaration and design of the
freedom of mankind. I have never read an author who can compact so much truth into one sentence as this master. Gandhi is
the greatest saint, Tagore the greatest poet of modern India, but
Sri Aurobindo is the greatest thinker, indeed has attained incomparable triune greatness, as poet, philosopher, and saint.'

F. Speigelberg of the Department of Asiatic Studies, Standford
University, California, author of a number of books on religion,
visited Sri Aurobindo Ashram early in 1949. On his return to
America, he told the Press that though he could see Sri
Aurobindo only for a few seconds, it was a never-to-be-forgotten
experience. While in India, in the course of an interview published
in the *Mother India* of Bombay, he said: 'I am very grateful that I
came into contact with Sri Aurobindo so late in life, for after
having wrestled with the ultimate problems of existence for years,
I am now in a position to appreciate his solutions to them. In
1947 I read his *The Life Divine* and was completely knocked
over. I have never known a philosopher so all-embracing in his
metaphysical structure as Sri Aurobindo, none before him had the
same vision.' In the course of an article in another issue of the
same paper Prof. Speigelberg wrote: 'I can foresee a day when
the teachings—which are alredy making headway—of the greatest
spiritual voice from India, Sri Aurobindo, will be known all over
America and be a vast power of illumination.' Prof. Speigelberg
introduced Sri Aurobindo's *The Life Divine* and *Essays on the
Gita,* and himself took their classes in the Standford University.
The Government of India, according to a Press note, have of late
been receiving numerous enquiries from various part of the world,
particularly from America, about the aims and activities of Sri
Aurobindo's Ashram. And the demand for Sri Aurobindo litera-
ture is rapidly on the increase. Giving his impressions of his tour
in America in 1949, Prof. S. K. Maitra of the Banaras Hindu
University, India, wrote: 'I found from my talks with many
American professors in New York and also in other parts of
U.S.A. and not only professors but also men in other walks of

life, that there was a keen desire in that country to know about Sri Aurobindo's philosophy.'

Sri Aurobindo touched the mind and heart of seeking souls in America, England and Europe through the work in recent years of the lectures and visiting professors from India who were often invited to address Universities and public institutions of the Western world on various aspects of Sri Aurobindo's poetry and philosophy. Among them were Pandit Rishi Ram, A. B. Purani of Sri Aurobindo Ashram, Pondicherry, S. K. Ghose of Visva-Bharati, Santiniketan, and A. Basu who for fifteen years from 1953 was Spalding Lecturer in Indian Philosophy and Religion at the University of Durham, England, Visiting Profesor at the Institute of Eucumenical Studies in Switzerland, and at the Hebrew University, Jerusalem, Israel, at both of which one of his subjects was Sri Aurobindo.

Many Yoga centres and institutions for the study of Indian cultural and spiritual disciplines in America include Sri Aurobindo as an important subject. One such is the California Institute of Asian Studies of which the President is Haridas Choudhury, internationally famous author of a number of books on Sri Aurobindo., Another is the Sri Aurobindo Centre at Crescent Moon Ranch, Arizona, started by Nicolas Duncan.

Of all the countries in Europe, it is France that is evincing the most lively interest in Sri Aurobindo and his gospel of the divine life upon earth. Some of his books have been already translated into French and there is a growing demand for them. Is there a spiritual affinity between India and France, a secret psychic kinship? The future is big with far-reaching possibilities and it would be wilful blindness to overlook this first flutter of the soul of France at the healing and delivering touch of India's light. We have already quoted the glowing tributes of praise paid by Romain Rolland and Paul Richard to Sri Aurobindo. Here is another no less glowing but undoubtedly more moving, from Maurice Magre, the distinguished poet, thinker and novelist of France: 'O Maitre Tu es assis dans la solitude parfaite, la sérénité divine, l'extase réalisée. Mon admiration s'élève vers toi dans le silence de la nuit, vers toi qui as franchi la porte de la perfection. Dis-moi comment doit s'élever la spirale de la méditation, donne-moi une formule de prière, même une syllable à laquelle je m'accrocherai comme un nageur qui à trouvé une

bouée.[9] These utterances are not passing effusions of a few senti-
mental lovers of India; they represent a real, insistent want felt
by the progressive section of humanity all the world over. They
are the cry of the resurging soul of man, a cry for peace and
harmony in a world torn by war and discord.

Besides the regions mentioned before, France, Germany,
Switzerland and Italy in Europe, and Japan, Hong Kong and
Singapore in Asia, have Sri Aurobindo Centres which not only
study Sri Aurobindo but help in the translation and popularisa-
tion of his writings.

This is how the Light is widening towards the 'Everlasting
Day' of the Master-Seer's vision when the Sun of Truth will shine
for ever on man's consciousness.

The empire of the Spirit of which India has dreamt for long
ages and which it is her sole privilege now to build up in the
mind and heart of mankind, will become a reality and take its
definite form when man turns towards the Word of the Master,
the last Creative Word of India which she has been waiting since
the dawn of her history to deliver for the redemption of the
human race, for its liberation into a higher life of Knowledge,
Bliss, Freedom and Harmony which are the very basis of the
One World, the Perfect Truth-born World of Tomorrow.

The deeper secret of India's soul is revealed today in its
wider implication because the time has come for man to realise,
both individually and collectively, his destined divine perfection.
When man does that, India fulfils her God-given mission, the
mission of establishing on the whole earth the universal empire
of the Spirit.

REFERENCES

Swami Abhedananda, *India and Her People;* Annie Besant, *India and
its Mission* (a lecture); Count Biornstierna, *The Theogony of the Hindus;*
Madame Blavatsky, *The Secret Doctrine;* Dineshchandra Sen, *Brihat
Banga* (Bengal); Will Durant, *Our Oriental Heritage, The Case for India;*
Enfield, *History of Philosophy;* Erdmann, *History of Western Philosophy;*
Richard Garbe, *Philosophy of India;* Heeren, *Historical Researches;*

9. *A la Poursuite de la Sagesse.* 'O Master, Thou art seated in perfect
solitude, divine serenity, realised ecstasy. My admiration rises towards thee in the silence of the night, towards thee who has crossed the
portals of perfection. Tell me how to ascend the spiral of meditation, give me a formula of prayer, even a syllable to which I may
cling like a swimmer who has found a buoy.'

Louis Jacolliot, *Hindu Origin of Hebrew and Christian Revelations*, *La Bible dans L'Inda;* Kalidas Nag, *Greater India;* A. A. Macdonell, *India's Past, Sanskrit Literature;* Thomas Maurice, *Asiatic Researches;* Max Muller, *Chips from a German Workshop, History of Sanskrit Literature, India—What Can It Teach Us;* R. C. Majumdar, *Ancient India, Greater India, Hindu Colonies in the Far East, The History and Culture of the Indian People* (ed.); Radha Kumud Mookerji, *Ancient India;* Okakura Kakuzo, *The Ideals of the East;* E. Pococke, *India in Greece or Truth in Mythology;* Sri Aurobindo, *Ideals and Progress, On the Veda, The Foundations of Indian Culture, The Renaissance in India;* Urwick, *The Message of Plato;* M. Winternitz, *History of Indian Literature;* Sir John Woodroffe, *Is India Civilised?*

9

Early Contacts of India with Islam[1]

I

THE COMING of the Muslims into India is generally associated with the first Arab invasion of Sindh early in the eighth century, but the part that the pre-Muslim Arabs played in the commerce between the East and the West had brought them into India long before Islam was born. It is said that these Arabs had settled in Chaul, Kalyan and Supara, and that for a long time they exercised great influence on the Malabar coast. The rise of Islam freshened up this intercourse which had previously been more commercial than cultural in character though a view is held that the *Sabaean* cult of the pre-Muslim Arabs had, to some extent, influenced the coastal people of Malabar. The new faith of Islam opened up new possibilities and India began to enter largely into the thoughts of the Caliphs. Questioned by Omar as to what he had seen in India, an Arab sailor said, 'India's rivers are pearls, her mountains rubies, her trees perfumes.' But Omar was against making any attack on India, since he believed that the followers of Islam as of other religions, were free to practise their faith in that country. As a matter of fact, he rejected every proposal that was made to undertake an expedition to India by sea.

---

1. For much of the basic material used in this chapter the author is indebted to Prof. M. Ziauddin, his colleague at Visva-Bharati, Santiniketan, during the thirties, thanks to his collection from the British Museum.

Nevertheless, the Muslim Arabs began to pay more frequent visits to the western coasts of India and their influence in Malabar was such that early in the ninth century the last of the Cheraman Perumal kings became a convert to Islam. A few years after his conversion he went to Arabia and died there. The Arabs whom he sent with instructions regarding the administration of his dominions were cordially received at Malabar and allowed to build mosques. This conversion of the king was remembered in the practice followed at the installation of the Zamorin when he had himself shaved and dressed like a Muslim and crowned by a Mapilla. The Maharajahs of Travancore on receiving the sword at their coronations had to declare: 'I will keep this sword until the uncle who has gone to Mecca returns.' The Zamorin became patron of the Arab traders who, in return, gave him every support in his campaigns. It is said that the Zamorin was so well-disposed towards Islam that he openly encouraged conversion among his subjects because sea-voyage being forbidden to the Hindus, local people were not to any extent available for manning the ships of the Arab merchants. He also gave orders that in every family of fishermen in his dominion one or more of the male members should be brought up as Muslims.

Appreciation of Islam by Hindu kings is testified to by Masudi who visited India early in the tenth century. He says: 'The king of Cambay was interested in religious discourses and exchanged ideas with Muslims and other people who might have visited his kingdom.' Regarding the Hindu king of Gujarat Masudi says: 'In his kingdom Islam is respected and protected; in all parts rise the domes of beautiful mosques where Muslims worship.' When the Hindus of Cambay attacked the Muslim masses, Siddha Raj punished the guilty Hindus and compensated the Muslims with money for building a new mosque.

After the invasion of Sindh by Muhammad bin Qasim, the administration was left entirely in the hands of the natives. The Hindus of Sindh appealed to Muhammad for freedom of worship. Muhammad referred it to Hajjaj, the governor of Irak, who issued the order: 'Permission is given to Hindus to worship their own gods. Nobody must be forbidden or prevented from following his own religion. They may live in their houses in whatever manner they like.' Von Kremer observes: 'The customary honour and deference due to the Brahmins and the three per cent share in the land revenue was maintained. "Build temples, traffic with the Muhammadans, live without any fear and strive to better yourselves in every way possible," was the law in Abul Qasim's days and later.' There cannot indeed be a better example of toleration than that which the Arabs granted to the Hindus of Sindh.

The first history of Sindh called the *Chach-Namah* is the work of an Arab historian. The Arab geographer Astakhri visited India about the middle of the tenth century. He is the author of many geographical works which contain a map of Sindh, the first of its kind. In his description of the important commercial towns of India which were inhabited by Hindus and Muslims, he said that in their social intercourse both the communities were tending towards a harmony of their manners and customs. The Hindus and the native converts dressed like the Muslims and spoke their language. In Multan, says Ibn Hauqual, the dress of the Hindus and the Muslims was the same. Politically, the Arab invasion of Sindh was not so important as its effect on the mind of the Arabs who felt attracted by the greatness of Indian civilisation and began to visit the country in order to be acquainted with the wisdom of the Hindus.

Buzurg bin Shahryar, who was in India in the ninth century, says: 'The Indian Rajahs are particularly well-disposed towards the Muslims. The Buddhists of Ceylon love the Muslims and are extremely kind to them. During the Caliphate of Omar they deputed two Bhikshus to Arabia to collect particulars about Islam. One of them died on the way back, and the other, on his return, expressed his admiration for the Caliph who led a simple and unostentatious life.' Sulaiman, an Arab merchant who was in India about the same time, said that none liked the Arabs more than the Vallabhi king of Gujarat. Buzurg bin Shahryar says that the King Mahrug of Alor in Kashmir had the Koran translated into Hindi and used to hear the translation read to him every day. The same authority tells us about a visit to Sairaf, a port on the west of Irak, of the Hindus—mostly Sindhis, Multanis and Gujaratis—who were invited there by Arab merchants to a dinner where special arrangements were made for their food. These Hindus impressed the local people by the fluency with which they spoke colloquial Arabic.

This is not of course the only instance of the intercourse

that then existed between India and Persia. About the tenth century when Persia was conquered by Islam, the Muslims came into contact with the Buddhist population of that country and evidently gathered from them some idea of the teachings of the Buddha. These Buddhists were gradually absorbed by Islam along with many others in Khurasan and Turkestan.

The Abbasid court of Bagdad was famous for its patronage of learning, and was keenly interested in Indian culture. It invited Hindu scholars and highly appreciated their incomparable gifts in medicine and astronomy. Many of them were appointed chief physicians in the hospitals of Bagdad and were asked to translate, from Sanskrit into Arabic, various works on medicine, philosophy, astronomy, etc. Yahya-ibn-Khalid, the Baramaki minister of Harun-al-Rashid, had a treatise on the various schools of religious thought in India, as also one on the plants found in India alone, prepared by a scholar whom he sent to India specially for the purpose. The Baramakis had been Buddhists having had their original home in Balkh, which came under Islam about the middle of the seventh century. Yayha was a Baramaki, and was, due to his Buddhistic inclinations, an enthusiastic admirer of Indian culture. He is one of the earliest to have furthered the cause of Indo-Muslim cultural friendship. And it was through his efforts as well as through the patronage of the Bagdad court that the interest of Arab scholars and historians in Indian culture was aroused and they began to visit this country in search of knowledge. These, as well those learned men who went from India to Bagdad, carried to that country much of Indian scientific knowledge which was subsequently assimilated to the lore of Islam, in which Indian influence is considered to be more pronounced than the Greek. But everything that the Arabs received from India was given by them a new character and a new garb in which it was later transmitted to Europe.

II

The appreciation of the religion and culture of the Hindus by the Arabic and Persian scholars shows the breadth of their out-

look and the sympathy and care with which they tried to understand things Indian.

Writes Al-Jahiz (9th century):

'The Hindus excel in astrology, mathematics, medicine and
in various other sciences. They have developed to a perfection
arts like sculpture, painting and architecture. They have collec-
tions of poetry, philosophy, literature and science of morals.
From India we received that book called Kalilah wa Dimnah.
These people have judgment and are brave. They possess the
virtues of cleanliness and purity. Contemplation has originated
with them.'

Writes Yaqubi (9th century):

'The Hindus are superior to all other nations in intelligence
and thoughtfulness. They are more exact in astronomy and astrology than any other people. The Siddhanta is a good proof of
their intellectual powers; by this book the Greeks and the
Persians have also profited. In medicine their opinion ranks
first.'

Writes Al-Idrisi (10th century):

'The Hindus are by nature inclined to justice and never de-
part from it in their actions. Their good faith, honesty and
faithfulness to their promises are well known and they are so
famous for these qualities that people flock to their country from
every side.'

Writes Al-Beruni, who was in India for thirteen years from
A.D. 1017 and who was of opinion that in the core of their
teachings Hinduism and Islam are almost one:

'The Hindus believe with regard to God that He is One,
eternal, without beginning and, acting by free-will, almighty,
all-wise, living, giving life, ruling, preserving; one who in his
sovereignty in unique, beyond all likeness and unlikeness, and
that he does not resemble anything nor does anything resemble
him.'

These revealing utterances of the Muslim scholars show how
deep was their insight into Hindu life and thought and how
correct their understanding of the Hindu character. They only
can build up unity who can appreciate the culture of others as
well as they do their own, for it is on mutual understanding alone
that unity can thrive. To these high-souled Muslims India should
remain grateful for the invaluable service they rendered to the

cause of cultural fellowship in those medieval times, the history of which has yet to be written. Not much is known about many of these seekers of knowledge. One name however looms large before our eyes. It is that of Al-Beruni whose visit to India is a notable event in the history of Indo-Muslim friendship in the world of learning. He came to this country in quest of knowledge about Hindu sciences and philosophy and visited prominent centres of culture in Northern India including those in Kashmir, Mathura, Prayag and Ujjain. He wrote a history of India in which he described the social and religious life of the country. It is noteworthy that nowhere in the book has he said anything that might offend the Hindus. Neither had he anything to say about the political turmoil that was then raging in the country beyond a casual reference to the havoc it did to the people. About his activities in India, Sachau, who collected and edited Al-Beruni's works, says: 'It was like a magic island of quiet and impartial research in the midst of a world of clashing swords, burning towns and plundered temples.' There is no doubt that in their exchange of views and in the daily talks that they had with Al-Beruni and with others who followed him and had preceded him in search of knowledge in India, the Hindu scholars had their first-hand information about Islam and the theology that was developed under its inspiration. Like an impartial scholar, Al-Beruni did not hesitate to criticise the defects that he noticed in the Hindus. He complained of their conceit and self-sufficiency, hoping at the same time that 'if they travelled and mixed with other nations, they would soon change their minds, for their ancestors were not as narrow-minded as the present generation is.' Al-Beruni 'studied Sanskrit diligently' and, as the first quotation from him shows, 'was fascinated by the philosophy of the Bhagavat Gita and the Upanishads.' For his encyclopaedic knowledge, the Hindus gave Al-Beruni the title *Vidyasagar,* 'the Ocean of Learning.'

The Muslim saints who visited India about this time were most of them Sufis, though many divines and *dervishes* had already been in India disseminating the tenets of Islam. Many of the Sufis settled in the country leading an austere life and devoting themselves to spiritual pursuits. For the catholicity of their outlook and for the loftiness of their doctrines they became popular among both Hindus and Muslims and earned their respect. It cannot be said that they were all of them pledged to a proselytising mission. Their saintliness and liberality attracted large numbers of Hindus, especially those whom the Hindu society neglected and would not give a human, not to speak of a respectable, status. The social organisation of the Hindus was suffering from many defects. It is to them that the cause might be traced of the growing discontent among a large section of people, which drove them to seek spiritual help from the Sufis. Many embraced Islam, and many became admirers of its liberal teachings.

Al-Hujwiri was one such illustrious saint who hailed from Ghazna and settled in Lahore which became a centre of his activities. Even today Hindus and Muslims come to pay their homage to his memory at his tomb in Lahore where he died in 1072. Hujwiri is believed to be the first teacher of Sufism in India. He emphasised complete annihilation of ego by which the seeker is to realise the all-embracing Unity and be the recipient of divine grace which will fill him with 'Godly idealism.'

Muinuddin's is another great name which is held in the highest esteem by Sufis in India. His tomb, eracted along with a shrine, is also a place of pilgrimage for both Hindus and Muslims. Akbar the Great is said to have travelled on foot to this place as a pilgrim. It is interesting that in this Sufi shrine, as in Hindu temples, music is played daily and professional female singers sing at the request of the pilgrims. The fame of Muinuddin and his spiritual activities spread over India, and even high-caste Brahmins fell under his influence. At Pushkar in Ajmer, a place of Hindu pilgrimage, where Muinuddin lived and passed his last days, there is even today a class of people who call themselves Husaini Brahmins, who are neither orthodox Hindus nor orthodox Muslims, having belief in Hindu customs and rituals along with Muhammadan ideas and practices.

The intermingling of rites and customs indicates the beginning of a new social outlook which was initiated through the influence of the Sufis. And by drawing adherents from among both Hindus and Muslims they were able to unify into a synthetic whole the two streams, Hinduism and Islam. Thus Sufism became one of those synthesis that came into being in the spiritual world of India under the inspiring influence of the lives and teachings of the saints and mystics in medieval times. The wide popularity of Sufi idealism among the Hindus is explained

among other things by the striking similarity between some of
its fundamental principles and Indian thought, especially Buddhism and Vedanta; and this was largely due to the influence of
the latter on the former. It is well known that the Sufis came
in touch with Buddhism in many important centres of the Muslim world. As early as the second century of the Hejra, the Arabs
translated many Buddhist works. The Sufi idea of *Fana,* i.e.,
of total self-annihilation, is distinctly a derivation from the *Nirvana* of Buddhism. The inspired utterance 'I am the Truth' of
Mansur, the well-known Sufi who visited India is only an echo
of the Vedantic '*Soham*', 'I am That.' The yogic breathing
exercises of the Hindus are followed in every detail by a section
of the Sufis and their practice of remembering God and repeating His name is the same as the *Japa* of the Hindus for which
the Sufi term is *Zikra.*

Such, in brief, was the character of the early contact between India and the Islamic world. It was principally cultural.
One might speculate on the turn that the course of Indian history would have taken if a closer political association had been
established during these early centuries between this country and
the enlightened court of Bagdad. But such speculation would
serve no really useful purpose. If subsequently Providence
thought it fit to introduce the stream of Islamic thought into
India through the agency of a swashbuckler like Mahmud of
Ghazni or a dashing cavalier of the type of Babar the Moghul,
it must have been done with a deeper design than appears on the
surface.

The two most remarkable qualities in Indian thought have
been its powers of reception and assimilation of new ideas.
These qualities have not always been externally perceptible in
the history of India's cultural evolution. But they have always
been there and working out a state of things which would make
India the pivot of human progress when mankind passes from
the stage of narrow mentality to that of a broad and divinely
illumined supramentality.

10

India—The Future[1]

I

THE FUTURE of India has in recent times been the subject of discussion among our thinkers. It is good that they should have a keen desire to think out the problem and indicate the lines on which it should be approached. Some of them have already expressed their views which throw much light on the various aspects of the subject as well as on the present trend of our thinking public. It seems that the India of tomorrow has entered their imagination. Many of them believe that for India to live and grow into the fullness of her being, a better social order must be built on principles of justice and equity, and completely free from any kind of social and economic inequality. The problem of India, according to them, is the problem of bread and an India well-fed and well-clothed will be an India happy and contented. Religion and spirituality are, in their opinion, hindrances to social progress, and are therefore tabooed in their scheme. Some speak of a new civilisation which they think is in the process of formation in India as a result of the fusion of cultures that has been taking place from the time of her contact with

---

1. Some views based on Sri Aurobindo's writings. The quotations in this chapter are all from his following books and writings: *Bankim-Tilak-Dayananda, The Ideal of the Karmayogin, The Life Divine, The Mother, The Renaissance in India, The Supramental Manifestation, The Yoga and Its Objects, The Foundations of Indian Culture, The Future Poetry, The Human Cycle, Karmayogin* (a Weekly paper, 1908-10) and from an unpublished letter to Dilip Kumar Roy.

foreign countries. There are others who hold different views about the shape and character of the future Indian civilisation. 'Back to the past,' 'Back to Nature' are the slogans of a large section which insists on a return to the old and simple forms of rural culture. They religiously cling to certain ethical ideals mistakenly taking them to be the ideals of Indian civilisation which is founded, not, as they think, on the varying and therefore imperfect codes of morality, but on the eternal truths of the Spirit. Some again are full of faith that a greater India recovering all that was best in her past and with new powers acquired through centuries of experiences will emerge in response to the call of the time-spirit for fulfilling some divine purpose. The birth of this India through a spiritualised order, they feel sure, is an inevitability in the inner scheme of things.

Whatever their differences, they envisage a better and brighter future for India. But what is striking in the first two views, especially in the first, is that they do not properly appreciate India's spiritual heritage, far less recognise its importance to her future rebuilding. And it is unfortunate that even an attitude of disdain is sometimes betrayed towards the spiritual genius of India which has all along been, and still is, the motive-force of her life and culture. The vision that India saw of the Infinite, the immortal truths that she discovered, the culture that she built up on her profound spiritual experiences have not only enriched beyond measure but have given its value, character and distinction to her civilisation. It is therefore imperative that in a discussion of what the civilisation of India is going to be in the future, the very first thought should go to that essential basis of her culture, the dominant tendency of her soul.

The norms and principles of sociology developed in the West may be helpful to such an undertaking. But they must not rule out any attempt to find out the methods by which to rekindle the soul of India so that a resurgence of her civilisation may be possible out of all the achievements of her great past. Sri Aurobindo's message has a significant bearing on this point. He has in many of his writings given clear hints as to what will be India's role in the future. His deep, penetrating and luminous exposition of her past has no parallel. The present chapter will, with the help of those writings, try to indicate the instrinsic values of Indian civilisation and show how indispensable they are to the rebuilding of India.

Europe gloried in her civilisation as the highest creation of the human mind. But she is bewildered today at the wanton destruction of her long-cherished social and cultural values, and at the brutal exhibition of barbarous instincts in a large section of her so-called civilised humanity.

The culture of Europe has undoubtedly advanced the cause of human progress. But in spite of all its great achievements, it has failed to solve her problems, and has, moreover, been largely responsible for throwing her and, through her, many other countries into the clutches of dark and undivine forces. True to her nature, Europe's quest has been for the truths of life and mind, and with whatever of them she succeeded in attaining, she developed her culture and her religion of humanism which sang the glory of man and extolled him as his own redeemer. But the quest of India has been always for God, for the truths of the Spirit.

The earliest aspiration of man to wake to the divinity within is recorded in the Rig Veda. 'That which is immortal in mortals and possessed of the truth, is a god and established inwardly as an energy working out in our divine powers.... Become high-uplifted, O Strength, pierce all veils, and manifest in us the things of the Godhead' (iv. 2.1; iv. 4.5.). To strive for and to adhere to the eternal verities is India's *swadharma*. Spiritual perfection has always figured as her one high ideal, and life to her was the field for its pursuit. Her civilisation has grown out of her inner realisations which she applied with wonderful success to the varied forms of her creative life. 'She saw the myriad gods beyond man, God beyond gods, and beyond God his own ineffable eternity; she saw that there were ranges of life beyond our life, ranges of mind beyond our present mind, and above these she saw the splendours of the Spirit.... She declared that there were none of these things which man could not attain if he trained his will and knowledge; he could conquer these ranges of mind, become the Spirit, become a God, become one with God, become the ineffable Brahman.' The whole of India's life is governed by this, her sovereign sense of the Infinite. It is indeed the very master-key of her mind. From the very beginning of her history, her spiritual adventures have flowed like a stream, fertilising her national life, implanting in it the seeds they carried from Truth's Himalayan heights, the seeds that have continuously sprouted and flowered in her art and literature, her religion and philosophy, her science and politics; but the most glorious flowering, the most surging tide is yet to come, and all that has preceded has been but the necessary preparation for it.

A section of our countrymen is inclined to think that the India of the ages is dead, that she has burnt out the oil of her life and now lacks the vitality to live again. The past is an anathema to them. They claim to be modern in their outlook. The Western ideas and institutions are easier for them to understand than the 'misty past of India' and her 'bullock-cart civilisation' as they contemptuously call it. They assert that India can best develop herself only by adopting Western institutions. It is curious that when Indian ideals are permeating the culture of many countries abroad, and are being increasingly admitted by them as influences that exalt and ennoble, and lead to a higher existence, when Europe stands dismayed at the failure of her own culture, we in India should reject our own ideals as 'old-world superstitions' and 'take up the cast-off clothes of European thought and life, and struggle along in the old rut of her wheels, always taking up today what she had cast off yesterday.'

India knows no death. She has become immortal by drinking *amrita*[2] at the fountain of her ancient wisdom. Neither has she exhausted herself by her great creations in the past. The vicissitudes through which she had to pass have always been a trial of her strength. By surviving them, while earth's oldest civilisations have gone into oblivion, leaving behind them nothing but their monuments, India proves her indomitable vitality, her deathless soul.

'India still lives and keeps the continuity of her inner mind and soul and spirit with the India of the ages. Invasion and foreign rule, the Greek, the Parthian, and the Hun, the robust vigour of Islam, the levelling steam-roller heaviness of the British occupation and the British system, the enormous pressure of the occident have not been able to drive or crush the ancient soul out of the body her Vedic Rishis made for her. At every step, under every calamity and attack and domination, she has been able to

---

2. Immortalising nectar, used figuratively.

resist and survive either with an active or a passive resistance. And this she was able to do in her great days by her spiritual solidarity and power of assimilation and reaction, expelling all that would not be absorbed, absorbing all that could not be expelled, and even after the beginning of the decline she was still able to survive by the same force, abated but not slain, retreating and maintaining for a time her ancient political system in the South, throwing up, under the pressure of Islam, Rajput and Sikh and Maharatta to defend her ancient self and its idea, persisting passively where she could not resist actively, condemning to decay each empire that could not answer her riddle or make terms with her, awaiting always the day for her revival. And even now it is a similar phenomenon that we see in process before our eyes. And what shall we say then of the surpassing vitality of the civilisation that could accomplish this miracle and of the wisdom of those who built its foundation not on things external but on the spirit and inner mind, and made a spiritual and cultural oneness the root and stock of her existence and not solely its fragile flower, the eternal basis and not the perishable superstructure?'

III

It is a short-sighted reading of Indian history to say that India fulfilled her mission through her great achievements in the past, and that the culture of India has nothing substantial to contribute to the reconstruction of her life for the future which will be a completely new creation. This is missing the central meaning of Indian culture as also its historical evolution. It is not merely its dominant spirituality, its living continuity and its stupendous life-force that are the only characteristics of Indian civilisation. There is about her a yet greater truth of which India is always conscious, and for whose fulfilment she has been preparing from the dawn of her history. The sense of that mission was always there as the motive-force behind every expression of her soul; and her culture has therefore been 'a continuously enlarging tradition of the Godward endeavour of the human spirit.'

'Indian culture recognises the spirit as the truth of our being and our life as a growth and evolution of the spirit in man. It sees God as the supreme and as the All and it sees man as a soul and power of the being of God in Nature. The progressive growth of man into self, into God, into spiritual existence by the development of our natural into our Divine being is for Indian thinking the significance of life and the aim of human existence.... Always to India that idea of Self, God, Spirit and the moulding of man into that have been the fundamental power of her philosophy, religion, civilisation. The formal turn and the rhythmic lines of effort of this culture have grown through two complete external stages. The first was the early Vedic in which religion took its formal stand on the natural approach of the physical mind of man to the Godhead in the universe, but the initiates guarded the sacrificial fire of a greater spiritual truth behind the form of outward religious worship and conception. The second was the Purano-Tantrik in which religion took its outward stand on the deeper approach of man's psycho-physical mind to the Divine in the Universe, but a greater initiation opened the way to the most intimate truth and living of the spiritual life in all its profundity and infinite possibility of uttermost sublime experience. A third stage has been long in preparation, its idea often cast out in limited or large, quiet or striking spiritual movements and potent new disciplines and religions, but not successful yet, because the circumstances were adverse and the hour not come, which will call the community of men to live in the greatest light of all and to found their whole life on some fully revealed power and grand uplifting truth of the Spirit. Not until that third enlarging movement has come into its own, a thing not so easy as the religious reformer, the purist of the reason or the purist of the spirit constantly imagines and by that too hasty imagination falls short in his endeavour, can Indian civilisation be said to have discharged its mission, to have spoken its last word and fully, *functus officio,* crowned and complete in its office of mediation between the life of man and the spirit ...'

'India of the ages is not dead nor has she spoken her last creative word; she lives and has still something to do for herself and the human progress. And that which is seeking now to awake is not an Anglicised oriental people, docile pupil of the West and doomed to repeat the occident's success and failure, but still the ancient immemorable Shakti recovering the deepest self, lifting her head higher towards the supreme source of light and strength, and turning to discover the complete meaning and a vaster form of her Dharma.'

It is held that ancient India excelled only in religion and spirituality, and neglected material pursuits, and thereby hastened her downfall. This view, wholly erroneous and unfounded, is put forward to advise against emulating the past of India in the matter of building up her future. The causes that led to India's decline are not for this article to go into. But the fact has to be borne in mind that India was considerably great in the varied richness of her life-expression. Her abundant energy, her inexhaustible vitality and joy of life, her almost unconceivably prolific creativeness have throughout the ages broken into a myriad vigorous activities that prove, if anything, the amazing virility of the race, its invincible puissance.

'India has not only had the long roll of her great saints, sages, thinkers, religious founders, poets, creators, scientists, scholars, legists; she has had her great rulers, administrators, soldiers, conquerors, heroes, men with the strong active will, the mind that plans and the seeing force that builds. She has warred and ruled, traded and colonised, and spread her civilisation, built polities and organised communities and societies, done all that makes the outward activity of great people.... It was not men of straw or lifeless or willess dummies or thin-blooded dreamers who thus acted, planned, conquered, built great systems of administration, founded kingdoms and empires, figured as great patrons of poetry and art and architecture or, later, resisted heroically imperial power and fought for the freedom of clan and people.'

The contact between India and Europe has been mutually fruitful. Europe has developed a tendency to subjectivism which has begun to effect subtle changes in her outlook on life; and India has felt within her an impetus to scientific and intellectual pursuits, and, what is more important, an urge to discover the truth of her own being. Here, India has not been a blind imitator of Europe, as unhappily she is now wanted to be by a section of our countrymen. Neither has Europe betrayed any sign of an external imitation of Indian ideas. There is an inner cultural interchange which is cultivated through the power of assimilation.

Blind imitation is slavish, and proves only the weakness and mental poverty of the imitator. In any case, the benefit which India derived from her contact with Europe was one of the forces that helped to bring about the awakening in India early last century. There were, of course, greater forces at work to rouse India to a conscious effort towards the renewal of her destiny. 'India has a secret Power that no nation possesses. All that she needs is to rouse in her that faith, that will. God has breathed life into her once more. Great souls are at work to bring about her salvation. The movement, of which the first outbreak was political, will end in a spiritual consummation. India is still in possession of her soul. The world will receive its message of emancipation from India.'

And 'Bengal was the first workshop of this Shakti of India.' Raja Rammohun Roy was the starting-point. The inception of the Congress movement in 1885 is a significant phase of this awakening. But it was a new light which dawned in the spiritual horizon of India when at Dakshineshwar 'the flower of the educated youth of Calcutta bowed down at the feet of an illiterate Hindu ascetic, a self-illuminated ecstatic and "mystic" without a single trace or touch of the alien thought or education upon him. The going forth of Vivekananda, marked out by the Master as a heroic soul destined to take the world between his two hands and change it, was a first visible sign to the world that India was awake not only to survive but to conquer.' Shri Ramakrishna saw the vision of the Divine Mother and released a stream of forces that through Vivekananda burst over India like an avalanche and gave a vehement impetus to her rebuilding on the basis of her spiritual heritage. It was a conquest of the spirit of India won for his Master by that soldier of the Light, that mighty warrior of God. 'Vivekananda was a soul of puissance if ever there was one, a very lion among men, but the definite work he has left behind is quite incommensurate with our impression of his creative might and energy. We perceive his influence still working gigantically, we know not well how, we know not well where in something that is not yet formed, something leonine, grand, intuitive, upheaving that has entered the soul of India and we say, "Behold Vivekananda still lives in the soul of his Mother and in the souls of her children".'

In 1905, the Shakti of India was invoked again by the united

voice of Bengal with the new-found *mántra* of *Vande Mataram.*[3]
It was not the physical India, but 'the Eternal and Timeless
India,' her Power, her Spirit, who was then worshipped by an
awakened people. The Mother revealed herself and responded to
their prayer, and infused into them a new strength, a new inspiration. And the whole nation was swept into a grim determination to win its freedom. But the actual political objective of the
movement did not detract from its ultimate spiritual intention.
The call went forth from its inspired high-priest: 'You must
know your past and recover it for the purposes of your future.
First, therefore, become Indians, recover the patrimony of your
forefathers. Recover the Aryan thought, the Aryan discipline,
the Aryan character, the Aryan life.... It is the spirituality of
India, the sadhana of India, *tapasya, jnanam*[4] and *shakti,* that
must make us free and great.... India's work is world's work,
God's work. Our captain is God Himself. He will lead us to
the goal.'

'India can best develop herself and serve humanity by being
herself and following the law of her own nature.' The following
are the three broad lines indicated by Sri Aurobindo on which
the work may be taken up: 'The recovery of the old spiritual
knowledge and experience in all its splendour, depth and fullness
is the first, most essential work; the flowing of this spirituality
into new forms of philosophy, literature, art, science, and critical
knowledge is the second; an original dealing with modern problems in the light of Indian spirit and the endeavour to formulate
a greater synthesis of a spiritualised society is the third and most
difficult.' But how to understand India's *swadharma,* the secret
law of her being? Mind will not take us farther than an objective knowledge of the past of India, her creations in the outer
court of life. In order therefore to get at the very heart of them
and find out how the drive is initiated there we must take to
the subjective method of intuition and introspection, and develop
an inward vision which alone can reveal to us the sacred sanc-
tuary of the flaming soul of India. Many of our countrymen
following exclusively the so-called scientific method of the West
make suggestions for the reconstruction of India which, they do
not perhaps realise, only expose the inadequacy of their know-

---

3. Bow to Thee, O Mother.
4. Spiritual knowledge.

ledge of that inner India which, let us repeat, cannot be fully understood by the intellect alone.

These suggestions are, as they are bound to be, nothing more than laboured elaborations of imported ideas without any connection with proper roots of Indian life and culture. But India must not cling to her past and refuse to move with the times. The truths of her great past she must rediscover and repossess for whatever strength they may give for building up her future. In any case, the Tomorrow is her immediate concern, and she must be alive to her mission which only her greater self can fulfil. 'A great past ought to be followed by a greater future.' The future, as the present, may well be the fruit of the efforts that have preceded it; but with every fresh stirring, the nature of the attainment will change, and change always for the better, the higher.

Even honest and unbiased opinions sometimes characterise the past of India as chiefly given to spiritual pursuits. A harmonious development of life, mind and body was not aimed at, they say. This is far from the truth. 'The ancient Indian culture attached quite as much value to the soundness, growth and strength of the mind, life and body as the old Hellenic or the modern scientific thought, although for a different end and a greater motive.... The new India will seek the same end in new ways under the vivid impulse of fresh and large ideas and by an instrumentality suited to more complex conditions; but the scope of her effort and action, and suppleness and variety of her mind will not be less, but greater than of old. Spirituality is not necessarily exclusive; it can be and in its fullness must be all-inclusive.... But the spiritual motive will be in the future of India, as in her past, the real original and dominating strain. To realise intimately the truth of spirit and to quicken and remould life by it is the native tendency of Indian mind, and to that it must always return in all its periods of health, greatness and vigour.'

But this high spiritual ideal, far less its integral character, is not sufficiently recognised and accepted, far less, affirmed in the aspirations of modern India. Many of those who are thinking about the future of this ancient country where spirituality was first born, do not appear to be fully conscious of this which is the foremost ideal of India and indispensable to her rebuilding.

Besides, whatever spiritual tendency there still is in India is more or less of an other-worldly nature, confined to the pursuit of individual liberation as the only aim of life, society and even life itself being regarded as hindrances to spiritual progress.

The problem today not only of India but of the whole world is essentially a problem of harmony. In India the ancient ideal of an all-embracing spirituality began to be dimmed in the racial consciousness when *mayavada* (the theory of the cosmic Illusion) was preached with all the vehemence that the human intellect could command, and was given a ready welcome possible only for a people which was then on the downward curve of its destiny. The ideal became more blurred in her vision when in a later period the glamour of a foreign culture blinded India—though temporarily—to the truths of her own self. In Europe the old Hellenic and the Christian ideals were gradually replaced by the complex forms of a materialistic civilisation which furnished man with enormous powers for satisfying his mental, vital and physical needs but widened the gulf between him and his God more than ever before. There have been attempts to reconcile these divergences, and solve the problems of mankind through religion, politics and science. But alas! true harmony is yet far off. It waits on other means.

III

Every religion is spiritual in its origin. But when an institution is made of it and more importance is given to the institution than to the spirit of the religion, it begins to deteriorate. An institution cannot thrive without popular support. And for a religion to be popular means its coming down to the ordinary human level and giving ordinary human satisfactions but with a religious colouring. Thus, while their lamps have been kept burning by the few earnest seekers of truth belonging to them, almost all the religions of the world have compromised with the vital needs of man and permitted in their bodies the growth of various codes and dogmas and rituals and other forms of sectarianism which choke the religious aspirations of man and stand in the way of his spiritual progress. The ethical bias in many religions is also no less responsible for their failure to solve the problem which is essentially spiritual. Morality is often confused with religion and spirituality. There is an element of morality in all religions, but the power of spirituality is a superior one. 'Morality is an attempt to govern the outer conduct by certain mental rules or to form the character by these rules in the image of a certain mental ideal,' whereas spirituality is a change into a higher consciousness through the realisation of the Divine within and without and making him the absolute ruler of life. It is to live in, and act from the truth of the Spirit, in a word, to live the Spirit. 'It is a growth or waking into a new becoming or new being, a new self, a new nature.'

The success of religion in India is due to its essential spiritual basis. But in spite of its broad and catholic outlook and a brilliant record of service in the cause of man's spiritual uplift, religion in India cannot be said to have reached that acme of greatness which her ancient seers expected of it. Its evolution was checked when it showed a tendency to mere externalism and failed to get out of a fixed social system in which it was cabined. It could not grow into that largeness of its innate spiritual character which is so necessary to the fulfilment of its original aim of liberating man into a higher existence. Yet for the seeker, every religion has its truths, and even ethical ideals have not been without their values to the social well-being of man.

Through politics man has tried to solve the problem of his external peace and freedom. But where is peace in the world today? and where is freedom? The chief concern of the State is to grow in power to fulfil its selfish ambitions, and be secure against aggression by the stronger; to serve these ends the resources of the country are blindly consumed, its nation-building works woefully neglected. A sense of war prevails everywhere. And when there is no actual hostility, there is at best an armed panicky peace, a panting lull before a burst of storm. And how can freedom thrive in a State which seeks to be absolute? Is it not beyond the power of a machine which the State has become to solve the problem of man who is not a machine but a complex being? One of the causes of this disharmony is the spirit of domination which is almost a concomitant of power when it is centralised in a system of government, whatever be its character. Conditions would not have been so distressing had the State been in charge of men with a larger heart and a wider vision. Instead, men, who are themselves subject to the worst of passions, form the powers that be almost everywhere. In ancient India these difficulties were to some extent obviated, the former by a popular system of local self-government, and the latter by selfless sages whose counsels were sought by kings on every important matter of the State. The spiritual bias in Indian character was no less a help in that direction.

Through the culture of science man has opened into new horizons of knowledge, into deeper truths of Nature. But since he has not been able to attain sufficient psychological development, he has failed properly to manipulate the vast potencies of the universal Force released by science, with the result that they are made to satisfy the insensate earth-grabbing of power-intoxicated peoples, and the whole world is thrown into a vortex of the dark Forces. Indeed, the amenities of life offered by science pale into insignificance before the disasters wrought by it in supplying man with deadly weapons of destruction which threaten to reduce him to savagery.

Though man was not fully conscious of the ultimate goal of his earthly adventure, yet all his creative endeavours have all the time helped his progress towards that goal of divine perfection which he is destined to attain as the next stage in his evolutionary ascent. This progress is shown in the height of mental power man has reached today. It is also seen in the growth of a seeking in him as well as of a feeling of discontent with the existing order of things. It is this seeking and this feeling of discontent which are the first signs of a spiritual awakening. But the problems remain unsolved. Man has not been happy; he has no peace, no freedom, no prospect, nothing that can lead to a better condition of life. His aspiration for the Kingdom of God upon earth is far from even a semblance of fulfilment.

The chief among the reasons of his failure is man's imperfect nature dominated by his ego. In religion the ego incites him to an attitude of superior separatism; and the image that he makes of his God ends by becoming a magnified image of his own self, and he would love to be pledged to a sect or dogma because it is his own creation. In politics it is symbolised in the State whose absolute power must be worshipped by all. In science it is glorified when man takes pride in his achievements and refuses to believe in anything that cannot be perceived by his physical senses. It is this ego which persists in every so-called triumph of human effort, and, as instrument of adverse and undivine forces, tries to tempt man away from God and chain him down to a life whose be-all and end-all would be a satisfaction of his mental, vital and physical needs only. But the ego is not the whole man. There is in him his Divinity. And by awakening to it he can replace the domination of the ego in him by the rule of the Divine and change into a higher nature. The reason why human creations cannot be perfect is that the power of mind by which man produces his art, literature, religion, science and politics is a dividing power and cannot go beyond finite constructions. How can he create perfect things with an instrument that is imperfect? Mind's is a separative function. 'It cannot have the total knowledge of the whole which is necessary for the right knowledge of the part' (*The Life Divine*, Vol I). This is a great source of error in all human knowledge to which may be traced the disharmonies in man's life and society. A creation is perfect only when it is the work of one who has himself become perfect by changing into a higher nature and being one with the Infinite Existence of which all finite things are embodiments.

It is this union with the creative Truth of the Infinite Existence and a dynamic living in it that can perfect humanity and build a perfect society. A true harmony and a true perfection is the only solution of all problems of mankind. 'And it is only India that can discover the harmony, because it is only by a change—not a mere readjustment—of man's present nature that it can be developed, and such a change is not possible except by Yoga. The nature of man and things is at present a discord, a harmony that has gone out of tune. The whole heart and action and mind of man must be changed, but from within, not from without, not by political and social institutions, not even by creeds and philosophies, but by realisation of God in ourselves and the world and a remoulding of life by that realisation.'

His failure to find a solution for the problems of life through the creations of his mind is not the only reason why man should turn towards spirituality and try to discover a higher than mental power for the reconstruction of his life and society. The social evolution of man is marked by four broad stages forming a psychological cycle through which a nation or a civilisation is bound to proceed.[5] The first of stages is called the Age of Symbol; the second, the Age of Convention; the third, the Age of Individualism; and the fourth, the Age of Subjectivism through which human civilisation in general is at present passing. Of course the progress has not been uniform everywhere. In Europe this spirit of subjectivism shows the promise of an awakening to deeper truths. In India indications are unmistakable of a spiritual renaissance, a rebirth of the old spirit into a new form of truth. Signs of an awakening are perceptible all over the world. The higher mind of humanity is gradually realising that it is only a life in the spirit, a total spiritual direction in all human affairs that can lift mankind out of the present chaos. But this consciousness has not yet gained sufficient ground. Nevertheless, the individuals in whom this new consciousness has dawned are the fore-runners of the great future. With the increasing aspiration of man, the growing stress of the evolutionary Nature and the pressure of external conditions, they will swell in number and form the community which will be the nucleus of the future world order, founded not on the absolutism of a dictatorship, but on the harmonic principle of an integral spirituality.

'In spirituality lies then the ultimate, the only hope for the perfection whether of the individual or of the communal man; not the spirit which for its separate satisfaction turns away from the earth and its works, but that greater spirit which accepts and fulfils them. A spirituality taking up into itself man's rationalism, aestheticism, ethicism, vitalism, corporeality, his aim of love and perfection, his aim of knowledge, his aim of beauty, his aim of power and fullness of life and being, revealing to them their divine sense and the conditions of their godhead, reconciling them all to each other, illuminating to the vision of each the way which they now tread in half-lights and shadows, in blindness or with a deflected sight, is a good which even man's self-sufficient reason can accept; for it reveals itself surely in the end as a logical, inevitable development and consummation of all for which he is individually and socially striving. The evolution of the inchoate spirituality in mankind is the possibility to which an age of subjectivism is the first glimmer of awakening

---

5. Sri Aurobindo has elaborately discussed this subject in his *The Human Cycle.*

or towards which it at least shows the profound potentiality of return. A deeper, wider, greater, more spiritualised subjective understanding of the individual and communal self and life and reliance on the spiritual light and spiritual means for the solution of its problems are the only ways to true social perfection. The free rule, that is to say, the predominant leading influence, guidance of the developed spiritual man—not the half spiritua-lised or the raw religionist—is our hope for the divine guidance of humanity. A spiritualised society is our hope for the communal happiness, or in words which, though liable to abuse by the rea-son and the passions, are still the most expressive we can find, a new kind of theocracy, the Kingdom of God upon earth, a theocracy which shall be the Government of mankind by the Divine in the hearts and minds of man.' This is Sri Aurobindo's vision of the future social and world order. In the spiritual age that is coming upon mankind, India will figure as the inaugu-rator of that spiritualised society. The time is therefore come for her to summon up all her inner powers and with their help to discover that new truth, that new harmony on which her future as well as the world's will be built. It is to India that the sole privilege is given of affirming that spirituality is the only panacea for all the evils that afflict humanity. Great in the past, she has to be yet greater in the future and accomplish the task given to her by God.

IV

The supreme need of India at the present moment is therefore to create such conditions as may be favourable to the birth of a greater India. The divine forces and personalities that have been working to bring about that consummation point to that propitious time when she will renew herself in a spiritualised social order founded on an integral harmony. A widespread spiritual awakening is the first and most necessary condition, of which a beginning has been already made in India today in that a definite turn has been taken towards the completion of the third enlarging movement (referred to before) in the spiritual life of India through which she will discharge her mission. India has discovered the complete meaning and a vaster form of her Dharma on which a larger synthesis will be built. She has found the harmony between 'the passionate aspiration of man upward to the Divine and the descending movement of the Divine leaning downward to embrace eternally its manifestation.' The confluence thus created of man's Godward longing and God's earthward leanings will be the perennial source of light, power and joy for a life in the Spirit which will be India's gift to humanity. A blissful union of heaven and earth will blossom into that greater life for man. And the power that will effect this union is the power of the Divine Shakti.

There are signs that conditions in life and nature are not only favourable to, but are pressing for, the emergence of a divinised humanity on earth. Sri Aurobindo is the Seer of a New Light which is descending upon the earth to effect through the Divine Shakti the supreme purpose of evolutionary Nature. He has shown the Path by which that new life will be attainable to man. He has spoken the supreme Word: 'As there has been established on earth a mental Consciousness and Power which shapes a race of mental beings and takes up into itself all of earthly nature that is ready for the change, so now there will be established on earth a gnostic Consciousness and Power which will shape a race of gnostic spiritual beings and take up into itself all of earth nature that is ready for this new transformation.' The revelation of this new truth today is among the signs that the time for its manifestation is come.

'A manifestation of the Supermind and its truth-consciousness is then inevitable; it must happen in this world sooner or later,' are the revealing words of the Master. How will this manifestation work in earth-nature and prepare man for his destined divine perfection? The Master, again: 'The descent of the Supermind will bring to one who receives it and is fulfilled in the truth-consciousness all the possibilities of the divine life. It will take up not only the whole characteristic experience which we recognise already as constituting the spiritual life but also all which we now exclude from that category but which is capable of divinisation, not excluding whatever of the earth-nature and the earth-life can be transformed by the touch of the Supermind and taken upto the manifested life of the Spirit. For a divine life on earth need not be a thing apart and exclusive having nothing to do with the common earthly existence: it will take up human being and human life, transform what can be transformed, spiritualise whatever can be spiritualised, cast its influence on the rest and effectuate either a radical or an uplifting change, bring about a deeper communion between the universal and the individual, invade the ideal with the spiritual truth of which it is a luminous shadow and help to uplift into or towards a greater and higher existence. Mind it will uplift towards a diviner light of thought and will, life towards deeper and truer emotion and action, towards a larger power of itself, towards high aims and motives. Whatever cannot yet be raised into its own full truth of being, it will bring nearer to that fullness; whatever is not ready even for that change, will still see the possibility open to it whenever its still incomplete evolution has made it ready for self-fulfilment. Even the body, if it can bear the touch of Supermind, will become more aware of its own truth,—for there is a body-consciousness that has its own instinctive truth and power of right condition and action, even a kind of unexpressed occult knowledge in the constitution of its cells and tissues which may one day become conscious and contribute to the transformation of the physical being. An awakening must come in the earth-nature and in the earth-consciousness which will be, if not the actual beginning, at least the effective preparation and the first steps of its evolution towards a new and diviner world order.

'This would be the fulfilment of the divine life which the descent of Supermind and the working of the truth-consciousness taking hold of the whole nature of the living being would bring about in all who could open themselves to its power or influence.'

This is the evolutionary Future of man, the vision of which came to Sri Aurobindo, the vision as well of how man will realise this his divine destiny in a perfect order of life through the instrumentality of the Supramental Gnosis which is the highest creative power of God. Not the liberation of man from Nature but the liberation of man in Nature—this is the unique message of the Master. This means that we are not simply to break the bonds of Nature in order to pass into a blissful state of silence but to divinely transform our natural being in all its members and enjoy the utmost freedom within Nature herself.

Sri Aurobindo's ideal consists not in a mere self-realisation and in an escape into the transcendental bliss of a far-off Heaven but in the dynamic self-manifestation of the Spirit in the conditions provided by Mother Earth. The fulfilment of this ideal lies in the evolution of man into superman who will represent Man thoroughly transfigured in every fibre of his being through the transforming touch of the Supermind.

This is the ideal for which Sri Aurobindo stands, the ideal of a divine life for man. Sri Aurobindo shows the Light when there is darkness everywhere. He shows the Path when there is none before man. The long night of human travail is going to melt before the sun of a new truth that is rising to remake man into a spiritualised being and enable him to start on a new career on earth. That turn of his is as certain as was his evolution into the mental life out of the animal. Mind has reached the summit of its possibility. The time has now come for the Supermind to be active in earth-principle and evolve out of man a supermental being. The only condition for this change is readiness for it on the part of man. And he would grow in readiness, if he could aspire with a passionate intensity of his soul, and have an unshakable faith burning upwards to heaven, and could sincerely and in every part of his being surrender himself to the Divine Shakti who alone can liberate him from his present bondage of Ignorance into the luminosity of a higher consciousness and transform his present imperfect and egoistic nature into the perfect nature of the Divine.

How true was what Tagore said to Sri Aurobindo when he met him in 1928: 'You have the Word, and we are waiting to hear it from you; India will speak through your voice to the world, "Hearken unto me!"' Sri Aurobindo speaks to humanity the last creative word of India in the same way as her Vedic Rishis spoke the first. He envisages a new Man, a new Society, a new Civilisation; and his message is indeed the greatest that man has ever heard from the Masters of the race. The initiation in India of this inevitable change in man's life and society surely means a brighter future for this ancient country. India possesses the key to the progress of humanity. It is with that key of Yoga that Sri Aurobindo has unlocked the doors of hitherto unknown spiritual treasures and made them available to mankind.

The future of India as also of the world will depend on how she opens to these truths and manifests them in the life of the individual and the community. The great civilisation of India's past which still glows in the memory of the race was built on the eternal verities discovered by the Vedic Seers. Her future will see a greater civilisation, because it will be built on a greater Truth which has come to the vision of Sri Aurobindo. That will be the most glorious flowering of India's spiritual genius, the fulfilment of all her dreams and aspirations, her strivings and seekings. This new civilisation will be a spiritual creation. It will be the beginning of a world movement, and will not therefore be confined within the geographical borders of India. It will have inherent in it the power of extending itself to the farthest limits of the earth; and wherever people will be ready, a nucleus of it will form and enlarge and gradually merge in one whole. One of its outstanding features will be its freedom from the rule of the individual as well as the collective ego. The present civilisation, as already seen, is governed by this undivine principle and has therefore failed to find a permanent solution for the problems of mankind. It has grown too big for man's limited capacity to manage. In the spiritual civilisation of the future this problem will not arise, since its corporate life will be reconstituted and reorganised by selfless spiritualised individuals and not by the semi-animal human beings, the slaves of the ego. The new and vast means of life of the present human civilisation will be utilised for higher and greater ends by the spiritualised society.

It is not possible to define what exactly will be the essential elements of this new civilisation. They will be determined by the Divine Shakti who will create it. But there is no doubt that they will be spiritual in their intention. Its poetry will sing of the New Dawn. 'It will be the utterance of the deepest soul of the spiritual man and of the universal spirit in things, not only with another and a more complete vision, but in the very inmost language of the self-experience of the soul and the sight of the spiritual mind.' Its art will express the truth of the spirit, the beauty and the delight of existence. Its education will embrace all knowledge but its whole trend will be to unfold the self in infinite directions. Its science will seek to know not only the world and Nature in all her processes and use that knowledge for material ends but also the workings of the Divine in them and His purpose that lies behind every natural phenomenon. Its

sociology will regard every individual as a soul growing to perfection and will seek help and power from the perfected ones
for the common well-being of the society, providing innumerable
opportunities for self-development of all according to their individual needs. Its economics will give all men the joy of work
according to their nature and free leisure to grow inwards as well
as a simple but rich and beautiful life. These will be the primal
aims of the principal forms of culture in the initial stage of the
spiritual civilisation, as indicated by Sri Aurobindo. It may be
repeated that in a life in the Spirit, possibilities of self-expression will be infinite. The creative life in the new society will
therefore go on enlarging its domain to greater and greater aims
along with its progress in higher realisations.

The future of India will be this new civilisation, this new
society. The Shakti of India was long preparing for this consummation. All the past endeavours of the race were directed to
this end. It is this great future of India that will explain her
hidden meaning. Every nation has a soul, a Shakti. So also has
India; but what marks her out is that, unlike other nations, and
true to her spiritual genius, she is conscious of her soul and also
of what may be called her over-soul, the Mahashakti. Herein
lies the secret of India, of 'the Eternal and Timeless India,' the
Bharata-Shakti that is the dispenser of her destiny. 'India is an
idea, a Truth, a Spirit,' 'Mother India is the Mother of the
world'—these are not words of vain dreaming, but utterances
of the soul, glimpses of a great truth. The sense of oneness of
all existence in the Mahashakti and of that Shakti guiding all
existence is ingrained in the racial consciousness of India. 'The
Mahashakti is the universal way of being of the divine Conscious
Force. She is the Universal Mother who creates all these beings
and contains and enters, supports and conducts all these million
processes and forces.... She works out whatever is transmitted
by her transcendent consciousness from the Supreme and enters
into the worlds that she has made; her presence fills and supports
them with the divine spirit and the divine all-sustaining force
and delight without which they could not exist.' In her transcendent way of being, the Conscious Force is the original
supreme Shakti, who stands above the worlds and links the creation to the ever unmanifest mystery of the Supreme. Through
the Mahashakti she guides the terrestrial evolution in which her

ultimate object is to effect 'the flowering of the life and soul and mind into the infinity of the Spirit by bringing down into this world of ignorance the Supramental light, the Truth life and Truth creation.'

India is the only country in the world to whom spirituality is the very breath of life. She has therefore been chosen by the Divine Mother as her suitable instrument. Not only that, she is even her conscious formation. Many a time has the Mother revealed herself to the vision of India. She was adored as Aditi in the Vedas and worshipped as the Mahashakti in the Puranas and the Tantras; and through countless other emanations she has illumined the hearts of her devotees and fulfilled their religious aspirations. But her manifestation in India today is of a completely different character. The stupendous work that she will accomplish this time requires the pouring of greater forces into the earth-consciousness and an action in it more direct and forceful than before. She has therefore in her infinite grace descended into the mire of ignorance in order to remould the human personality into the divine Nature; for, that is the purpose of the individual way of being of the Conscious Force in which 'she embodies the power of the Transcendental and the Universal, the two vaster ways of her existence.'

It is indeed fortunate that this holy land should once again be the centre of a spiritual activity which is guided by divine personalities and the like of which has never before been witnessed in human history. In fact, it is the very summit of man's spiritual endeavour and is going to make a new history for him. A greater future for India is not its only aim; it seeks to help in the redemption of the whole human race and ensure a greater future for the whole world.

The inner meaning of the supreme Shakti's descent as an incarnation will be fully revealed to those who will feel within them a deep spiritual urge and take a plunge into the currents of a new life that are streaming into India today from their springs in a higher world brought down by the Mother out of compassion for her distressed children of the earth. And an awakening is already there. The glimmerings of the dawn at the advent of the Mother are already there on the horizon for those who have heard her call to see. In her sacred temple her children from far and near are beginning to gather to re-vision the Ancient

Mother in a new way of her being, to worship her by offering themselves and all that is theirs at her feet and be prepared for her work. 'The One whom we adore as the Mother is the divine Conscious Force that dominates all existence, one and yet so many-sided that to follow her movement is impossible even for the quickest mind and for the freest and most vast intelligence. The Mother is the consciousness and force of the Supreme and far above all she creates. But something of her ways can be seen and felt through her embodiments and the more seizable because more defined and limited temperament and action of the goddess forms in whom she consents to be manifest to her creatures.'[6]

The world today is under the shadow of a threatening catastrophe. Dark and undivine forces are at work. Driven by the pressure of the Light that has descended upon the earth they have surged up and, taking advantage of man's egoistic ambitions, are desperately trying to destroy all higher values and frustrate the purpose of the Divine. But as the victory of the Light is certain, so is their fall; and their present rise is like the last flare of the dying lamp. For, when God hits He hits straight and hits hard; and His triumph is resistless. Who then will present the divine front and baffle the asuras?[7] And who else can do that but India where the supreme Shakti has manifested herself and where the source of a tremendous spiritual power, unknown before, has been discovered with the means of putting it at the service of the world? It is the Divine Mother who by that power will usher in a higher order of life and build a greater India and a greater world, liberated once for all from the clutches of undivine and hostile forces.

A new age is coming upon mankind. And as always in history, the dawn will first be heralded in the East, and this time in its very heart, in India, who, reborn into her Shakti as the gracious and majestic Mother of the world and crowned with the sun-laurels of a unique spiritual conquest, will bring in order where there was chaos, light where there was darkness, love where there was hatred, truth where there was falsehood, beauty

---

6. The Mother's three ways of being, the Transcendental, the Universal, and the Individual, and her four Powers, Maheshwari, Mahakali, Mahalakshmi and Mahasaraswati, which are her four outstanding Personalities, as well as some of the basic principles of his Yoga, Sri Aurobindo has revealed in a little book called *The Mother*.
7. Demoniac forces.

where there was ugliness, peace where there was strife, joy where there was sorrow, freedom where there was bondage, immortality where there was death, and will that way create a new world, establish a new heaven on earth and lead mankind to its divine perfection. This is how India will fulfil her ancient vision and fulfil herself in the soul of humanity.

Says the Master: 'The sun of India's destiny would rise and fill all India with its light and overflow India and overflow Asia and overflow the world. Every hour, every moment could only bring them nearer to the brightness of the day that God has decreed.'

11

Towards a New World

I

AGAIN AND again in his history man has found himself forced into a condition of war by circumstances over which he could have no control. When he was not the aggressor he had at least to be the defender of his rights and of his *lebensraum* against the encroachment by a powerful invader. Anyway, violent hostilities have come to be a recurrent phase in the community-life of man. There can be no gainsaying the fact that war is an evil, but it has not been in the past an unmixed evil. If to the path of peace man owes much of his progress, not a little of it he owes to the path of war, notwithstanding all the miseries it has brought upon him. From a longer view of its ultimate effects, war would appear to have been a useful factor in the growth and expansion of human collectivities. But why war at all? 'Wherefore God hammers so fiercely at His world, tramples and kneads it like dough, casts it so often into the blood-bath and the red hell-heat of the furnace? Because humanity in the mass is still a hard, crude and vile ore which will not otherwise be smelted and shaped; as is his material, so is his method. Let it help to transmute itself into nobler and purer metal, His way with it will be gentler and sweeter, much loftier and fairer its uses.'

Indeed evolutionary Nature cannot stop in her upward movement; she must go on fulfilling herself in and through the cosmic process, regardless of the nature of the means she employs for the achievement of her supreme aim. Yet conflict is not always her favourite method. Human history is not throughout a black record of war and hostilities. It had its periods of light when the world was illumined by the advent of saints, seers and prophets who, by their life and teachings, proclaimed to man that in peace alone lies the true foundation of life and that it can thrive only on Truth, Love, Freedom and Unity which are the very nature of his soul 'in which Peace hath its eternal abode.' They emphasised in unmistakable terms that for his growth towards the Light, towards the higher destiny of which he is capable in his terrestrial evolution, man must live in his soul and realise these ideals in his life. This is Nature's way of balance and harmony.

It is not that these teachings were slow and uncertain in working their way into the heart and soul of man. Some of them have produced in his inner life more revolutionary changes then have actually been caused in his outer life by any violent conflict of the battlefield. But they are of a different character, and have always helped forward the spiritual progress of man by intensifying his Godward endeavours, his soul's aspiration for a greater fulfilment that would take him to the goal for which he, or rather Nature in him, is always striving.

There is no doubt that man, especially so far as his spiritual evolution is concerned, has been immensely enriched and exalted by the truths revealed to him by those true uplifters of the race. But the fact also cannot be overlooked that his progress and civilisation have been not inconsiderably accelerated by the clashes that have taken place in his collective life as a part of Nature's plan, made inevitable by the stress of those forces which dominate man when he gravitates exclusively towards vital satisfactions, when he panders to his individual and collective egos, and forgetting his high destiny, ceases to make any serious effort to actualise in his life the ideals held aloft by the great masters. This is a state in the affairs of man which tends to dry up all springs of real progress and threatens to imprison the soul, rendering all spiritual endeavour difficult. The death of many civilisations in the past has been more or less due to such retrograde movements of the collective being to which they belonged. War, therefore, is in the nature of a battery charge or a sharp galvanic shock.

History from its very dawn testifies that even a long and

unhampered period of peace has very rarely proved a guarantee of continued cultural advancement. Often enough it has been found to beget such ease-loving, and therefore, demoralising tendencies as benumb or destroy in the nation or the people all its grit, vigour and initiative, so much so that it soon shows signs of decadence precluding a new going-forth, a fresh adventure. What has happened in many instances to serve as a way out of such a moribund state is an incursion or onslaught from outside by barbarians or by a stronger power whose impact has infused a new energy into the people, or thrown up a far-sighted states-man or a heroic builder who by his power, sometimes derived from a higher source, has quickened into activity the whole people, holding before it a glowing ideal and inspiring it to live and die for that ideal, with the result that the people has been reborn into virility and greatness. But this again has led to an excessive self-glorification resulting in conflicts with others who happened to stand in the way of its political or regional expansion. Lust for world-empire has been no less a cause of such conflicts.

Thus it seems that war is a phenomenon which has been unavoidable in the order of things in which man has so far found himself. Human groups and collectivities have in most cases been formed and organised through clashes and collisions in the earlier stages of man's social development bringing home to him the necessity of strengthening his community-life, so that when necessary—and there has never been any dearth of pleas for that —it might extend the sphere of its existence or defend it against attacks from outside. But what is more is that, apart from the various constructive movements and institutions which conflicts between nations or peoples throughout history have been found to have brought into being, they have served a yet greater purpose—that of giving an amazing impetus to the creative faculties of the peoples involved, stirring them into a new life, into new ideas, into new channels of self-expression by which they produced what turned out to be so many steps forward in the general progress of mankind. The English historian utters a great truth when he says that civilisation advances by powder-carts. A yet profounder truth is suggested in the saying of Heraclitus, 'War is the father of all things; War is the king of all.'

There is another reason why Nature adopts this drastic method when she finds peaceful means not fully effective. It is that she is against the old order of things to continue for a long time and that she abhors unnecessary delay in the completion of her work in the terrestrial evolution. She is here the Mahakali, 'the Warrior of the Worlds who never shrinks from battle, who has in her an overwhelming intensity, a mighty passion of force to achieve, a divine violence rushing to shatter every limit and obstacle. All her divinity leaps out in a splendour of tempestuous action; she is there for swiftness, for the immediately effective process, the rapid and direct stroke, the frontal assault that carries everything before it.'

II

It seems that some kind of strife is at the root of everything by which Nature keeps up her progressive movement towards her evolutionary goal. The world itself, it may be said, is born out of the clash of material and other forces, and it proceeds by perpetual struggle against those that oppose its onward march, ever creating new things, ever destroying the old, and leading through whatever trouble and apparent confusion towards an approximate to some divine revelation. Whatever that may be, 'this is certain that there is not only no construction here without destruction, no harmony except by a poise of contending forces, won out of many actual and potential discords, but also no continued existence of life except by a constant self-feeling and devouring of other life. Our very bodily life is a constant dying and being reborn, the body itself a beleaguered city attacked by assailing, protected by defending forces whose business is to devour each other: and this is only a type of all our existence. The command seems to have gone out from the beginning, "Thou shalt not conquer except by battle with thy fellows and thy surroundings; thou shalt not even live except by battle and struggle and by absorbing into thyself other life. The first law of this world that I have made is creation and preservation by destruction."'

War and destruction, it would seem, are a universal principle of our life. They also appear to be unavoidable. Their necessity in the plan of Nature is indicated by the fact that, since evolution is a kind of rebirth of the old into newer and better forms, the old must go; and when, as often, it does not, but rather clings and persists, Nature is forced to use her deadly weapon of war to destroy the old and the effete, so that the new may come into being and grow in freshness and vigour. In this way the cycle goes on, war helping to keep up this continuous flux of things towards greater and unrealised possibilities.

In every field of human activity no movement has ever made any progress without a struggle, a battle between what exists and lives and what seeks to exist and live. 'It is impossible, at least as men and things are, to advance, to grow, to fulfil and still to observe really and utterly that principle of harmlessness which is yet placed before us as the highest and best law of conduct.'

The power of the soul can of course obviate any such external clashes. But it cannot be so easily evoked, and when its effective use is possible, it is found to be more terrible and destructive in its results than the sword and the cannon. The triumph through the soul-force of Vashishta over the military power of Vishwamitra is an appropriate instance. Anyway, infliction of violence on others cannot be stayed by an external method. To abstain from violence simply because it involves killing is to deny the very law by which humanity is at present guided. The debt of Rudra must be paid, the Lord of destruction must be appeased so long as the Asuric force in men and nations, the enemy of the Divine, is not completely annihilated. The promised Dharmarajya, the Kingdom of Truth and Righteousness, of which God will be the sole ruler, can be founded on earth only when it is freed from the influence of the demon.

But the deeper root of all conflicts in his inner and outer life, into which man finds himself dragged by an inscrutable fate, lies in the very nature of the terrestrial existence whose inward meaning remains hidden so long as an approach is not made to it in consonance with the secret aim of Nature in the evolutionary unfolding of the earth consciousness. That aim is the progressive emergence in man of the Light which is involved in the ignorance, inertia and division of the inconscient material substance. Nature chooses man as a special field for her work, because he has arrived at a stage in his evolution at which he must be made ready for the next higher one through the victory of the spirit in him over his lower nature, for which the conditions on the earth are becoming more and more favourable. There is in man an ascending urge which is rekindled by Nature into a flaming aspiration towards the Light whose instrument he is destined to be in order to take part in its manifestation on earth. Man, as he grows in his aspiration, grows also in his spirit and in his readiness for that consummation.

Man will have, therefore, to discover in himself his psychic being, that entity of his soul in his life, mind and body, which derives its evolutionary motivation from the supreme Shakti who, in one of her aspects, is the evolutionary Force herself. It is his psychic being that seeks through the cycle of births to fulfil itself in the process of evolution. Man must open to the supreme Shakti and be plastic enough for her Light to come and descend into him and purge him of all his turbidities and mould him into an expression of the Divine. But being at present conditioned by Ignorance and by all that it has erected in its dark region for the maintenance of its domination over him, man, when he hears the call of the Mother and takes the decision to respond to it, finds himself confronted by formidable odds presented by the evils which he has allowed to rule his present existence. These evils try with all their might to keep him under their subjection and frustrate his endeavour to turn towards the Light and to find there his perfection. Yet they have their value in the scheme of things, since they give man an opportunity to fight and thereby gather the experience and evolve the strength by which he can win his ultimate victory and possess its fruits and assimilate them, to the enrichment of his whole being.

Struggle, therefore, is a necessity and its importance in any spiritual effort, no less than in any secular, cannot be ignored. Though, in fact, it is not the human individual, but the divine Shakti herself who has always done and is always doing every bit of upward climbing for her creatures, yet nothing proves wholly effective in the process of evolution unless and until a conscious co-operation is given to her in the spirit of a complete surrender to her Will, so that she may perfect the instrument and divinise it. This is how Nature goes on fulfilling the purpose of the Mother both in the individual and in the collectivity. And when there is opposition from the earth due to its unwillingness to change, Nature renews her effort with greater vehemence, hastening thereby the revelation to man of the luminous world of the heavenly Light. Man grows nearer to this Light as his seeking after it becomes more and more intense. And the urge to renew this quest comes to him so often from the conflicts, whether inner or outer, which are like the friction in the Vedic image of two pieces of sacrificial wood, out of which leaps forth the flame, the flame of man's aspiration towards the Light. The flame represents the Divine's Will in man, the Will of the Mother-Power, to uplift him to his highest spiritual perfection. The Sempiternal Fire from above leans down to meet its own spark in man which then darts upward to find its fulfilment in its supreme Source. This is the Mother's way of reclaiming her lost children of the earth. This is how she prepares them for the peace, freedom and power of a divine existence.

Viewed from this standpoint, the phenomenon of war springs from no external cause, nor is it meant merely for the accomplishment of an external objective. The supreme Shakti wants it and will continue to want it so long as man does not obey her Law and accept her as the sole ruler of his life and become the willing field of her work in the terrestrial evolution. War has therefore a role, not insignificant, to play in the evolutionary plan of Nature.

Life has been characterised as a battle. And indeed a battle it is, as it was to the Vedic Seers who in a mystic image represented 'the life of man as a thing of mixed truth and falsehood, a movement from mortality to immortality, from mixed light and darkness to the splendour of a divine truth whose home is above in the Infinite but which can be built up here in man's soul and life; a battle between the children of Light and the sons of Night, a getting of treasure, of the wealth, the booty given by the gods to the human warrior, and a journey and a sacrifice.'

In every Godward endeavour, in every upward striving, man is assailed by hostile and undivine forces, the *panis,* the coverers of light; and if and when he gives in, as he often does, he loses the battle for the time being. If, instead, he wakes up from his sleep in Ignorance, becomes conscious of his high destiny, responds to the call of the indwelling Mother—the only source of his strength—and gives a straight fight to the enemy in the name of the Mother, then alone will victory be his and all the riches of a heavenly life.

War will for ever be banished from the earth not when man will realise not merely its futility, as he has already begun to do, and try by the power of his mind to make it impossible, but when he is able to conquer the foes—the Sons of Night—grown in him out of his baser instincts, which are responsible for all the conflicts in his community-life and have developed in his individual life all those obscurities that obstruct the birth in him of the consciousness of his infinite existence for which his present life in Ignorance, as also many before it, has been in travail.

Nevertheless, war is an evil, a monstrous evil, and it must go. It has existed long enough having fulfilled the purpose of Nature in the making of what man and his world are today. Time has now come for man to outgrow the stage when war was a contributory factor in his own growth as well as in the growth and expansion of his civilisation and collective being. But it will not stop only by our wishing it. The mechanical way in which it was sought to be ended has failed and will always fail because, as we have seen, war has its origin deep in the inner laws that guide the evolution of the cosmic system and direct the procession of humanity towards its divine goal.

The modern mind is so much obsessed with its achievements in the outer court of life, so much dominated by an exclusive inclination to be satisfied with mere externalities that it is incapable of looking beyond the surface-view of things, and is only too prone to rely on the values of science and reason, the values of all extrinsic attempts to solve a problem which is fundamentally intrinsic and intrinsically fundamental. Science has provided man with enormous powers which are proving far beyond his present capacity properly to manipulate. And if man is not able to attain sufficient psychological development, he will either be crushed out of existence by the deadly weapons he has himself forged with the help of his science or revert to a stage of barbarism.

There are thinkers who believe that science may make war of the present type with shot and shell and mine and battleship and atom bomb an impossibility and yet develop or leave in their place other and simpler means which may bring back the type of ancient warfare. But that is no solution of the problem.

The terrible horrors of war may lead human reason to make a long peace possible, based on common community interests and mutual well-being; but so long as the nature of man remains as it is, such peace will sag or break under the stress of human passions.

Biologically, war may cease to be a necessity. The fullness of life into which the modern world has developed may, if reason so wants, bring about an equilibrium in the material life of man; but that will not change his heart. So long, therefore, as war is not made psychologically impossible it will recur, and the utmost that the superficial efforts towards its elimination can do will be to shorten or lengthen the interval between its recurrences according to the nature of the effort and the acceptance of its results by humanity. The fact is that what is within must be out. The hostilities that break out in the open field of man's collective life will cease for ever only when man attains a decisive victory in his inner individual world over the forces of his lower nature. Disarmament will defeat its own purpose if man is not disarmed of his baser instincts. The explosion of a bomb does invariably have behind it the explosion of the passions that rage in man and burst forth when ignition is given to them by a conflict of ideals or clash of interests in the external sphere of human activity.

The pity of it is that every consideration of the problem has ignored the one thing that matters, the remoulding of the human nature. The first World War stimulated the mind of man to think out the problem, but not a single plan for the reconstruction of the world from which, it was hoped, war would be tabooed, pointed out, far less emphasised, that the root of the evil lay deep in the very nature of man. It is exceedingly unfortunate that every scheme or plan so far put forward for bringing about a new order after the cessation of the Second World War should consider only the political and economic aspects of the problem and never the spiritual aspect of it, thereby repeating the same mistake as before. Nay, it is no longer a mistake. It will prove to be a colossal blunder since the future of humanity depends so much on how the problem is tackled, and how real and lasting is the solution arrived at. And why only the problem of reconstruction? All major problems, those of freedom and unity in particular, man has not as yet been able successfully to handle.

But what is deplorable is not so much his failure to find out a solution—because that is difficult, if not impossible, with even the highest of his mental powers that he can possibly possess, —as his incapacity to trace it to its proper origin. The march forward is certainly there in everything that man has so far achieved by the power of his mind. But our estimate of it must be revised in the light of what it has resulted in. No wonder that the brutal exhibition of savage instincts that we are witnessing before our eyes today should make us question the much-vaunted superiority of the modern civilisation whose sponsors are themselves bewildered by the destruction that is taking place and that is threatened, of many of the higher values which have so long sustained man's urge towards perfection. The root of the whole trouble is the unregenerate nature of man and the problem of problems is how to reform it.

III

In the midst of the thick gloom that envelops the world today the gleams of a coming dawn are beginning to be visible. The higher mind of humanity, represented by a very few individuals, is opening to the truth that man as he is now is unequal to the task of saving himself from the disasters that are growing every day; he must therefore change in his consciousness to be able to get at the true truth of things and to rebuild on it his life and society.

This touches only the fringe of the solution. The greater truth has yet to come, or rather, is in the offing and has yet to enter the consciousness of humanity, at least, of its thinkers who are open to new truths. Nevertheless, the idea that a change must come in the outlook of man so that a better order of things may emerge, as well as the fact that man is feeling the shock of war to be too severe and is trying by all means to remove it from the face of the earth are evidences of the possibility that the days of war are numbered and that a new turning-point in the history of man is very likely to be reached indicating a greater future for him. But the difficulties in the way appear to be formidable. How can man by himself change into a higher consciousness with his present nature remaining imperfect? And how can he perfect his nature if he cannot liberate himself from his bondage to Ignorance, if he cannot emancipate his spirit from its sordid identification with life, mind and body? The answer to these questions must come from within, and it will depend largely on the readiness of man to hear the call of the Divine and seek the guidance of the supreme Shakti.

IV

Exclusive pursuit of life impulses and feverish desire for their satisfactions, and an unexampled mastery in the world of matter have on the one hand given man enormous powers by which he has erected the vast structure of his civilisation, while on the other hand, the same powers have enslaved him to the Asuric forces which are always on the alert to pander to his egoistic impulses that exhibit themselves in the glorification of man above everything else, above even his own spirit whose call he has heard in rare moments but has never had the strength to respond to, lest he should lose his credit as the creator of his world of dazzling wonders which proclaim his unique victories and lure him into the conviction that it is he and none else who is its sole builder. Thus is man tempted away from God and is encouraged to worship the Titan whose hold on him increases in proportion as he receives his help and allows himself to be ruled by him. Not only life, but mind also has in the same way grown into an undivine power. So also has matter to a still greater extent. And all of them are being used by the dark Forces to strengthen their domination over humanity. Man duped by the glitter of the material possessions that he has acquired with the help of these demoniac powers, has readily played into their hands and as their instrument, gives them his co-operation so that more treasures may come to him and more pleasures, little knowing that along with them will inevitably come a grinding, a corroding slavery and a palsied poverty of the soul.

This is indeed a very dismal scene in the human drama. The sorrows of man seem to be at their worst in spite of his being the possessor of almost every kind of material prosperity. But he cannot remain for ever a victim of these Forces. There is a higher destiny for him, a greater perfection, and to realise that is the true purpose of his life. A child of Light, he has the power inherent in him, the power of the Shakti, by which to baffle and beat the sons of Night, and be the victor. But he cannot by his own effort evoke that power in him. He must aspire for the Grace of the Divine Mother who alone can do that for him and lead him to his evolutionary destiny. Whatever the impediments, they have to be overcome, since it is the law of Nature that evolution must proceed, realising itself progressively till its ultimate goal is reached. It cannot stop short, neither can it take a wrong course.

The signs are clear that in his evolution man has arrived at a stage where he seems to have attained the highest point of his mental possibility. And the vast successes that he has achieved by his mental and vital powers are beginning to prove too heavy for him, and their dead weight is about to kill his soul. Man has also started to feel, however vaguely, that an exclusive reliance on the creations of his ego-driven mind has, instead of helping him to solve his problems, rendered them more difficult. This feeling will possibly bring about his disillusionment and there will grow in him a seeking after the true truth of his life and the deeper intention of Nature in it.

V

The time is propitious today; and the conditions in life and Nature are not only favourable to, but are pressing for, the emergence in the vision of man of that great truth and also of the 'sunlit Path' that will lead him to its realisation. This will be the dawn of a new life for man whose birth is signalised by the world-wide travail through which humanity is at present passing. Forces of darkness and evil are rampant everywhere. Falsehood reigns supreme. Death is abroad. All these show a condition of things which, according to the assertion of mystics and prophets, must precede the Manifestation and is even a sign of its approach. Says the Master: 'The end of a stage of evolution is usually marked by a powerful recrudescence of all that has to go out of the evolution.'

Wherein then is the secret? Where is the Light? The secret has begun to be revealed to those who have heard the Call. The Light has been seen. The strength has come. The darkness will pass away, and the Sun of Truth will burst into the magnificence of a heavenly glory on earth. A higher than mental life is the promise for man; and that is the only way out of the evils which afflict humanity.

A new Light from above is descending upon the earth by which will be effected the desired change in the nature of man as also in his consciousness, a change that will take place as the next inevitable stage in the evolutionary process of Nature. It is the pressure of this Light that has driven the forces of evil to invade the earth in all their riotous orgies. But their fall is certain, because the Light is decreed to come down and manifest on the earth, lifting man beyond himself into a higher order of being. Man must, therefore, be ready for this transformation. He must turn inwards, live within and live in his spirit. He must aspire for the Grace of the Mother, the Divine Shakti, who herself guides and directs the evolutionary march of man and who only, and not any human *tapasya,* can liberate him from the clutches of the Asuric powers and, by releasing the Godlike elements in him so long veiled by Ignorance, mould him into an expression of the Divine.

Seers of the Supreme Truth, bringers of the Light, they are also the leaders of the Way who unfold before man the splendours of a new and higher life into which he is going to be born. Bearers of a world's burden, its greatest saviours, they intensify the ascending urge in man, and in their divine way are preparing him, so that he may recognise and receive the Light and be illumined and exalted into the higher consciousness in which he will find the perfection of his whole being.

That 'divine event' is going to happen in the life of man; the end of his human journey is in sight. For, has not the Light descended upon earth? And have not the liberators come? and their Call? and the Assurance?

> 'A new light shall break upon the earth,
> A new world shall be born,
> And the things that were promised shall be fulfilled.'

The Mother recorded the above in her Prayers and Meditations on 25 September 1914, six months after her first meeting with Sri Aurobindo.

On 24 April 1956 the Mother made the historic declaration:

'The manifestation of the Supramental upon earth is no more a promise but a living fact, a reality.

'It is at work here, and one day will come when the most blind, the most unconscious, even the most unwilling shall be obliged to recognise it.'

On the same occasion the Mother declared:

> 'A new light breaks upon the Earth,
> A new World is born,
> The things that promised are fulfilled.'

Man now has the happiest assurance in the Mother's own words:

'A constant action is going on in the world. It is spreading and it is effective everywhere. Everywhere it gives new pushes, new turns, new ideas, new will-formations.' 'Through the apparent chaos of today a new and better order is being formed, but to see one must have faith in the Divine Grace.'

The broadening of outlook and co-operative effort in matters of human concern beyond national limits, to the international, even to the universal, is a promising sign. If the world today is heaving to higher ideas and awakening to newer truths, hitherto considered strange or fantastic, one can well imagine how the fuller picture will emerge with the growing action of the Supermind, now always at work.

Says the Mother: 'Once more we are at this moment at a decisive turn in the history of the earth.... All the aspects of man's progress unite with yet many others to form a more total and complete progress, a more perfect understanding of life, a more integral approach to the Divine. Even this unification is not sufficient. One must have faith, a vision of the future, of the goal towards which humanity is moving, of the future realisation of the world, the last spiritual revolution of which Sri Aurobindo speaks, that which will open the new age, that is to say, the Supramental revolution.... That will not be a new religion which will not only be useless but harmful. A new life has to be created, a new consciousness has to be expressed, something which is beyond intellectual limitations and mental formulas. It is a living truth that has to manifest.

'But all that is of the future, a future that has begun but will take some time before realising itself integrally. In the meanwhile, we are in a very special situation, extremely special which has had no precedent. We are attending on the birth of a new world, altogether young, altogether weak—weak not in its essence, but in its external manifestation—not yet recognised, not yet felt, denied by most; but it is there, it is there endeavouring to grow and quite sure of the result. Yet, the road to reach there is a new road, that has never before been traced; none went by that way, none did that. It is a beginning, a universal beginning.... It is no longer a hope, it has become a certainty.'

What place has India in the new Divine set-up? Why has the Universal Mother, the Mother of all, and of all the worlds, why has Sri Aurobindo with his infinite expanse of divine wisdom, chosen to fix upon India as the centre of their work? Let every Indian, every man in general, infer the answer from what they have said of India:

Says the Mother: 'In the whole creation the earth has a place of distinction, because, unlike any other planet, it is evolutionary with a psychic entity at its centre. In it, India, in particular, is a divinely-chosen country.' And further, 'The future of India is very clear. India is the Guru of the world. The future structure of the world depends on India. India is a living soul. She incarnates the spiritual knowledge in the world.... India is very conscious of her mission in the world. She is waiting for the exterior means of manifestation.... India must maintain the spiritual leadership of the world.'

We have quoted Sri Aurobindo extensively in the previous chapter on how India's great past points to her greater future. Here are a few more words from the Master: 'India is the *Guru* of the nations, the physician of the human soul in its profounder maladies; she is destined once more to new-mould the life of the world and restore the peace of the human spirit.'

Therefore, with India as the centre, the Mother has been carrying on her divine work of world-transformation.

As seen in the previous chapter and in Chapter Eight, seeking souls and forward-looking minds in many parts of the world are opening to the Truth and Light of Sri Aurobindo and the

Mother whose dynamic working on earth prepares man for the
fulfilment in him of the purpose of evolutionary Nature. The
Divine Grace is: 'A New World is born.'

REFERENCES

Sri Aurobindo's *Essays on the Gita, The Life Divine, The Mother,
Thoughts and Glimpses, War and Self-Determination, On the Veda, Bande
Mataram* (Weekly). The quotations are from the above books. The
quotations from the Mother are from her *Prayers and Meditations* and
from the *Bulletin of Sri Aurobindo International Centre of Education.*

12

The Vision in History

THE DISCOVERY of his past opened before man a new world of knowledge. It made him conscious of his own heritage and inspired him to the study of his early story. Soon, however, he wanted to know how the story developed, how it attained its coherence and ensemble. The result of it was the idea of the 'History of History,' the concept of a method and manner in the historical recordation of the course of human affairs. The idea varied according to the approaches made to the subject by different minds. But whatever the nature of this divergence, the evidence of archaeology and other kindred sources has proved beyond doubt that culture in the past was always, as it is today, an all-embracing development, an integral flowering of the many-sided genius of man. And no one form of it—however important to his progress— can fulfil its purpose if it is not given scope enough to fructify along with the other forms, all of which are the component parts of an organic whole.

Indeed, culture can achieve its true aim only when it conduces to the growth of man into his higher possibilities, when all his expressions converge towards a greater than his present life in the Ignorance. Man's first impulse to create and the dawning sense in him of his own power initiated and impelled that ceaseless striving through which he has been gaining new masteries and proceeding, now with sure, now with faltering steps, towards the distant divine goal of his earthly existence. History begins with a portrayal of his aeonic pligrimage and goes on increasing in content as man advances, enlarging the sphere of his creative activity. Thus with the progress of man the idea of history also becomes wider and more defined: history however will achieve its crowning success when it is able to interpret this march of man in the light of its inner significance.

Man by his mind builds stories about his adventure on earth, vaguely suggesting various kinds of future for himself; but none of them is complete, inasmuch as they fail to take into account the real intention in those adventures. Besides, being limited within its own range, mind cannot rise into the world of perfect knowledge; neither can it have a total view of things. And it is beyond its power to have a clear idea of the ultimate destiny of man. The key has, therefore, to be sought in the integral vision of the Truth, glimpsed by the early mystics but now fully seen and possessed by the Master-Seer of the race. It is the vision of the one infinite Reality unfolding itself in the drama of cosmic evolution and seeking to manifest in man the delight, harmony and perfection of its own transcendence. To depict the story of how evolutionary Nature endeavours through the ages to prepare man for that glorious consummation will indeed be the truest function of history.

What follows is an attempt to point out the vast scope history offers for a comprehensive envisaging of its aims and objects, and to study through it the growth of an integralising historical idealism, and, lastly, to show from that standpoint how man as a race marches on in his journey towards the fulfilment of that vision. It is not possible within the compass of a single chapter to give even an outline of a large subject such as this. The present therefore can only be a brief introduction.

I

A biography usually describes the life of a great man. It shows how he lived and worked for a noble cause. It is thus a record of those activities of his for which he is loved and remembered. History may be called a kind of biography, not, however, of a particular man but of people or of the whole of mankind. All the different stages in the life of a heroic soul—his childhood, youth, manhood and maturity—come to be told by one who portrays them in their proper perspective. But there comes a time in that life when the curtain is rung down on its play on earth, the person having made his exit from it leaving behind him the legacy of the golden deeds he performed to the everlasting benefit of the race, especially of the people among whom he was born. It is, then, his biography that helps to perpetuate his memory. Likewise, there are many great peoples in history, such as the Egyptians, the Sumerians, the Babylonians, the Assyrians, and later, the Greeks and the Romans, who did live a long and fruitful life during which they built up the splendid structures of their civilisation which are regarded as definite landmarks in the cultural progress of mankind. But nothing of their achievements remains today except the relics and antiquities most of which lie buried under the earth. They have departed from the stage never to appear on it again. It is the voice of their history—the old monuments articulating it—that defies time and proclaims what they did to weave the many-coloured texture of their creative life.

But it is not that the same thing has happened to all the civilised peoples of the ancient world, that after they had lived their span of life they were overtaken by decadence and death. There are peoples however who were contemporaries of those oldest ones, and yet keep burning to this day the lamp of their ancient culture, notwithstanding the vicissitudes they have passed through in the long course of their history. History differs from biography in the sense that the latter ends with the life of one man, whereas the former does not or need not do so, because it is concerned not with the life and work of a particular individual but with the aspirations and struggles, the failures and victories of the never-ending stream of humanity. There are peoples—the Hindus, for instance—who now live the life they lived at the very dawn of civilisation. Indeed, China and India continue in history as the inheritors of a magnificent past whose spirit still lives in their creative strivings which right down the ages have never known a full stop: that is to say, both of them yet retain their old strength and energy and are able to make ever-new endeavours with results not short of the marvels of their ancient heritage. Nevertheless, the histories of all the peoples of the world, dead or living have their place in the larger conception

of history, being one unbroken record of the whole life of
humanity and of the manifold deploying of its powers in every
sphere of its activity from the very dawn of its civilised existence
on earth. It is World-History which is 'One' in its actual and
ultimate values.

What then are the elements that make up history or form its
contents? and how are they woven together?

A biography, as already seen, helps us to learn about the
various ways in which a heroic soul expresses himself. But,
generally speaking, all these expressions are more or less tuned
to one particular theme or subject. It is rarely that a genius proves
many-sided in the higher sense of the term. A Leonardo da Vinci
is certainly an exception in the annals of human greatness; for,
as a matter of fact, every great man has but one song to sing,
one message to deliver. And everything else that he does may have
in it something remarkable and worthy of him, but it is not that
for which he is immortalised in history. Rabindranath Tagore,
whatever his contribution towards the rural and educational
uplift of his country, will be remembered by posterity more as a
master-poet and singer than as a champion of joy and freedom
in education or a pioneer in the field of rural reconstruction.

Obviously enough, history cannot limit itself to a particular
subject. It has to speak about the creative expressions, not of one
man, but of a whole people consisting of individuals of various
natures, such as saints and sages, prophets and philosophers, poets
and mystics, artists and scientists, rulers and statesmen, and
so many other kinds of men, great and small, all of whom play
their respective parts in the common corporate life of the people.
It may be noted that history cannot ignore the work of ordinary
men whose silent services keep life going and lend colour to it.
To be a complete picture of every phase of man's activity history
must include the man who tills the soil, the one who builds the
house, the one who by his labour makes the earth fit for man
to live in happily. But all these find their place in history not
as they merely are but by virtue of the contribution they make to
the general progress of mankind. And it is for history to show
how nations or peoples advance the cause of that progress, each
following the law of its own being, its own line of self-development.

History therefore is a symphony of many tunes, an orchestra, as it were of many notes. It brings to light every effort of man to better and elevate himself both in his individual and collective life through the cultivation of the faculties that lie dormant in him. The progress of man means the progress of his culture, and man grows in culture in proportion as his upward endeavours become fruitful. It is not that these efforts of man have always been crowned with success. Man has had to face failures; the obstacles in the way have many a time proved too difficult for him to overcome; and it is not unoften that he has himself forsaken the ideal and strayed into devious ways, lured by the desire to satisfy the lower aims of life. History will belie its function if it fails to take cognizance of all these aberrations of man. It must at the same time point out that what was regarded as impossible in the past has already become a fact of present achievement, and that the ideals of today are likely to be the realities of tomorrow.

History's is thus a comprehensive picture, an all-embracing panorama, epitomising on its canvas the vast and variegated drama of man. It tells us how in the past he built his society, how he responded to the call of the Spirit, how he worshipped his God, how he lived his life as a householder, how he evolved his culture, what dreams he dreamt, what visions he saw. It has therefore to speak of the spiritual seekings of man, of his religious impulses and his endeavours to cast them into forms, of the high ideals he expressed, of the arts and sciences he developed. It is thus a record of the spiritual, religious and aesthetic life of a people as well as of its literary, scientific and political life. The religion and spirituality of a people give intimations of its soul. Its arts are the flowering of its inner aesthetics, an expression of its cult of the Beautiful. Its science and literature indicate the growth of its mental life. And its political strivings exhibit the evolutionary stages through which its vital physical being passes, acquiring more and more competence to organise and strengthen its corporate living, the chrysalis of the future unity of the race. History in this sense is a study of all the various creative activities of man. But in order that it may be a living organic whole it must point to the common ultimate goal towards which all these activities are leading and probing beyond its normal depths, discover those deeper springs in man from where comes to him the impulsion to undertake his adventures in the world of 'sweetness and light' in which lies the seed of his ultimate perfection.

II

It is unfortunate that history today should in most cases be so apathetic to its own high ideal and unable to discharge fully its noble mission. Of the many external forms in which the collective being of man manifests itself, that of politics has become most powerful and governs almost every field of human activity. And the integrity of history is one of those things which are being sacrificed at its altar. The idea that a nation's well-being depends solely on its political capacity and that history has very little to do with anything which has no bearing on the political affairs of a people is largely responsible for the narrow outlook that regards history as nothing more than a mere narrative of political happenings, of the rise and fall of kings and empires. Freeman's view that 'history is past politics and politics is present history' reflects almost correctly the present-day trend of historical thinking. Politics in the past did help to create conditions favourable to the growth of culture. But the democratic institutions of ancient India, in spite of the fact that they are the prototype out of which similar institutions in various parts of the world have evolved, cannot certainly be called the most remarkable feature of her true greatness. It is her unparalleled spiritual genius that marks her out as the one country in the world where every expression of life is inspired and motivated by the godward tendency of her soul.

Of what avail is history to India if it has in it no place for that which constitutes her real glory? The Mauryas of old did indeed build up the largest empire in their contemporary world and the system of polity they followed was an equally striking example of their political wisdom, yet it is not so much for these as for the unique religious idealism of one of their emperors that they deserve the particular attention of the historian. The triumph of Confucian thought over the imperial might of the Chinese emperors is one of those significant events which give character to the whole history of China in which the masterly works of her artists, poets and philosophers have always found greater prominence than the services of her jurists, rulers and statesmen, eminent and constructive though they were. The history of ancient Greece will not only be incomplete but also a far from correct presentation of her great achievements if it speaks only of her democracy and nothing of the splendour that she was in art, literature and philosophy. And even today a modernist would resent a picture of the corporate life of his time if it describes only the brilliant successes and equally brilliant or dismal failures of the political experiments of today and makes no mention of its contribution to the world of culture.

In the early days of India and China, the ideology of politics was based on sound ethical principles. It did not show any such aggressive tendency as is found in many political organisations of the modern age. In India a *chakravarti-raja* would mean the lord paramount of a vast empire who must, as the term connotes, successfully discharge his twofold function of the king and the preserver of the Dharma. The king had moreover to declare himself as the servant of the people. It was his chief duty—dereliction of which might bring about his dethronement—to uphold the ideals of the race and promote them by providing the necessary opportunities, so that his people might strive to live up to them both in their individual and collective life. In their idea of the State the ancient Indians conceived a perfect social order in which perfected individuals would live in freedom and peace, and in complete harmony with the soul of the collectivity. The early monarchs of China were called 'statesmen-saints' who would never do anything without prayers invoking the aid of the gods. During later ages the 'scholar-officials' were the real rulers of the country whose sole care was to put into practice the democratic and ethical ideals set forth in the teachings of the great sage Confucius. Since the very dawn of their civilisation, the Chinese people have never considered national government the highest form of social organisation. Their political thinking has always been in terms of all mankind, with world-peace as the final goal, and family and nation as transitional stages in the perfecting of the World-Order. Besides, 'the Chinese civilisation is most decidedly organised for peace....: And China is the one country in the world where it is considered disgraceful to be a soldier.'[1] Plato propounded the ideas of 'philosopher-king' and 'virtue-state,' and, according to Aristotle, a king is a king only when he furthers 'the highest good' of his subjects. Thus the world, in three of its greatest culture-centres, China, India and Greece, passed through a common cycle or age of Dharma when the vision of its external form came to their thinkers mainly as a State founded on righteousness, the ideal rule of living. There is no evidence however to show how far the Greeks were able to give any practical shape to the Platonic or Aristotelian ideals, not to speak of later Europe which seemed to have broken away from Hellenic traditions; but history is certain that the Indians and the Chinese had been ever alive to what in the past their seers and law-makers had laid down, and that they tried to follow them in all their social and political endeavours.

If the history of a people should be concerned with nothing but its political activities then the history of many countries, especially of China and India, will have very little to say about their marvellous creations in the domain of culture, creations which have immensely enriched the civilisation of mankind. History books on these two countries, written from the political standpoint, do them a great injustice by presenting only one aspect of their creative life in which they fared perhaps not as remarkably as in those higher enterprises which, according to them, are the true aim of culture. And this narrow, truncated presentation proves all the more effectively misleading by the very reason of its being based upon a one-sided truth. It cannot therefore be accepted as a correct and complete study of the historical evolution of these two oldest peoples of the world. Politics alone cannot be the sole content of history, at any rate, of the history of China and India. In other countries too, as in these, it has been almost always only one of their many activities. How can history, pledged to that one phase of a nation's life, be called an authentic record of all the multiple expressions of its soul, far less a revealer of the secret intention of Nature in it?

The connotation of the term politics cannot by any stretch of ingenuity be so widened as to include the various efforts that

---

1. H. A. Davies, *An Outline History of the World*, p. 77.

a people makes to accelerate its national progress. Man is of course not a 'political being' only. And an 'Ideal State' is neither possible in the existing order of things, nor can it be a solution for all the problems with which he is confronted in his collective life. Rather, it is his politics which, more than anything else, is the cause of the evils that afflict him today. It is true that politics has developed into a great force in the community-life of man and that without it the latter would not have attained its present organised form, but it is also true that the political ambitions of powerful nations, accentuated by exclusive materialistic tendencies, have blinded them to the higher values of life, leading them to aggrandise their collective ego, with the result that in his international life man has arrived at a stage—a critical stage, no doubt—in which he finds himself thrown into a vortex of continuous conflicts and clashes, deliverance from which or from the like of which is becoming more and more impossible for him to think of. What part history is playing to help in inciting nations to these disasters will be for the future historian properly to judge.

But the most deplorable fact is that history has lent its pages to the propagation of things which are anything but wholly true. Facts freely distorted, falsehoods wantonly fabricated, fill and desecrate the pages of history, so that they might subserve the so-called political purposes which disguise the selfish attempts of human groups to satisfy the egoistic demands of their body-politic. History must be rescued from its abject slavery to such low aims. It must cease to be guided by any parochial leaning, any ulterior motive, but stand out as the sovereign voice of truth, and nothing but the truth, about the whole life of man, about his ideals and aspirations and the various ways in which he tried to fulfil them.

Indeed, an integral outlook in history is impossible to develop so long as it does not present a complete picture of all the activities of man, so long as its writing is dominated by considerations other than purely historical. The historian has therefore to be above all petty passions and prejudices. He must discriminate between the true and the false, the genuine and the spurious, and accept nothing that does not stand the test of impartial scrutiny. His is the sacred task, he must never forget, of telling the whole story of man in its true perspective, the story of his historical evolution, of the forces and personalities that have helped to guide it through the ages.

III

Generally, the cultural achievements of man come into the pageant of history through the epochs and ages which are often associated with those great souls who compel universal homage not only by the dynamic excellence of their life and teachings but also by the service they render towards the intrinsic uplift of humanity. It is they who are the true creators of all that is of permanent value in the cultural expressions of the race. It is they who hold up the ideal and inspire man to make the endeavour. Was it not the Rishis of ancient India who evolved the basic principles of Indian civilisation? and are they not still cherished by the people with deep veneration? Does not Shri Krishna with his message figure more than anything else in the racial consciousness of India? The Buddha came and won his incomparable victory for all time. So did Christ. So did Ashoka, the emperor whose unexampled concern for the moral welfare of mankind made him immortal in history. To the thinkers of ancient Greece, Europe owes all the great beginnings of her philosophy and idealism. The teachings of Lao-tze and Confucius as well as those of the Buddha are the very bed-rock of Chinese culture. All these and many others—lesser luminaries—are the torch-bearers of truth and light, the harbingers of new dawns in the life of humanity. Little doubt that their life and work should form part of the history of the world, particularly of the countries hallowed by their advent. It is these leaders and pioneers of the race who make up the biographical element in history.

But again, history is not these heroic souls only. There is no gainsaying the fact that to them will always go the glory of being the discoverers of the goal, the explorers of the path which they had often to hew out of enormous rocks of resistance. But when humanity accepts the goal and follows the path, its leaders then become one with it and form the vanguard of its victorious march. History should be pre-eminently concerned with this march of man through the ages and deal with other things as subsidiary to it. These great souls come into its pages not so much for what they are by themselves as for what they do to further the cause of human progress. Every great epoch in a country's history represents the cultural advancement made during it by that country through the efforts to which it is inspired by the teachings of the master-spirits born in it. It is generally the development of the mind, its mastery of powers by which to fulfil its higher possibilities that is indicated in the results of these endeavours. History here is the mirror that reflects the various stages of this progress of man from age to age. But to be true to its aim, it must also be a deep and penetrating study of every such activity as enlarges the domain of man's mind, helping him thereby to grow in readiness for the greater illumination that is to come to him in the future as the crowning event of his sojourn on earth.

To the Chinese of old, history was like an ending scroll of pictures depicting the procession of humanity, and the scroll unrolls itself as man marches on, let us add, towards the destiny assigned to him by God. Ibn-i-Khaldun, the eminent Muslim thinker of the fourteenth century, discerned in historical ideology a world-view, an integral standpoint from which, he said, the progress of man as a whole should be assessed. But it was Voltaire, Condorcet and the French Encyclopaedists of the eighteenth century who gave a more definite form to this idea. Condorcet declared that man individually, and society as a whole, are capable of 'infinite improvement,' and that history must show in bold relief the various stages of man's growth towards that 'destination.' The French group of 'philosophers' believed that absolute freedom in every sphere of life is indispensable for man to be able to achieve that progress. G. V. Vico sees the history of all nations 'running', that is, evolving according to the Ideal Eternal History of the Spirit. Emerson, the transcendentalist, saw in history the works of the one mind common to all individual men. Frederick Morrison called history an exponent of human affairs unfolding the oneness of mankind that perennially fulfils itself in time through every expression of its creative life. Gooch says that the stuff of history is the whole field of human experience. Its subject is the making of civilisation, the ascent of man. To Croce freedom is the keynote of man's historical evolution. History is nothing if not a record of man's struggle for liberation from the evils that stand in the way of his progress. There are historical writers who think that the process through which human collectivities have evolved into their present forms tends to culminate in a real and lasting solidarity of the whole of mankind. A more recent utterance is that of Nicolas Berdyaev who posits the idea of universal history as being the description of man's approach to his destiny through the interaction of Nature and the spirit in him. The emancipation of the spirit is therefore a necessity for man to achieve, the aim of his terrestrial existence.

An ancient Indian definition regards history as a record of those endeavours of man through which he seeks to satisfy 'the four legitimate motives of life—his vital interests and needs, his desires, his ethical and religious aspiration, his ultimate spiritual aim and destiny, in other words, the claims of his vital, physical and emotional being, the claims of his ethical and religious being governed by a knowledge of the law of God and Nature and man, and the claims of his spiritual longing for the Beyond for which he seeks satisfaction by an ultimate release from an ignorant mundane existence.'[2] The psychologists and social thinkers of ancient India showed their deep insight into human nature when they discovered these fundamental motives of life and pointed out the need for man to fulfil them so that he might grow in readiness for greater perfectibilities. The ultimate end however has always been an ascent and liberation into higher and higher states in the world of the Spirit, which have to be approached through a disciplined fruition of the essential inclinations of man, that is to say, of his nature—a fruition held as *sine qua non* for his all-round development. For history to study and analyse how man exerts himself to that end in the course of his earthly career would mean its being a synthetic delineation of all the stages of his labour and journey towards the goal in different periods and in different countries.

What exactly is the meaning of this march of man? What is its destination? and how is history to accomplish its purpose as an interpreter of this world-movement of humanity? History so far cannot be said to have tried in all seriousness to give any definite answer to these questions that arise in the minds of those who see in the annals of man the working out of a 'predetermined

---

2. *The Life Divine,* Vol. ii, p. 583.

Plan,' the study of which, they think, might lead man to an understanding of his future possibilities whose seeds lie embedded in all that he now is and in all that he does. The condition in the world today makes the demand for an answer all the more insistent. Indeed the time has now come for history to present a revealing picture of the meaning and purpose of man's adventure on earth. Most of the appraisements, cited above, do indeed point, however vaguely, to an integral vision in history, but they are not at all clear as to how to actualise it. They state the ideal, at least many important aspects of it, but they seem to be far from the way to realise it.

That a march forward is always inherent in everything man has done and is even now doing does no doubt suggest some kind of progress, a going forth, a venturing on from that which is known towards that which is in the womb of the future. An idea of change from one condition to a better one, a growth, mental, moral or spiritual, seems to be envisaged in almost all the above views on the march of man in history. But none of them throws any light on the process through which the change takes place, neither do they indicate the ultimate purpose of such progressive changes. The historical synthesis defined by India during her Age of Reason made a nearer approach to the ideal, but it also was unable to offer a satisfactory solution because it emphasised a withdrawal into the Spirit, the Beyond, as the end of all human endeavour: all the expressions of life were recognised in it but that they should be one in their intention to grow into a greater, a more harmonious fulfilment was not within its scope.

The many ways in which mankind, whether in groups or in totality, has taken part in that movement of change seem to be bewildering and make the principle of oneness in history somewhat difficult to discover. Indeed, a singleness of purpose is not so easy to trace in the various achievements of man. It is not only its many-sidedness but also the dissimilarity among the various forms of it that often hinders the correct preception of a common higher objective in all human strivings.

But a more fundamental reason is that the power of the mind by which we try to penetrate into the secret mystery of the world-drama is limited to a plane which is veiled by the power of Ignorance. Mind is thus unable to give us a deep, complete and integral view of things. Unless the Light from above breaks upon that plane and rends the veil and opens it to its native splendour of Knowledge from which it originated, mind remains confined to its own narrow groove, taking the parts for the whole, the fragments for the vast. And instead of tending towards a solution, the problem becomes more complicated.

This is indeed a crisis in the realm of historical thinking. The way out may be sought, as has always been done whenever mankind has been faced with a similar situation, in the teachings of the Pioneer-Souls of the race, who by rising into a higher consciousness have attained to the integral vision of the supreme truth of existence. An attempt is therefore made here to study the ideology of history from the standpoint of what Sri Aurobindo has laid down as the basic principle of an evolutionary manifestation on the earth. History here is a reflector of the dynamic process by which the divine plan fulfils itself in man through all the progressive stages of his life on earth.

IV

That history is a record of the progress man achieves through his multifarious activities, mainly those of his creative life, has been already discussed. But the function of history is not merely to make up and keep an inventory if those activities as they outwardly are. It must also discover in their development a principle of organic growth that evolves with the progress of man; and when history does that it becomes its true self. As dry bones do not make a human body, but flesh, muscle, blood and so many other things and, above all, vital energy are necessary to make the body complete and living, so also a mere conglomeration of facts and events does not build history; it is the way in which they are presented so as to bring out their hidden meaning, the intention of Nature in them, that gives history its integrality and its force of life. It has already been seen how the various forms of the culture of a race become the contents of its history, not as so many isolated units pieced together but as expressions of the creative soul of that race, through whose impact they coalesce into a historical wholeness mainly as its extrinsic phenomena.

This is how the objective integration in history has taken

shape, to which a definite impetus was given by the French Revolution that roused the nations of the world to a new sense of their rights and liberties and also of their past glories, providing a most favourable condition for their independent growth and evolution. Following the French Encyclopaedists, the nations started to prepare their histories in which a place was found for all the many ways through which they tried to express their souls. And these registers of national achievements became more and more enriched and accentuated as archaeology and other allied sciences began to bring to light hitherto unknown evidences of the nations' antiquity and ancient heritage, whenever they were available. But what is missed in these early efforts is a world-standpoint, a global outlook; and they betray a tendency to self-limitation in their scope and purpose, resulting in what are known as the so-called national histories of today. These regional records of human affairs have often been found to be stamped with a local colour which becomes deeper and louder as the particular human group inhabiting that region takes to a more and more egoistic and exclusive line of self-development. There is a centre in them and a force as well, but it is a force that is too concentric to allow anything within their orbit to widen and expand. All purely objective studies suffer from this defect, and history, whenever committed to this aim, finds it difficult, if not impossible, to transcend its limitation.

This 'realistic' trend in historical thinking took a better turn when the first rays of a new idealism began to be visible on the intellectual horizon of man. If the previous stage had been one of individualism in which the peoples of the world proclaimed their new-found nationhood as a criterion of their distinctive historicity, the one that followed may be characterised as a subjective stage in which the study of human affairs was in the main directed towards the discovery of those laws and forces that seem to guide and motivate the destiny of man as a whole. The world-history came into existence and with it the concept of 'One History.' It is a kind of historical romanticism, as it were, which based its rationale on the essential unity of the human race and on the idea that the highest aim of all social endeavours is to achieve that unity by which alone can permanent peace be made possible. This is certainly a great advance in the idealising of history; and it became more definite when the catastrophe of

1914-18 compelled man to think that the world could not be saved from such disasters in the future unless there was a real solidarity among all its peoples. It went so far that even Utopia, that is to say, a perfect world of peace and plenty, seemed to figure in the imagination of the historical idealists. It would not of course be true to say that these two stages are separate. In fact, as in the general cultural cycle of mankind, so also in the cycle of its history, the age of individualism has always in it certain elements of subjectivism. While therefore the nations were trying to find their own selves, they came upon the discovery that the force or forces that governed their destiny were everywhere the same and that there seemed to be a common goal for them.

These ideas found more prominence in, and gave meaning and motive to, the writings of those historians of the present century who took up the entire field of human activity as their subject and the whole world as their canvas on which to depict the theme in all its variegated colours. But their vision was not deep enough to catch the inward significance of the human affairs, for which a higher than mental power is necessary. Hence they could not get out of the constructions built up by the mind and founded in the norms of humanism that had its birth in the Renaissance of Europe. Man dominates the scene. It is he who is the master. It is he who is the poet, the artist, the thinker, the scientist, the builder of the State. He is the creator of the splendid things that make the fabric of his culture. He will therefore be the harbinger of the new world of peace and freedom that is to come in the future. It is a brilliant picture no doubt that the best of the history books, written in recent times, make it their business to give about the past, present and future of the human race.

Yet the solution of the problem is as distant today as it was before. Night sits heavy on the world without any prospect of the dawn. And man gropes about in the darkness that thickens everywhere. It is true his subjective thinking has opened him to the truth that every noble deed he does, every beautiful work he produces, every great thought he expresses, is always for the whole human race with which he is one both in his cultural and social life, and that there is a common goal, the goal of freedom and unity towards which the whole humanity is moving through all its trials and travails. But this only gives a wider meaning to his ideal of humanism, and does not bring to him in its fullness the truth he needs.

The question is, whether it is only man with his human drama that should be the be-all and end-all of his earthly existence, whether the stage is set only for him to people all its scenes and through them to sing the paeans of his own triumphs. If that is so, if that is the sole implication of what man has been in the past and is today, then it is difficult, if not impossible, to conjure up a bright future for him. And does not the gloom that envelops the world today point to the same conclusion? What then is the solution? And how is history to light the chequered march of man through the ages? The march has its moments of struggle with adverse forces, of exhaustion and failure and distress, when wrong paths are taken; and of joy and victory, when his steps are on the right.

It is this march of humanity in all its stages that integrates itself first into the objective, and then or simultaneously with it into the subjective elements of history. But the journey does not end, neither does the traveller show any sign of exhaustion. It has rather been a ceaseless one; only its continuity is marked by upward and downward movements. Thus, every period of decline is followed by a fresh endeavour into which man is stirred by the unfailing force of his life. Every deviation from the ideal is followed by a return to it, the sentinel-light of the past helping him back to the right track. And what is most glorious is that when man is faced with a crisis and has to take a decisive step, there appear on earth for his deliverance the Vibhutis[3] and the Avatars[4] of God who awaken man to the light of the Spirit in him, the light that leads his soul on to greater possibilities. It is to be aware of and live in it that the call has again and again come to him from the saviours of the race. Indeed, Christ's 'The Kingdom of Heaven is within you,' the Buddha's 'Be a lamp unto yourself,' Shri Krishna's 'Seek refuge in the Lord seated in the heart,' the declaration of the Rishi in the Upanishad, 'Thou art That,' are verily the same gospel in the teachings of all God-men and seers. It is this divinity of man, then, that is the key to his journey on earth, and its meaning fully unveils itself when the

---

3. Emanations or manifestations of the Divine.
4. Incarnations of the Divine.

divine spark in the finite being flames forth into the supreme
Fire of the Infinite.

V

During her age of the Spirit the early mystics of India discovered
—and Sri Aurobindo today has re-visioned and revealed its
deeper and wider significance—the hidden truth that, in order to
have delight of manifestation, the One Reality becomes Many by
plunging into the 'shadow of its own Light' and through it, first
organises the form of matter, itself remaining in it to create by
its own upsurging Force conditions for a higher formulation of
itself. And when Matter is ready the Force breaks into a splendour
of living forms. When, again, these forms prove capable of a
still higher evolution there appears man, the mental being,
possessing a power by which he is distinguished from the animal
even as life is distinguished from matter. Matter, life and mind are
thus the three fundamental principles in and through which the
Supreme has taken forms and entered into the terrestrial becoming.

But man as he now is, imperfect and subject to the Ignorance,
cannot of course be the last term of evolutionary Nature. There
must be yet higher statuses for her to ascend to as the culmination
of her evolutionary career on earth. And man being the highest
point so far reached by her in her upward drive, she is preparing
him for that consummation. 'The animal is a living laboratory
in which Nature, it is said, worked out man. Man himself may
well be a thinking and living laboratory in whom and with whose
conscious co-operation she wills to work out the superman, the
god. Or shall we say, rather, to manifest God?[5]

That is why there is always in man the urge towards perfection, the urge to exceed himself, which is a force in him derived
from the Will of the Divine. He seeks perfect beauty in art,
perfect truth in philosophy, perfect law in science, perfect health
in his body, and, above all his own perfection in all his spiritual
endeavours. And it is the business of Nature to keep burning the
fire of this quest in him and provide conditions in which he may
give full play to his creative faculties, the cultivation of which

---

5. *The Life Divine*, Vol. i, p. 5.

has helped him through the ages to grow and to increase, to widen and to expand in all the members of his being. Indeed, any true progress would have been impossible if man had not within him this impulse to search for his own perfectibility. 'All man's agelong effort, his action, society, art, ethics, science, religion, all the manifold activities by which he expresses and increases his mental, vital, physical, spiritual existence, are episodes in the vast drama of this endeavour of Nature.'[6]

Nature's purpose in human evolution is fulfilled when man is ready for emergence into superman. But Nature only prepares. It is the Paraprakriti, the divine Conscious-Force, who is the ultimate Source, the supreme Fashioner of things. It is Her Light whose manifestation in man will change his imperfect nature into the perfect Nature of the Divine. Beyond this triple world of Ignorance are the worlds of Cosmic Knowledge, and beyond them again are the supernal planes of Light from where the divine Shakti—of whom this Nature is an executive Force—creates and directs the whole system of worlds.

Indeed, the Mother stands even above all these worlds, bearing in Her eternal consciousness the Supreme Divine. The Supreme is manifest in Her as the everlasting Sachchidananda and through Her in the worlds and planes which are Her immediate embodiments. In Her own mystery She stands as the Infinite Mother of the gods and projects Herself into all that forms the Great Play. All is She, because all are the parcel and portion of the divine Conscious-Force. This world of Ignorance and imperfection is upheld by Her and it is She who guides it to its secret aim. She is here as the Mahashakti, seeking by Her creative Light to build in the nescience of Matter of godlike Life—the flowering of the life, soul and mind in matter into the infinity of the Spirit. She works through Her Powers and Personalities, governing and leading the lines of development for their forces so that the world may progress towards its goal. But also She prepares and shapes things of the earth that 'She may manifest in the physical world and in the disguise of the human consciousness some ray of Her power and quality and presence. All the scenes of the earth-play have been like a drama arranged and planned and staged by Her with the cosmic Gods for Her assistants and Herself as a veiled actor.'[7]

---

6. Ibid., Vol. ii, p. 597.
7. *The Mother,* pp. 45-46.

And it is always Her aim on this earth to create a new world of
harmony and perfection and evolve out of the mental man the
supramental being.

This is the way in which the Divine who has descended into
the material consciousness recovers in it His own splendour in
man transformed and perfected by the luminous dynamism of His
own Force. Whatever might the humanist say about the unsur-
passable glory of man, however emphatic might the rationalist
be about the absolute value of human reason, a deeper knowledge
proves to the intuition of man that the real player in the world-
drama is the divine Shakti Herself—She alone is the play, the
player and the playground. All are Her forms which She creates,
develops and leads to their highest efflorescence. And man being
Her chosen vehicle for a greater manifestation, She works in him
through Nature that he may wake up from his sleep in the Ignorance and open to Her Influence, to Her Presence and Power
in him, and thereby grow into his perfection—the blossoming of
his inherent divinity. For, if man is God self-involved and progressively self-evolving in form, the conclusion becomes inevitable
that his perfection and fulfilment can be nothing short of a full
emergence of that Godhead in him. And it is only the power of
the divine Shakti, not any human endeavour or *tapasya* that can
effectuate this consummation in man. Indeed, She alone 'can rend
the lid and tear the covering and shape the vessel and bring down
into this world of obscurity and falsehood and death and suffering Truth and Light and Life divine and the immortal's Ananda'[8]
—the most perfect of things into which man in his life, mind and
body, is destined to be new-born. This is the meaning of the
Supreme's earthly adventure, the meaning also of man's heaven-
ward journey on earth.

The divine Conscious-Force is infinite in Her powers and
personalities. But it is in Her four great Aspects[9] that She is manifest in the earth-consciousness for the accomplishment of Her
immediate purpose in it. The first is Her aspect of calm wideness
and comprehending wisdom, which in man is the inspiration
behind all his spiritual enterprises, the works of majesty and
greatness. The second is of power and passion and force, which

8. Ibid., pp. 84-85.
9. Maheshwari, Mahakali, Mahalakshmi and Mahasaraswati, as described in *The Mother*, pp. 48-50.

exhibits itself in the dynamic and heroic activities of man. The third is of beauty and harmony and rhythm, which in man is his aesthetic impulse that seeks to make the earth an abode of the beautiful. The fourth is of practical knowledge and flawless work and exact perfection, from which come science, craft and technique of things for the perfect organisation of all kinds.

These powers by their insistent pressure from above have not only helped the growth of man, the mental being, but they have also been sometimes sought after by him and admitted into himself and assimilated in proportion to his developing capacity. Because they are also within him—latent, involved and steadily pressing for evolution—man feels a natural impulse, an irrepressible yearning for their discovery and possession. And in epochs of resurgent creativity he has at times broken beyond the normal confines of his mind and created right out of the very heart of his experience of them. Indeed, his art and literature, mysticism and spirituality, religion and philosophy, science and politics are but expressions, plenary or partial, of these powers to which he has ever turned, consciously or unconsciously, at all stages of his evolution. The progress of man is the progress of his evolving Spirit which is effected through his culture, the outcome of his cultivation of these powers in him of the divine Shakti. And it is for history to study this progress and portray the rise and growth of the nations and peoples of the world, unravelling the various ways in which they incarnate and give form to these powers, and thereby prepare for a greater destiny in the future.

VI

The historian has been a realist concerned mainly with facts and events that constitute the cultural life of humanity, and his work has resulted in the integration of the objective elements in history which constitute the foundation of all historical undertakings. He has also been an idealist, roaming in the world of thought which has given him the vision of freedom and unity, and in the light of this vision he has tried to reconstruct history, though still on the basis of the objective realities, demonstrating the essential oneness of the various creative activities of man, by which, as the truth of it becomes more and more evident to him, the diverse factions of the race would be forged into a homogeneous whole. The history of man has been and is still being written from the standpoint of this cultural synthesis, however inchoate in form it may appear to be; but where are the ideals of unity and freedom it inculcated? Have not all its golden dreams remained dreams till now? Nevertheless, ideals are not chimeras; they are potential realities and they have in them a truth which the race is certain to realise, but only when a radical transformation of man's nature is effected by his ascent into a higher than mental consciousness wherein alone peace, freedom and unity take their perfect forms. It is to this inevitable destiny of his that man is being led by Nature as an evolutionary necessity.

The great epochs of history, its golden periods, are the decisive stages through which this march of man has been accelerated. Even periods of decline and darkness with all their chaos and conflict have not inconsiderably helped forward the growth of man towards that many-sided achievement. To attain this consummation it was necessary that man should reach the very summit of his earthly possibilities by developing to their utmost all the powers that lie dormant in him. And when he himself does not do so and unconsciously gives way to sloth, Nature jerks him out of it and gives him a new start.

Thus, when life stagnates, progress is clogged, and there is no new going-forth, war becomes a necessity to open for man fresh channels of self-expression—war at once on subjective and objective planes of existence. Many such blood-baths result in the regeneration and remoulding of the old and effete human material, even as the arts of peace exalt and increase the cultural content of the national being. The aim of history will be to discover how in every one of her workings in man through the ages Nature has been seeking to accomplish her revolutionary purpose. And in order to be able to do that successfully the historian must have an integral vision of the whole plan and working of Nature as well as of that ultimate end towards which she is inevitably advancing.

Objective history has tried to answer the question, 'What are the contents of History?' Subjective history's attempt has been to trace how they come into being and what they lead to. The turn has now come for the student of the Spirit in history to explain the why of them by bringing out their inner implications. The historian has therefore to be a seer. He must have an intuitive insight into the very source of the human drama, the *karan jagat*, the world of types and causes, where Nature fixes everything before she works it out in the outer world, and where she initiates the movements that are the pageant of history. But beyond Nature he will have also to go into the world of basic forces, of fundamental realities, into the flaming heart of things where all actualities are born and take first shape. It is to a vision of this world of the Mother that the seer-historian must first rise, and illumined by its Truth, he will proceed to his task of reconstructing the history of man in which he will describe how Nature fulfils the Will of the supreme Shakti in the terrestrial evolution, what are her manifold steps and how she takes them in order to prepare the earth for the Mother to manifest in it the Light of the Supermind, and evolve the gnostic being. The creative activities of man—so many milestones on his onward path—will be for the historian to assess as the expression of Nature's striving in man to cultivate and refine, to exalt and elevate the various parts of his being, so that they may be plastic enough to the influence of the Mother and change into their divine counterparts.

When his physical being became sufficiently developed through the strenuous exertions into which man was forced by the unavoidable conditions of the primitive phase of his life, his vital began to reinforce the efforts that he made to enlarge the sphere of his actions and interests, economic, social and political. The higher vital in him growing through his creative action has been always behind those activities of the mind which produce all that is of value in his culture. Mind, however, is the most cultivated of the planes in man; and nearly every one of his cultural endeavours has contributed to its growth which is so important to his evolution.

It is remarkable that man's quest of truth is almost coeval with his civilised existence. Thus religion, occultism, mysticism, and spirituality have through the ages helped in the emergence of the spiritual man. The moral content in religion as well as other mental and moral disciplines have promoted the growth of his ethical being. His art, music and poetry have in their pure forms brought down light from the deeper reaches of consciousness and by it refined and enriched his aesthetic and emotional being. His philosophy and science have increased the light of reason in him, the latter giving to his mind the power of precious observation and masterful manipulation of matter. It is not that this process has gone on uniformly throughout the ages. There have been aberrations, deviations into wrong paths and retrogressions as well, when the race forsook the ideal and ran after lower pleasures and ceased to create things that could tend to further its collective well-being. The historian here will show this aspect of the process with its inner cause or causes no less vividly than the bright one which he will depict, illustrating how man's co-operation with Nature has always resulted in the advancement of his culture, and therefore, in his progress towards the goal.

It is true that the past dawns of human culture were the dawns of real glory and greatness, but it is also true that a blazing moontide waits for the advancing man in the near future. 'A great past must be followed by a greater future.'[10] For if the morning shows the day, the splendid mornings of the past are a sufficient promise of the ambient warmth and illumination of the coming day. Man, as he grows, resumes and integrates all his past and moves forward creating the greatness of the future.

Progress, therefore, is the whole drift and purport of human evolution; and it is to a delineation of this spiral progress and to a discovery of its hidden springs and pregnant, prophetic significances—to a reading of what has been and a revealing of what will be—that history should apply itself with the integrality of its subjective and objective resources.

VII

The historic development of mankind is too complex a phenomenon to allow of any clear division into separate periods which may be presented against a common background. That history is fundamentally the working out of a 'predetermined Plan' or a 'creative Idea' is even more difficult to discover in what externally the epochs in it appear to the student of human affairs. But a deeper

---

10. Sri Aurobindo in a letter to a disciple.

view of things vouchsafed to the seers reads in history a pur-
posive process through which man is led from age to age so that
he may rise to the summit of his possibilities individually as well
as collectively. History reflects the integral vision when it studies
all the efforts and achievements of man as a manifold organic
progression; and the vision finds its wider meaning in history
when the latter depicts the story of how man as a race moves
forward in his chequered march to that goal.

A perfect order of collective spiritual living is the hidden
aim intended in the evolution of humanity. Perfection of the individual fulfils itself in the coming into being of a perfect community. The core of all human progress is an inner preparation
of man for that great end of his social existence. Sri Aurobindo
sees in the story of this progress several broad stages[11] through
which man passes in order to arrive at the highest point of his
evolution on earth.

The first of these is the symbolic stage which began in India
when the earliest and the most luminous of the spiritual dawns
lit up its immortal fires in the intuitive horizon of the Rishis
who saw in them the infinite splendours of the Supreme and that
supernal Light of His which was to come down on earth and
new-create man into a divine perfection, or rather to manifest
the divinity that is already there in him, because that is his
inevitable destiny for the attainment of which Nature in him has
been in constant travail. It is to these early fathers of Knowledge
that the race is indebted for the profoundest truth-visions that
have ever come to any mortal. The various cults of India, all
her social and religious institutions are significant symbols of the
eternal verities seen by the ancient mystics.

An entire self-giving to the Godhead for the manifestation
of His power in the human aspirant is the central discipline of
the Veda. This is symbolised in the cult of sacrifice which governed the whole society, all its hours and moments. Similarly,
the gods in the Veda are, each of them, various powers of the
Godhead. The worship of so many deities—facets of the One—
has its origin in the Vedic pantheon. In the same way, the system

---

11. Sri Aurobindo takes up these stages as the basis of a most illuminat-
    ing discussion on the Psychology of Social Development in the *Arya*
    (Vols. III & IV), published in book from under the title *The Human
    Cycle*. A bare outline of them in their historical setting is attempted
    here.

of caste and the fourfold motive of life are institutional expressions of truths about man and his higher possibilities, which in their essence were first revealed in the Veda, rightly called the very bedrock of Indian civilisation. Spiritually, these institutions, when living, did exert subtle influences on their adherents, helping them to grow in their inner life. Socially, they united the race into a co-operative unit to live up to the ideals set forth in them. And culturally, they provided scope for the development of the various faculties of man, particularly those of his mind and heart.

This growth and fruition of the mind and heart, it may be incidentally mentioned, is an evolutionary necessity and it has not always and everywhere been a straight upward movement: it has had its inevitable periods of decline when the growth was effected even through the fulfilment of their downward inclinations which fundamentally described a curve of descent in a spiral of progress. Neither is it that man has always taken the right path. His frequent deviations caused his difficulties—unnecessary prolongation of his journey, its arduousness, its complexity.

Whatever that may be, the fact is there that each phase of the symbolic stage and that of the later ones has used for its characteristic self-expression a special faculty of the human consciousness developed during the period of that stage. We may classify them by saying that it was intuition that gave its stamp to the Vedic age, the intuitive mind to the Upanishadic, and the ratiocinative mind to the period of the Dharma-shastras when the social institutions were given their final forms and attempts were made to explain and justify things in terms of reason.

The symbolic stage and the subsequent ones did not, however, arrive at the same time everywhere; neither was the Ideal seen by all the countries in the same way. This stage in China was represented by her greatest classic, called the *I-Ching,* or the 'Book of Changes,' dated a little earlier than the first millennium B.C., which contains mystic trigrams about the oneness of heaven and earth in a universal rhythm, called *Tao,* the heavenly Way. According to it, man becomes truly himself when he realises his harmony with heaven. About six centuries later, the great mystic Lao-tze reaffirmed the same truth in his idea of 'Cosmic Unity in the Universal Mother.' The *I-Ching* is to China what the Veda is to India. To it China traces the origin of all her mysticism and thought. And it was mainly her intuitive mind that was at work during that age. Her great sage Confucius called himself 'a transmitter of the wisdom of the *I-Ching.*' Taoism occupies a very important place in the early thought of China out of which her culture has evolved. As a creed it symbolises for the race the truths about the perfectibility of man, that came to her mystics millenniums ago. Many of her higher endeavours were inspired by it. To the Chinese the 'Ways of the Ancients' are always the best, since they aim at the 'Perfect Man,' the 'Higher Man.' Out of these grew their ancestor-worship which has been religiously followed by the whole people from time immemorial as the symbol of their traditional belief in the spirit of the past, that is to say, in the 'Ways' discovered by the pioneers of the race and handed down from generation to generation for its collective well-being. In this common instinct of the people to adore their forbears lies the secret of China's national solidarity.

The esoteric doctrines of the early Egyptians made a near approach to the symbolic stage, and in Greece it was echoed by her fathers of knowledge who founded the mystic rites of Orpheus and the secret initiation of Eleusis, both of which are said to have influenced the numbers and figures of Pythagoras and Plato. The Greek thinkers expressed in these symbols their ideas of perfection which they conceived with the help of their disciplined intellect. The age of symbols is indeed a glorious phase of human adventure; and its history has yet to be written showing how as a result of their incomparable spiritual enterprises the ancients had the vision of the Ideal and evolved those institutions through which man was to prepare himself for the great future when the Ideal would become real in his individual and collective life. The symbolic is an age not only of great beginnings but also of wise path-findings.

The later days of the symbolic stage are marked by a tendency towards the interpretation of the ideals and institutions of the past from a philosophical and ethical standpoint. Through the increasing growth of this tendency the age of symbols merges into the typal phase of human history, represented in India mainly by the *Ramayana* and the *Mahabharata.* The age of the *Ramayana* was the flowering of moral idealism, of the ethical mind; the age of the *Mahabharata,* that of a puissant intellectualism, of the intellectual mind: but both were inspired by the Godward bent of India's soul. Buddhism, built later almost on the same ideology, was another notable effort to cultivate the ethical side of human nature. The call of the Divine upon the Aryan man, rung in the trumpet-notes of the Gita, was the greatest social ideal of the age. To see God and to see Him in one's self is not the only aim. To be perfectly equal to all beings and to see and feel them as one with oneself and one with the divine; to feel all in oneself and all in God; to feel God in all and oneself in all—this was then, as it now is, the true aim of the spiritual seeker. In China the typal phase was that glorious age which was heralded by Confucius who gave a clear and bold definition to the ideals of life and conduct and laid down the foundation of her social and collective life. It was this great sage who preached the message of *jen,* or universal love, and propounded the doctrine that in order to live one must let others live, in order to develop one must let others develop. Both China and India are at one in their conviction that there can be no freedom for the world so long as a single soul remains in bondage. The Buddha turned back from the threshold of Nirvana and took the vow never to cross it so long as a single being would remain subject to sorrow and ignorance. Greater social ideals have never been before in any other country of the world. History must tell the story of how China and India tried to live up to these ideals and how by their effort to do so they built up for all time a marvellous spiritual unity which is a unique social phenomenon in the history of mankind. Even in their political thinking both these peoples, as already seen, were guided by their high religious idealism. The early Christian of Europe was prone more to the old Greco-Roman mentality than to any religio-ethical adaptation of Hebraic traditions. Besides, the spiritual elements in the teachings of Christ were not fully understood by their exponents. And the mystics who had glimpses of the truth have scarcely been an influence in the life of the people.

In the typal age itself it was the outer institutions and traditions that began to be given more importance than their original spirit and intention, although the idea of their being a cohesive force in the collective advancement of the race emerged clearer than beforce. When this tendency grew stronger the typal phase passed into the next age of convention during which everything in society was regarded as a sacrament and therefore, inviolable. Attempts were made to fix everything into a system, to stereotype religion, to bind education down to tradition, and to subject thought to infallible authority. And the result of it was that the whole social system became petrified into particular forms and structures which admitted of no renovation, no readjustment to changing conditions in the external life of the people. The custodians of the society made it their sole business to preserve those forms to that end, to interpret the texts in their own way. The ordinance of Manu, the code of Confucius, the injunctions of the Pope, were held as supreme and sacrosanct, and that too not for what they were worth in their spirit but only for the very letter of them. The claim of capacity was gradually replaced by that of birth in the determination of caste, and the religious life lapsed into a soulless formalism having lost touch with its spiritual foundations. The four *ashramas* or motives of life, existed merely as a mechanical routine, instead of as necessary aims to be fulfilled for the all-round development of man. The worship of ancestors took the form of family exaltation. And much worse things happened in Europe in the name of religion. Yet, is spite of all these rigidities, the conventional stage in India, China and Europe was marked by long periods of great cultural revivals that proved the immense vitality and wonderful creative energy with which Nature had endowed these countries so that they might be able to live fruitfully and advance steadily towards their future destiny. Another saving aspect of this stage was that in its effort to preserve the shell it helped in a way to preserve the kernel too. Thus, beneath all excrescences there was always the shining core of the ancient vision, though for a time hidden from the human view.

The conventional is a remarkable phase in the historic evolution of India. It is the longest and culturally the most creative epoch in Indian history. A period of over a thousand years of it is known as the classical age when the highest point was reached during the time of the Guptas which witnessed a most brilliant outburst of the literary and artistic genius of the race, almost incomparable in history. After going through the experiences necessary for a greater rebirth India evinced all through this period ample signs of preparedness for a renewal of her life. But it could not then come about as the true significance of the ancient Ideal was not reaffirmed and the people had already opened themselves to the reactionary forces of decline. Nevertheless, the conventional mind of India during this period was largely responsible for the protection of her religion and society from disintegration and through them of all the past achievements of the race, and that at a time when they were being interpreted in a dry formalistic way. Almost the same thing happened in China. An exclusive regard for everything of the past was then the dominant tendency of the Chinese mind. This conservative attitude is ingrained in all Eastern peoples.

As in India, so in China, elaboration of formulas out of the ancient teachings was during this period the main activity in the world of thought. But in art and poetry China rose to classical excellence when the T'ang and the Sung dynasties were ruling over the country. The conventional stage in Europe was the Middle Ages, and the Renaissance—not the Reformation, for reasons already stated—was the zenith of its cultural expression. The Renaissance opened before Europe the treasures of the Greek learning, the study of which did on the one hand rouse her interest in the beauty of life and Nature, so gloriously articulated in the arts and letters of the period, and on the other, kindled in her a spirit of enquiry and research, the spirit of a rational approach to things that was to break into a passion for truth, a demand for reason in the age that followed. It is because of this that the Renaissance is often called the inaugurator of the modern age. Indeed, all later upheavals in Europe, religious, social and political, are in a deeper sense different expressions of the spirit that took its birth in Italy in the fourteenth century when Petrarch was writing his odes and sonnets.

The age of convention had other aspects that deserve mention as having had a bearing on the historic evolution of humanity. Generally, it gave the conventional and conservative mind of man its round of experiences, but during its epochs of revival his creative and aesthetic mind also received its growth and fruition. And its finest works of art showed man's openness to higher levels of consciousness, and that in a manner which has no parallel in the whole history of art. It was the light of the Spirit that glimmered in them, waiting for its hour to reveal itself fully in the cultural expressions of a perfected future humanity. Indeed, it was the same light which has always been there in every true creation of man as an evidence of Nature's endeavour to sustain the various forms of culture till they attain their highest excellence in a greater future.

The last days of the conventional stage however present a dismal picture of human history. There was the society, perhaps more defined in its aims than before, but it was so much hedged in by irrational rules and cramping restrictions that it could not function as a living organism. There was also the larger collectivity, better organised than before, but its real being had yet to develop into a governing force in all its activities. The religious life was choked with the fungus growth of blind practices, meaningless dogmas and superstitious beliefs. And the intellect was forced to engage in empty logomachies for the defence of those unwholesome accretions. These are not certainly the conditions in which any progress is possible, or any new going-forth. The only way out was the liberation of the mind from its subjection to the dead or dying forms of the past and to the prevalent reactionary forces. The key of knowledge had to be repossessed with which to unlock the door of the future. Nature, therefore, called upon the individual, the individual who is always the pioneer and precursor, to shake off all slavery to the past, to steer clear of the chaotic ferment of the present and to rise up in his own strength and right and freedom to know and to master, to conquer and to create.

The first response to this is witnessed in the revolt of Reason against the absurdities so much rampant everywhere in the name of religion and learning. The awakening individual began to feel that the widespread rule of those degrading tendencies had to be overthrown, all old notions shattered, the barriers—the walls of unreason—that thwarted the free development of man broken down; and man must go in for 'fresh fields and pastures new.' Thus began the age of individualism whose culmination was the triumphal progress of physical Science. Man denied everything that would not satisfy the evidence of the senses. He questioned the validity of things that would not stand the test of reason. He ventured into the unexplored. He set out for the unknown. And to all these he was impelled by a search for knowledge, a quest for truth, that gave the individualistic age its real sense as a necessary phase in the historic evolution of mankind.

The achievements that crowned these mighty efforts of Europe where the age had taken its birth—since she was a more suitable field for that than conservative Asia—proclaimed her conquest of matter, her mastery over the potencies of universal Force, that brought to man a rich harvest of new knowledge—the knowledge of the physical, of the external order of things, through which his materialistic and scientific mind had its growth and fruition and his earthward desires their satisfaction, if there could be anything like that for them. But is it not a going to the one extreme of things? And the other extreme, we know, is the knowledge of the supra-physical pursued and attained by the East, by India in particular, where in later times an exclusive emphasis on it led to a recoil from life, a refusal of its values, which slowed down the tempo of her progress for many centuries. If Europe accepted nothing but life and matter as the only truth and denied everything else, even God, India rejected everything, even life and accepted nothing but God. The truth as revealed to the vision of ancient India was that matter and life are as much real as God. Matter is verily the body of the Spirit, and life the expression of its energy, and in the discovery and possession of their harmony lie the true meanings of things.

Yet the value of critical and rationalistic attitude that Science developed in man can never be over-estimated. It is because of his insistence on reason that man is becoming more and more free from his infra-rational instincts, impulses, blind fervours, crude beliefs and hasty prejudgments, and that he is today nearer 'the full unveiling of a greater inner luminary.' Science is indeed 'a right knowledge, in the end only of processes, but still the knowledge of processes too is part of a total wisdom and essential to a wide and clear approach towards the deeper Truth behind.'[12] That Science has already begun to open to a higher order of things is evident from the views of many of its eminent votaries that scientific discoveries have always behind them some kind of intuitional experience and that beyond the world of sense-perception there exist other worlds of 'Thought' or 'Ideas' which are no less real than the former. Thus Science which ushered in materialism seems itself to be paving the way for its exit.

The age of individualism carries in it the promise of the

---

12. Sri Aurobindo in *Evolution*, p. 29.

next age of subjectivism. Nay, it even suggests the latter and passes through phases in which the two become indistinguishable. When his Science makes man conscious of his latent capacities the cultivation of which brings to him the knowledge of the external world, he feels an urge to know what he himself is. As this seeking grows, man begins to turn inward and glimpse, however dimly, the truth and law of his being to which he finds he could relate the truth and law of the cosmic process, a rough mental picture of which being already there before him presented by physical Science. But a clearer conception of these things, of the secrets and profundities of the soul in man and the soul in the world is beyond the ken of intellectual reason. 'Knowledge waits seated beyond mind and intellectual reasoning, throned in the luminous vast of illimitable self-vision.'[13]

Rationalism has had its day and it was also a necessity in the mental evolution of man. It has guided him so far, illumining his path with whatever light it was capable of. But any further help reason seems unable to give him. What man needs now is intuitional knowledge, a deeper self-awareness, for which he must develop higher than mental faculties. The awakening individual therefore begins to betray his subjective inclinations. He must know and be in complete possession of all the powers and possibilities that lie hidden in him. And he must have scope enough for that in life. So he demands utmost freedom for his growth and widest opportunities for self-development. New ideas begin to stir him to new activities, and the result is a remarkable advance in art, literature, education and thought, every one of which attests the trend of a mind more and more waking to the intrinsic meaning of things.

Like individuals, peoples also gradually begin to discover their own selves, their own genius and possibilities. And this new-found consciousness incarnates itself in the nation which bids fair to be the living embodiment of the collective aspiration of human groups. The communal soul of humanity seems to be awakening. But the nature of these groups is not everywhere the same. An overstress on equal rights of man to satisfy his physical needs leads some of them into those dark recesses of a sheer ravenous materiality where they are caught in the toils of lower undivine forces. In one case, as it appears, the ego of life got so

13. *The Life Divine,* Vol. i, p. 183.

much enmeshed in the tangle of matter that it regarded man as
nothing more than a human animal. In another, it is the ego of
mind that combined with the ego of life only to become the instrument of a dangerous evil. And these were responsible for
the rise of that dictatorial totalitarianism which threatened to
destroy all superior values of life, all prospects of further advancement of the race, since the individual in it had no separate
status and, therefore, no freedom to express his higher self. And
in the collectivities elsewhere the vestiges of their egoistic aggran-
disement linger in the forms—though much weakened—of 'earth-
hunger, gold-hunger and commodity-hunger.'

   To save the world from the disastrous consequences of these
and other aberrations of the groups, Nature rouses in the progressive nations the democratic impulse and reaffirms to them the
ideals of peace, freedom and unity. Indeed, these ideals have
always been there before man inspiring his onward march; they
have been accentuated at critical times by the pioneers of the
race or by world-shaking cataclysms, but never before so much
as after the First and the Second World Wars. And these ideals
are certainly not those that exist only in the imagination of man.
Today they are much clearer in his vision than at any time in
history. And there are signs that Nature insists on their acceptance by man as the governing principles of his collective life.
Whatever the politicians might say or do, the race has begun to
be moved into an earnest aspiration for a life of permanent peace
and freedom. That is how nations and peoples are called by
Nature to wake up and be ready for a greater future.

   The world-wide influence of European culture is a phenomenon as unique as it was inevitable. Never in history has the
whole of civilised mankind had such a common cultural experience as it is having today through its contact with the dynamic
culture of the West. And it is an experience that man everywhere
must go through in order to be fit for the subjective stage that
follows the individualistic. Control of matter, discipline of life,
organisation and method, enlightened reason, emancipation of
mind, search for knowledge and truth, are its outstanding contributions that do help in strengthening the foundations of life on
which the future has to be built. It is these again that prove to be
cohesive factors in the collective life of man uniting him with a
common outlook, common endeavours, common corporate acti-

vities that constitute in history the movements of the human whole.

Individualism always carries in it the seeds of subjectivism. And the future depends on how the latter thrives in conditions made favourable by the former. In the materialistic mind of Europe and in other countries these seeds did not sprout as easily as they did in the inward mind of Asia, particularly of India. In fact, the impact of the West did not take long to quicken in the East the beginnings of the subjective age. It served as an incentive to Japan to discover her national self, her creative genius which flowered into manifold expressions. China, the Mother of the Far East, could not so easily respond to the Western influence. When, however, she came to realise the elements of truth in it, she lost no time in receiving whatever of value there was in Europe, and was soon able to rouse herself into a national awakening which is comparable to few of its kind in all history.

Like conservative China, India also took some time to derive the intended benefit from the European impact. But the very moment she was on the path of self-discovery she began striving for the resuscitation of her national genius, and the result was resurgence of her creative soul in every sphere of her life. Her in-born spiritual impulse, thus rekindled, broke into many stupendous efforts not only to re-vision the truths of the past but also to bring them to bear on the life of the race for an all-round harmonious uplift. After a period of glorious striving crowned with many achievements, the vision of the highest Ideal has now come to her as also the power to make it real on earth. The Master of the race has spoken the Word. The Light which the Rishis of old had glimpsed shone full upon him in all its supernal splendour, and the hour of its Manifestation on earth is NOW. It is the power of this Light that will lift humanity beyond itself and new-mould it into a divine perfection. Says the Master: 'As there has been established on earth a mental Consciousness and Power which shapes a race of mental beings and takes up into itself all of earthly nature that is ready for the change, so now there will be established on earth a gnostic Consciousness and Power which will shape a race of gnostic spiritual beings and take up into itself all of earth-nature that is ready for this new transformation.'[14]

_____

14. *The Life Divine*, Vol. ii, p. 1028.

Conditions in the world today do not seem to indicate the coming of such a spiritual change in the life of man, at least in the near future. But the ways of the Divine are inscrutable. Out of the worst of evils He brings into being the highest Good. Mystics and prophets of all climes and ages have averred that the brightest Dawns are always preceded by the darkest Nights. Indeed, the greater and nearer the Manifestation, the fiercer becomes the resistance to it by the hostile forces that have their empire already established on earth which they would not part with. It is this resistance to the descending supramental Light that has thrown the world into such gigantic conflagrations.

There are other signs, too, not externally perceptible, but equally, if not more, suggestive of the conditions of the earth being ready for that Light to come down and be active in its consciousness. True, the essential nature of man has not improved in proportion to his cultural progress and that the civilisation he has built up and the control his Science has given him over the potencies of universal Force are proving beyond his limited mental capacity to utilise and manage, but it is also true that through the progress he has so far made his mind has reached the very summit of its normal possibilities—a thing so necessary for the next evolutionary ascent of the race. Thus is the condition created for a higher power than the mind to descend and manifest on earth and effect a new saltus of evolution. And it is for this that man is waking up from his agelong sleep in the Ignorance, from the evil dream of an unquiet desire-driven existence, and is catching the first golden glints of a dawning glory. Large ideas, vast thoughts, wonderful visions, matchless dreams are stirring his heart and soul, and he is beginning to feel that out of the present convulsive throes a new world is at last going to be born—a New Heaven, as it were, which evolutionary Nature has long been patiently building in secret. But the most heartening promise of that 'divine event' is that they who would liberate man are at work on earth today—they who are the Leaders of the way, the Bringers of the Light.

Spiritual forces, the Light and Force of the Supramental Truth-Consciousness, are at work in the world, in the life of man. Forward-looking minds are tending to visualise a new future for man, 'a new world of uncharted possibilities in which man will transcend himself' (Julian Huxley), 'man's emergence into a new type of cosmic consciousness' (Arthur Koestler), 'the first symptoms of an aggregation of a still higher order' (Lacomte du Nouy), 'an integral culture based upon intuitive foundations' (Pitirim Sorokin). Sri Aurobindo revealed the truths of man's divine destiny more than fifty years ago. Even Science today seems to be very near Sri Aurobindo when he says that the knowledge of the physical completes itself in the knowledge of its origin in the supraphysical.

Not only these, there is all over the world today an awakening of a unique kind which indicates that the Force is preparing the earth for a decisive change of its consciousness. This phase of its working, though revolutionary in its results, is more or less peaceful in the inner life of man. However crude and violent sometimes, the reactions of youth to its pressure are bursting out almost everywhere in the world, the youth whose soul, discontented with the old and the effete, is ardently aspiring after a new order of things, a better arrangement of the affairs of the world. Not that they are all of them conscious of what is impelling them to such vehement expressions, but it is true they are passionately in search of 'The Future.' It is a kind of 'divine discontent,' 'a spiritual anarchism' which is inevitable when 'the Ideal is nearing its realisation.' True, the past has given man many eternal truths but these will be of use to him not through their old forms but through newer ones from the new vision of his greater Future. Newer ways of life must be there for man that he may consciously new-make his life for the new World of Tomorrow. One of the organised moves in this direction, in recent times, is the World Future Society which held its first world assembly in Washington, in May 1971. Attended by 700 scientists, teachers and sociologists, who are members of its 9000 strong parent-body, the assembly discussed, from an integral standpoint, various problems of life including those of science and technology, and concluded that man could choose his future and consciously participate in his evolution towards 'noumenal man.' Almost similar is the aim of the 'Prospective' movement in France. Thus is developing Futurology as an important discipline.

These are among the signs of the subjective period of humanity through which humanity is at present passing and which, says the Master, 'is marked by a definite tendency to-

wards inner seeking. . . . and thinking, new attempts at mystic
experience, groping after the inner meaning of things, a reawakening to some sense of the truth and power of the spirit.'
As this tendency deepens in man, his vision becomes larger and
larger, opening him to the secret aim of his life on earth as well
as to the truth that he will attain his highest spiritual perfection
—for that is God's intention in him—only when, with the descent
into him of the Light from above, he rises into the supramental
consciousness which alone can effectuate a total conversion of his
present imperfect nature into the perfect Nature of the Divine.
Thus emerges the superman, and man having completed the
human cycle enters upon the new cycle of a divine living. A greater age of the Spirit dawns on earth. It is not that the whole race
will be raised at once and *en bloc* to the Supramental level. The
individuals ready for it will first attain to it and form the
nucleus of the gnostic community, the earnest of the perfect race
of the future. Founded in the Knowledge of the Truth, the
gnostic being will be one in the Spirit, one in the consciousness
of the supreme Shakti, and will live and act in Peace, Freedom
and Unity that are for ever. This is how man fulfils his highest
individual and collective destiny and how a spiritual, a perfect
social order, as envisaged by Sri Aurobindo, comes into being.

What is this perfection? And what is this freedom? Says the
Master: 'To be made one self with God above and God in man
and God in the world is the sense of liberation and the secret of
perfection.' 'The perfection of man lies in the unfolding of the
ever-perfect Spirit.' 'An eternal Perfection is moulding us into
its own image.' 'It is by the perfection of the soul within that the
outer environment can be perfect.' 'Man's true freedom and
perfection will come when the spirit within bursts through the
forms of mind and life, and winging above to its own gnostic fiery
height of ether, turns upon them from that light and flame to
seize them and transform them into its own image.' '. . . the individual exists not in himself alone but in the collectivity and
that individual perfection and liberation are not the whole sense
of God's intention in the world. The free use of our liberty includes also the liberation of others and of mankind; the perfect
utility of our perfection is, having realised in ourselves the divine
symbol, to reproduce, multiply and ultimately universalise it in
others.' The universalisation of perfection being the ultimate aim

of evolution, the perfection of the various cultures of the world
will fulfil itself in a perfect world civilisation, since 'perfection is
the true aim of all culture.'

VIII

History finds its deepest and widest meaning when its writing is
guided by the vision of how man as a race grows towards the
heavenly Light which is the eternal abode of his spiritual existence. To trace the chequered march of man through the ages,
outlined above mainly from the standpoint of his social development, will be the great task of the historian, to discharge which
in the best way he will have, among other things, to unravel the
inmost significance of the cultural movements of each of the
epochs, showing from a larger view how all of them converge
towards the one goal—attainment by man of a Godlike life. Not
only that, he will have also to show that every one of man's activities has been a step forward to the same end. His art and
science, his religion and philosophy, his mysticism and spirituality, his dreams and visions, his aims and aspirations, his society
and politics, his trials and sufferings, his struggles and failures,
no less than his peace and happiness, his victories and triumphs
—all these are but kaleidoscopic scenes in the wonderful drama
of man; and all reveal in the last analysis the one evolutionary
intention of the Supreme Shakti, who indeed is the real veiled
Player in them, upbearing and directing the labour of man towards his divine perfection.

When the historian becomes the exponent of this grand spiritual integration of humanity, the interpreter of its triumphal
progress towards Unity and Harmony, towards the termless
luminous bliss of an infinite and immortal Perfection, he not only
extends to their utmost the frontiers of his own province but also
achieves the consummate greatness of his function. Croce said that
history should be written only by philosophers, because 'they will
look at things in the large.' We may add that history should be
written by the seers who command an integral vision of the cosmic existence and its aeonic evolution. And what is this cosmic
evolution but a progressive self-revelation of Sachchidananda—

Infinite Existence, Infinite Consciousness, Infinite Bliss? These supernals of the supreme Shakti are for man to realise when he awakens to Her secret intention in his evolution, and grows into Her light and force, the light and force of Her supramental Truth-Consciousness, and thereby perfects his life, mind and body—the derivates of those supernals in the lower hemisphere of Ignorance. As man does this, the civilisation which he has built with these imperfect derivates, takes its perfect spiritual form, and a New Age of the Spirit dawns upon earth, heralded by the Supramental Manifestation.

This is how the Ancient Vision of India is fulfilled, the vision with which she began her march in history. This is how man attains his divine destiny, his integral perfection in the Spirit.

Says Sri Aurobindo: 'The history of the cycles of man is a progress towards the unveiling of the Godhead in the soul and life of humanity.' History so far has been the history of preparation: from now on it will be the History of Fulfilment.

And the most significant phase of these divine fulfilments will be the historic emergence of a Perfect Man, and through him, a Perfect Society and a Perfect Civilisation, and all these as the ever-progressive self-deploying of the Infinite Shakti in the endless march of the evolutionary world.

'Slowly the Light grows greater in the East,
Slowly the world progresses on God's road.'[15]

REFERENCES

M. P. Pandit (ed.), *Gems from Sri Aurobindo;* H. A. L. Fisher, *A History of Europe;* Hu Shih, *A Short History of Chinese Civilization;* J. H. Breasted, *Ancient Times;* Kiang Kang Hu, *Chinese Civilisation;* J. H. Robinson, *Medieval and Modern Times;* Tan Yun-Shan, *Modern China;* F. S. Marvin, *The Living Past;* F. Morrison, *The Meaning of History;* Nicolas Berdyaev, *The Meaning of History;* H. G. Wells, *The Outline of History;* F. J. C. Hearnshaw, *The Science of History;* (in *An Outline of Modern Knowledge*); Will Durant, *The Story of Civilisation;* Vol. I, and *The Story of Philosophy;* Toynbee, *The Study of History;* Sisirkumar Mitra, *Evolution of India—Its Meaning; History as the Future; The Vision of History;* (in the *Modern Review,* Jan. 1938); B. Croce, *Theory of History and Historiography;* The works of Sri Aurobindo quoted and referred to in the footnotes.

15. Sri Aurobindo, *Savitri,* Book VII, Canto IV.

Index